Somewhere Over the Rainbow

A Soul's Journey Home

Gloria Chadwick

Mystical Mindscapes
Palatine, Illinois

Somewhere Over the Rainbow
A Soul's Journey Home

Publisher's Cataloging-in-Publication Data

Chadwick, Gloria

Somewhere Over the Rainbow / Gloria Chadwick.
ISBN 1-883717-33-7
1. Reincarnation 2. Spiritual Reawakening
3. New-Age Fiction 4. Novel I. Title.

Library of Congress Catalog Card Number: 93-91601

Published by Mystical Mindscapes
P. O. Box 5424 • Palatine, Illinois 60078

Printed on recycled paper in
the United States of America

Cover Design by Lange Design

Cover Photo © H. Armstrong Roberts

Somewhere,
Over the Rainbow, Clouds are Clear.

There's a Place That I Dreamed of,
Once in a Time Now Here.

This book is dedicated to Rainbow

Acknowledgments ...

Loving thanks to both my daughters: To Jenny, who shared her power when I first became aware of my experiences as the philosopher, and who found the rainbow for the cover. To Jaime, for listening to the early versions of the chapters over and over again, and for all the spiritual walks and talks.

Thanks to Arthur Burt, for being the first person to buy my book several different times.

Thanks to Joan Czerneda, for her very generous loan and her belief in rainbows.

And a very special thank you to all those souls, visible and invisible, past, present, and future, who helped me see inside my rainbow dreams.

Contents

Introduction

In every sense of the word, I'm a free spirit. I'm also a real person, learning how to synchronize my energy vibrations into all my experiences. Being physical and spiritual at the same time, and in the same dimension, is an exciting and challenging adventure. Sometimes I wonder what life is all about and what's real. I wonder who I really am and if I'll ever know all there is to know about the true nature of my soul.

The idea for this book was born inside a rainbow that whispered to me in my dreams. As a little girl, I loved walking barefoot through the rain and looking for rainbows. (I still do.) I thought rainbows were magical because they only appeared in the sky when the clouds cleared and the sun began to shine after it rained. Whenever I'd see a rainbow, I'd feel an incomparable sense of awe and joy within myself. It was like opening a wonderful gift and discovering a beautiful treasure.

Somewhere inside me, I knew that rainbows were real and magical at the same time and I shared a special secret with the rainbow. I knew the rainbow had really been there all the time, just waiting for the sun so it could magically appear.

When I grew up, I left my rainbows and sunshine in the sky and lived in what everyone told me was the real world for awhile before I saw how unreal it was. I felt lost in a world that I thought belonged to other people, not to me. Deep inside, I knew something very special and important was missing and that I wasn't being true to my real nature.

Then one morning I woke to the sound of raindrops tapping softly on my window. As I listened to the rain, I remembered that the rainbow was centered between both worlds as it blended into the earth and the universe. I returned to the world of my imagination and dreams, and began a journey into myself to look for my soul. As I walked through the rain and traveled within the quietness of my mind, I found my rainbow again and I knew what was real.

Exploring the true nature of reality and rediscovering my spiritual essence is such an awesome experience that I'd like to share the thoughts and images with you that I believe to be very real. Mystical knowledge can always be found hidden in the light, waiting to magically appear to anyone who knows the secret. The key is to look for the light within yourself.

Although this book is based on a past-life memory, in a world where tangible things seem to matter, this book is termed fiction—a fantasy created in my imagination and in my dreams, but I know it's really much more than that. It's a down-to-earth, mystical search for truth—a quest for knowledge—that every soul, at one time and in one form or another, will experience as they embark on a journey to see what life is really all about and to understand who they truly are.

Because I feel that spiritual knowledge is to be taken seriously, I thought the best way to write this book would be in a light-hearted manner. Appearances aren't always what they seem to be, and in this way I sincerely hope you'll see how special the characters and their experiences really are because they bring the joy of knowing and the treasure of truth into your awareness through the magical avenues of your imagination and dreams.

At first glance, it may appear that Rainbow, Lavender, Amanda, and the other characters in the book are imaginary—especially the ones you'll find running through the pages and hiding in the paragraphs—but they tend to become real when you see them in your mind. If you read between the lines and look below the surface, you may feel their thoughts and see their experiences vibrate with energy. You might recognize parts of yourself in their personalities or see familiar pieces of their experiences in your life.

Many of the situations and scenes portrayed in this book are symbolic of spiritual reawakening and represent the mystical knowledge I've acquired through many lifetimes. But some of the stuff is merely my interpretation of what I've found to be true for me. There's more to truth than meets the eye and to see it clearly, you have to see it for yourself. That's the joy of knowing. If you look within the mirror of your thoughts, feelings, experiences and dreams, you'll see the reflection of your spiritual knowledge and rediscover the essence of your soul.

As I hope you'll also discover in the magical world of your inner knowledge, Rainbow is more than she appears to be—just as in your world, you're more than you appear to be. As you open yourself up to seeing who you really are, and you begin to travel a mystical journey into your soul, keep in mind that the book only appears to be a reality and the characters only seem to be an illusion. The truth of the matter is: The words are an illusion, but the world they've created is real.

Prologue

Somewhere Over the Rainbow ...

"Lavender, what are you going to name yourself this time?"

"I'll call myself Amanda. I like the energy vibration of the name." Looking at the misty images in her mind, she saw that Amanda's parents, Beth and Jim Millenum, were anxiously awaiting her arrival but she kept procrastinating, trying to find a good excuse not to be born. Time was running out and she knew she'd have to make her entrance soon.

"On second thought, do I really have to experience the reality of reincarnation on earth again?" she asked. Rephrasing her words, she said, "I'd rather go to school in the universe. There are a few more things I'd like to know about my true spiritual nature."

"You chose another lifetime on earth to evolve your soul and you've agreed to be born now," Rainbow said. "Besides, you've just opened up a separate space for a parallel vibration of energy and you have to put it *somewhere*. Amanda will need your help as she learns how to apply her spiritual knowledge in the physical world." Rainbow shimmered in the sunlight. "And then there are the experiences in Egypt you said you'd take care of."

A foreboding sense of fear began to slowly surround Lavender as shadowy images loomed in her thoughts and wove silently through her mind. "But I thought Egypt was scheduled for another lifetime," she whispered, hoping to postpone it.

"It's scheduled for right now, but you think it's later. When you're done with your doubts about remembering Egypt and your second thoughts about experiencing life as Amanda, I'll meet you over at the school. You can register for classes as soon as Amanda decides to be born. And you don't have much more time to play around with," Rainbow said pointedly.

"*Time—?*" Lavender repeated suspiciously, stretching the word and watching it bounce into what seemed like a never-ending vibration of energy as she listened to it echo through the space of all eternity. "You're not going to try to teach me how to synchronize time and space again, are you?"

Rainbow smiled. "You'll learn about time and space for yourself in your earth experiences and through your nearly-remembered knowledge. When you clear up your thought perspectives, and see the light within yourself, you'll see the truth about your spiritual nature. Then you'll know who you really are and you'll be able to find the way home." With those words, she disappeared into a misty cloud somewhere above herself.

Watching the ethereal mist in the universe circle around Rainbow, Lavender knew she hadn't really disappeared. It just looked that way. But even though she knew that, she felt a sinking sensation in her soul and thought she'd somehow lost touch with her.

How do I get myself into these predicaments? she wondered, feeling as if she was falling through time and space somewhere between the universe and the earth. She began to think that Amanda's earth experiences weren't going to be any fun at all. Understanding your true spiritual nature sounded serious.

One

Raindrops

Twenty-one years later ...

"Follow your dream," the rainbow said.

Amanda heard the rain tapping softly on the window as if it were inviting her for a walk. Rubbing the sleep out of her eyes, she dressed in blue jeans and an oversized sweatshirt, then opened the door and stepped barefoot into the rain.

Walking through the rain, she pondered the questions and thoughts that had prompted her dream. What is life all about? Who am I? Why am I here and why do I feel so lost? She shivered, feeling as if she was a ghost walking through a foggy mist. Sometimes it seems as if I'm not real, as if my life is just a dream.

The raindrops were like warm splashes of misty memories drifting through time. Looking into the images, she saw herself as a child running free and happy through the rain, loving the feel of the gentle raindrops on her face and the soft, wet earth beneath her feet. Rainbows had been her most special treasures. She smiled, remembering her feelings whenever she'd seen a rainbow shimmering in the misty sunlight.

When she was fourteen, her science teacher told her that rainbows were composed of the seven natural colors of the energy spectrum. Red, orange, yellow, green, blue, indigo, and violet. Rainbows were an optical illusion—prisms of color reflecting sunlight, air, and moisture from the rain. But she'd known that rainbows were really much more than that; there was a magical essence about them. She remembered telling her teacher that you couldn't define a rainbow in scientific terms. Somewhere inside your soul, you just had to believe that rainbows were real.

Looking up at the sky, she searched for a rainbow but clouds covered the sun. Listening quietly to her thoughts, she heard the rearranged words of her favorite song play in her mind.

Somewhere, over the rainbow, clouds are clear.
There's a place that I dreamed of once in a time now here.

Someday I'll wish upon my star and wake up with a rainbow all around me.

Where clouds are clear and light is bright, that's where I'll find me.

"I wonder if there really is a place somewhere over the rainbow where I can find myself?" she whispered.

The clouds began to clear—becoming iridescent, then luminous and then transparent—and a rainbow appeared in the sunshine, showing her a path inside its colors. Stepping into the rainbow, she saw a golden key in the sunlight and heard herself say that she wanted to understand her true spiritual nature.

A buzzing noise interrupted her dream, scattering the images into fragments. The color at the top of the rainbow, she thought drowsily. The color is lavender and a door was opening into a sphere of light. "This time I'll remember who I am," she promised. Half-awake, she scribbled a few words in her dream journal then drifted back to sleep, falling into a blur of misty images in a timeless and almost-forgotten world.

A loud clap of thunder rolled through the clouds and lightning flashed across the universe. "Follow your dream," Rainbow said. The words sounded like a whisper, echoing through the winds of time.

Listening to the raindrops tap softly on her window, she wasn't sure if she was dreaming or if she was awake. Looking at the digital clock, she saw that time had disappeared. The thunderstorm must have blown out the electricity and the clock stopped sometime during the night, she thought. More than anything else, she wanted to follow her dream—to go walking through the rain and find herself somewhere inside the magical world of a rainbow.

Kicking off the covers, she wondered what was real. Walking in the rain and traveling through the colors of the rainbow looking for herself had seemed to be the most natural thing in the world. She smiled as she saw an image of herself standing at the top of a rainbow. If the dream was real, she thought, I'd fall through the colors and plummet to earth.

Getting out of bed, she mumbled, "This is real life and I have to go to work today. If I'm late one more time, I'll get fired." But the dream had held a promise she wanted to discover. She sighed and stretched. The dream will just have to wait, she thought, until I can find the time to explore it.

Two

Circles and Parallel Perceptions

"She did it again," Lavender said to Rainbow. "She remembered, then forgot as soon as she knew. When is she going to wake up and listen to me?"

"You have to make sure she's paying attention to you and focusing her awareness into your energy vibrations," Rainbow said. "She thinks you're a ghost and she sees me as a misty dream image and a childhood memory."

"But she said she wanted to understand her true spiritual nature. She felt it was very important to find out what her life is all about and she was on the verge of knowing what's real and remembering her promise to me."

"Maybe you could look inside her dream, Lavender, instead of only observing it from one point of view," Rainbow suggested.

"Maybe her dream is how she'll remember who she is. Then she won't feel so lost and she'll be able to find her way home," Lavender said. "Maybe she isn't ready to see the light within herself and that's why she can't seem to clearly see you or me, or find the time to understand herself."

"Maybe Amanda is a little lost in earth energies," Rainbow replied, leafing through the pages of an open book. "Lately I've noticed that she's been going around in circles." She looked at Lavender. "I think she needs your help to remember the reasons for her reincarnation."

"Isn't the purpose of life, and the whole earth experience, to come full circle so you can completely understand yourself on every level of awareness and evolve your soul into a higher vibration?" Lavender responded. Her voice dwindled to a whisper and she barely heard a parallel thought about expressing your true nature.

"Maybe you've forgotten the real purpose of Amanda's existence in this lifetime," Rainbow said.

"I tried to remind her of her purpose in this life by opening the book for her, but she got lost in one of the pages," Lavender replied. "I think she got stuck *somewhere* in the real world and now I have to read the book to find her." She sighed, remembering that it wasn't the only time she'd lost her. "Keeping track of your parallel self is very challenging at times," she muttered quietly.

A memory tumbled into her mind. "And then there was the time that I, uh, sort of tripped her, but it was an accident." She looked at the image in her thoughts. "Umm, to be perfectly honest, it wasn't an accident. I did it on purpose. It was either her or me, so I tripped her and watched her fall." She paused, seeing it happen all over again. "I feel so guilty about it now," she added, remembering that confession was good for the soul.

"I know all about that," Rainbow said. "She lost her balance for a moment but she survived the fall. The only thing that got hurt was her pride and her sense of harmony is still a little out of sync. She forgave you a long time ago and was actually very grateful for the push."

Lavender lightened up immediately. It was such a relief to let that burden of guilt go. She smiled at Rainbow. "In Amanda's dream, I noticed you showed her how to find the way home."

"It's no secret," Rainbow replied, shimmering in the misty sunlight.

An image of a golden key illuminated by a ray of light appeared in Lavender's thoughts. She turned the key over in her mind, wondering what it opened. Someone—a philosopher or a writer, she thought—had once said that realms of enlightenment were worth reaching for.

"Sometimes the earth experience is only a test to help you remember who you really are," Rainbow said. Appearing to change the subject, she continued, "I think you might be letting your perceptions get in the way of Amanda's thoughts. Maybe you're the one who is going around in circles."

Rainbow's comment about circles made Lavender's thoughts spin. "Wait a minute," she said. "*Your* perceptions seem to be influencing *my* thoughts."

"Why wait?" Rainbow asked. "You have all the time in the world but Amanda still believes in linear time and thinks that the world is exactly what it appears to be. Since a major part of your homework assignment in the Reality Awareness class is to help her remember who she really is so she can see what her life is all about, it might be a good idea for you to begin at the beginning and explain circles to her. And while you're doing that, try not to get her any more confused than she already is."

"Okay, but I'd like to do one thing at a time," Lavender replied. "Helping her find herself so she can remember who she is might prove to be a bit difficult. Every time I say hi to her, she gets confused." But that's because gravity pulls down her thoughts, she reminded herself, thinking about the time she'd tried to raise Amanda's thoughts above that lowly energy when she'd wanted to know what everything is relative to by explaining that thoughts are lighter than air and energy is always in motion. She grimaced at the image of Newton-Einstein, sitting beside her in the Energy and Matter class.

But that's neither here, there, nor anywhere right now, she thought, remembering where she was and seeing that she'd jumped into the middle of things again. She didn't want to misplace her awareness by letting herself get sidetracked away from the current conversation. In the first place, she didn't want to miss anything. And in the second place, it didn't look good for appearances if you faded off into space or floated in and out of the picture when someone was talking to you. She tried to straighten out her thoughts as she focused her attention on Rainbow's words.

"As you're explaining simultaneous spaces and circular time to Amanda, don't linger too long with linear thought perspectives and logical image perceptions," Rainbow said. "They can be very limiting and tend to tie up your thoughts and cloud your images. And you know what happened the last time you misunderstood time/space energies. You fell through your dimension and got stuck in the vibrations of matter."

"Yeah, I know," Lavender replied. "It was awful. Being lost and living on earth without my real knowledge was a terrible experience. I forgot that I was truly a spiritual being and I wasn't able to really accomplish anything, anywhere, no matter where I turned. I just kept going around in circles and it seemed to take forever to remember my knowledge and find myself again." She shuddered at the memory, not realizing that she was seeing future images that presented themselves in a past frame of time. "I'll be careful to keep my thoughts clear."

"By the way, Lavender, thanks for dedicating your book to me, but are you sure I'm your teacher? What if I can learn a lot of things from you?" Rainbow asked. "What would you think if I told you that you're more than Amanda's parallel self? And have you ever considered the possibility that we're all much more than we appear to be?"

"The thought has crossed my mind once or twice," Lavender replied.

"Maybe you're not seeing the whole picture all at once. What if I'm the future, you're the past, and Amanda is the present?" Rainbow continued. "Or what if we're all one and the same? And while we're on the subject of synchronization, why do you think Amanda feels out of tune with herself?"

There she goes again, Lavender thought, wondering what she meant and half-thinking that she was either out of her mind or dreaming. Some of the things Rainbow says every now and then have double meanings and can be confusing from time to time. She's probably playing mind games with linear time and logical thought perspectives to see if I can keep all the vibrations of energy in my here and now perceptions of reality.

But when she says *present*, does she mean a gift or is she talking about time? Rainbow knows very well that she's my present. And what does *we're all much more than we appear to be* mean? Maybe we just don't see all of ourselves at the same time. And it's obvious that Amanda feels out of tune with herself because she doesn't remember who she really is.

Rainbow smiled at Lavender's thoughts. "Intellectualizing thoughts is quite different from intuitively knowing that those same thoughts are true," she said. "There's a world of difference between the two."

A light flashed through Lavender's mind. "I know what she's trying to do. She's testing me to see if I'll trip on my thought perspectives. I'm not going to fall for that again," she said to herself, gathering her energies around her. Surrounding herself with boundaries made her feel safe, like a caterpillar in a cocoon.

Despite her seemingly clear thoughts, she felt a little dizzy and disoriented as if she was wandering through a foggy cloud somewhere in her mind. Thoughts of nearly-remembered knowledge began to slowly weave through her mind as misty images painted words with colors of light that splashed through her awareness.

She sensed that her energies were beginning to vibrate in a circular motion as thoughts, misplaced in time and space, now spun to the surface. Images of the sunrise seminar she'd attended with Amanda spiraled into her thoughts as she watched her manuscript rearrange itself again. Paraphrased words and revisions ran like illusions of reality through the pages, playing a game of hide 'n seek between the lines, jumping in and out of paragraphs and dancing with images of energy and matter through the chapters.

As the words whirled through her mind, she watched her images start to scatter and saw that her thoughts were coming apart at the seams. She tried to line up her thoughts with their images but before she could catch them all, her thought/images fragmented into multicolored prisms of light and showers of knowledge.

She dashed for cover, but wasn't quick enough and the energy expressions of all her experiences reverberated through her mind at the same time. She looked at the myriad motions of matter and sighed. "Sometimes life is much easier to understand if you don't try to look at everything all at once," she said. The thought/images began to slow down and pieces of the picture began to fall into separate spaces.

That sounds like something Amanda would say, she thought. It sounds limiting and linear. Plus the whole idea of *one thing at a time* is too far out of the realm of logical possibilities because I know from past experience that more than one thing is always happening at the same time, even if I'm not aware of all of it or can't keep everything centered in my mind. I have a feeling Rainbow would tell me that the only way to see things clearly is to look for myself, she thought. She didn't miss the implication of looking for herself; she chose to ignore it. It was just too much to handle all at once.

I hope she doesn't remind me that I'm a mirror image of myself or that parallel perceptions are really the same thing, viewed from separate lines of thought that vibrate to similar levels of energy and awareness in the same space, she thought to herself. "The earth and the universe vibrate in harmony with one another." Rainbow's words echoed in her mind.

"The only thing that distinguishes all your thought/images for you is that you see them happening in different dimensions and you're placing those dimensions into parallel places in your mind. You're looking at separate frames of time/space energies and motions of matter, but it's all the same reality. When you view yourself from clear thought perspectives, you see your image perceptions about yourself change."

"Are you enjoying this conversation with yourself?" Rainbow asked.

Lavender reflected on the thoughts and images in her mind, just now realizing that she'd been talking to herself again. "Yes, I am," she replied. "And I think I'm learning a lot."

"The round-about way you have of looking at things is making me dizzy," Rainbow said, smiling at her. "Just watching you go through your motions is very entertaining and at times, it's quite enlightening."

Lavender emerged into the sunshine, sparkling into vibrant prisms of color. "I really love being a free spirit," she said, smiling and stretching her arms open wide. "I imagine Amanda enjoys being a butterfly as much as you enjoy being a rainbow. And the illusion is fun, don't you think?"

Rainbow burst out laughing, just for the joy of knowing.

"I'd like to get Amanda straightened out on circles so I think I'll begin at the beginning," Lavender said, suddenly becoming very serious about her spiritual studies.

"If there really is a beginning, and if there ever was a beginning to begin with," Rainbow replied, "then it would probably be a good place to start."

"If there really is and ever was a beginning to begin with," Lavender repeated slowly to herself, looking into the words to see what they said, "then it would probably be a here and now parallel perception of its own past/present/future image."

But how do you know which image is real if they're reflections of one another? she wondered. And if time is simultaneous, and all experiences are occurring in the same dimension of space at similar vibrations of energy, and reality is happening on every level of awareness concurrently, then how in the world would you know where to begin to look for yourself?

"This could be confusing," she said, trying to synchronize her thoughts and center her awareness at the same time. She wondered if Amanda would think the beginning was the end or if the end was really the beginning, hoping that she wouldn't get stuck somewhere in the middle.

Three

A Lavender Sphere of Light

Before the Dream; Before it all Began This Time ...

Lavender stretched and shimmered in her sphere of light, watching highlights of her earthly experiences flash through her thoughts. "It was only a dream," she said. "It wasn't real."

Floating through time and space within the multi-dimensional realms of her experiences, she focused her thoughts into her spiritual evolvement. Visions of wisdom not yet acquired, and experiences not yet understood and balanced, were reflected in karmic destinies to be explored. She woke with a shock, realizing she'd have to return to earth. It was an awful thought. Of all the places she could go, earth was the last place she wanted to be.

She sighed with despair. It seemed like only yesterday she'd left there and now today, it looked like tomorrow she'd be right back where she started. Opening the images of almost-forgotten memories, she saw that the pictures of her two previous lifetimes were shrouded in a cloudy mist. Africa drew muddy images and Egypt inspired shadowy shapes of fear. She didn't know what she was afraid of, but just the thought of experiencing another incarnation on earth made her shiver deep inside her soul.

Dreary thoughts began to crowd her mind. Earth is too limiting; it seems there's never enough time to do everything. Gravity drags you down, energy vibrates too slowly and there's not enough space to move around in. Things—real, tangible things—get in the way and matter up your thoughts. You have to abide by the rules of illusion and the question of what's real keeps coming up. Worst of all, you're stuck in a physical body; you're not a free spirit anymore.

An image of a butterfly soaring somewhere over a rainbow into the universe fluttered into her thoughts. She wanted to be that butterfly, free in spirit and form, flying through the clouds into the sunlight. Despite her reluctance to reincarnate, thoughts of exploring new vistas and expanding her horizons flowed into her mind. She wavered ambivalently. Although living on earth—actually being there in person—wasn't something she was looking forward to, she remembered that some of her experiences had been wonderfully exciting and illuminating. Wondering what to do with her life and what experiences to create, she saw part of a page from a book appear in her mind.

A soul can choose to experience the earth environment in a spiritual vibration to gain knowledge, and that same soul can choose to be inside the physical energies of their experiences to acquire understanding. To evolve into enlightenment, a soul must harmonize spiritual knowledge with physical understanding.

Earth is like a school where you learn how to master the energies of all your experiences. If you do it right, you advance into higher vibrations of knowledge. If you do it wrong, part of your essence and the energies of your experiences are left hanging in the balance and you must return to see the truth within yourself and to put your experiences in their proper places.

If a soul views all their experiences in a clear and positive way, life can be enjoyed as a wonderful adventure and a magical, mystical journey into awareness and light. Life on earth can be freeing and empowering, as well as fun and rewarding.

Yeah, like hell, she thought darkly. Life can be disastrous if a soul applies negative energy into their thoughts or if they misunderstand the meanings within their experiences. And too many souls get lost in earth energies because they don't remember who they really are.

Wavering images of her soon-to-be life on earth began to focus blurrily in her mind. The scenes fluctuated and fragmented in an ever-changing flow of energy. Trying to look at all the expressions of her possible experiences, she couldn't clearly see what they were or what they might become. Not that it mattered right now, but she did want to know how the images would probably take shape and form in her life.

Not knowing what to expect, she began to get worried. What if the spiritual signposts that showed the way to wisdom and enlightenment, or the inner images that would guide her on her journey home, were hidden or safeguarded in the light of the universe and she couldn't remember how to read the images or recognize the signs?

The more she tried to see through the cloudy images in her mind, the more she became aware that—for some unknown reason—she couldn't tune into the images properly.

Shifting her focus, she watched abstract idea/pictures float through her mind. Earth could be a masterpiece of colors drawn on your thoughts or a mosaic of fragmented images. It could be a magical world of imagination or a mystifying land of illusion. It could be a golden sunrise or a majestic sunset. The colors could be clear or clouded. It was always your choice, as a creator, of how you wanted to paint and color the images of your life. You decided how to focus your feelings and how to shape and sculpt your thoughts and their forms into expressions of energy.

When you imbued your images with your essence, they came to life. When you were in the energy of your experiences, you could change their vibrations to create new images and expressions. You could put finishing touches on interrelated situations and scenes you'd created in other time/spaces. You could enhance and enrich all your experiences with flairs of previously-acquired learning and talents, and add flourishes of universal light and sparkles of spiritual insights.

You could even introduce a touch of drama or humor to the events and experiences you'd envisioned if you got bored with the way the picture was playing out, or if you just wanted to create more excitement and variety in your life. It was as easy as changing your mind and as quick as rearranging the energy of your thoughts and their images. You always had free will to do anything you chose to do with your creations and circumstances, but you had to accept the consequences for your attitudes and actions in all your experiences. On earth, it was known as *Creating Your Own Reality.* In spiritual realms, it was referred to as *Balancing Your Karma.* Some souls misunderstood the concept, not recognizing that they were working with universal power.

Lavender laughed in spite of her dilemma about how she wanted to shape and color her earth experiences. In a previous lifetime as a teacher she'd learned from one of her students that creating your own reality was, in real life, playing with the images of your illusions.

Floating on a cloud between the earth and the universe, and centering her energies into the present, she saw a misty image of a rainbow holding an open book. Looking at the blank pages, she began to pencil in phrases and magical metaphors as she watched sketchy shapes of future events and shadowy images of past experiences loom in her mind.

Looking into a nearly-forgotten lifetime where she knew she'd acquired a vast amount of spiritual enlightenment and mystical knowledge, she saw that she'd either lost or misplaced those experiences. The missing memories have to be *somewhere;* they couldn't just vanish into *nowhere*, she thought to herself. Two things were clear: She wouldn't be able to bring her spiritual knowledge with her into this lifetime because she simply couldn't remember it and if she wanted to find her knowledge, she'd have to look into the shadowy images that moved silently through her thoughts.

Bravely focusing her awareness into the shadowy images, her throat began to hurt. You're not supposed to feel pain unless you're physical, she thought, wondering how that had happened. An image of an old, bearded man holding something in his hand emerged from the shadows and she heard an echo of a voice that was strangely familiar. "To be a free spirit on earth—really free—you have to remember who you are."

"But it's so difficult to **remember** who you are when you're there," she said. "Once you're burdened with a body, you're subject to earthly laws of energy. You tend to forget that you're truly a spiritual being and life turns into a game of illusion because you think that you're only a physical being."

The image began to fade and float away. It seemed that he had nothing more to say. The dark, menacing shadows began to surround her and she felt an almost-overwhelming sense of fear.

Quickly she brushed the shadowy thought/images and feelings aside, replacing them with the energy of universal light. She felt better immediately and saw that she was now traveling through a bright, warm ray of sunshine. Everything was clear and shimmery, luminous and transparent all at once and she knew her soul was vibrating in harmony with the light.

"Words just can't describe the light; to really see and understand the light, it has to be experienced," she whispered, wishing that everyone could experience the joy of knowing and feeling and being in the light. If you knew that universal light was a reflection of the light within yourself, you could recognize your soul.

A thought sparkled in her mind. It would be a novel idea to create a magical world of images drawn from words. Looking into the thought, she saw an image of a scroll and read the opening words. *From the pictures in your mind come words* ... She heard an echo of a silent voice say, "Share the secrets of spiritual knowledge with words." Her throat began to hurt again.

A cloud obscured the light, drifting into her thoughts and weaving through her images. Sinking into the clouds and bouncing through turbulent air in the earth's atmosphere, she sensed that she'd lost touch with herself and was now out of sync with her spiritual energies.

She noticed that the sky was changing and that she was beginning to wander through her thoughts about living on earth as images of experiences began to take shape and form into the vibrations of solid matter. This is getting real, she thought.

A rainbow shimmered in a misty ray of sunlight. "I want to remember my spiritual knowledge and harmonize the energy vibrations of my soul with universal light," she said, feeling as if she was in two separate worlds at the same time. Trying to rise above the ethereal mist over the rainbow, she saw that she'd been falling through time and space and was now entering the energies of earth.

"It must be later than I thought," she said to herself. "This is not a good way to begin a new incarnation," she added. Entering a physical life without clearly knowing what she was going to do or how she was going to do it, and with only a glimpse of why, she felt like crying.

"Are you ready to be born?" Rainbow asked.

"No, not yet," Lavender replied. "I have some serious doubts and second thoughts about my upcoming earth experiences," she said, feeling very frightened by the shadows that surrounded her.

"I'd feel more spiritual if I could bring my knowledge with me," she whispered. An image of a golden key flashed through her mind. "This time, I'll remember who I am," she promised herself, wishing with all her heart that she knew who she'd been before.

Four

Down to Earth

Lavender watched Amanda fall backwards through the rainbow. Swirling, spiraling forms of energy spun all around her as she catapulted without rhythm and harmony through colors of light, doomed to crash into whatever awaited her. Misty memories and shadowy images rushed past her awareness as she plummeted toward earth.

Lavender breathed a deep sigh of despair. Looking into her energies, she saw that her thoughts were cloudy, her images were scattered and everything seemed to be out of sync. Lightning flashed somewhere in the universe, illuminating a rainbow and Lavender floated above herself.

Amanda felt totally disconnected. It must be an accident, she thought. I must have fallen. A misty image of a lavender sphere of light floated through her mind and she sensed that someone had tripped her at the top of a rainbow. But who? she wondered. And more importantly, why?

Feeling lost, she looked around trying to see where she was, but everything was foggy and seemed unreal. Thunder rolled through the clouds as lightning flashed across the universe. With a shock that reverberated through her soul, she realized that she was stuck in the energy vibration of a physical body. "Let me out of here," she screamed.

Someone else must be masterminding my fate, she thought. I know I wouldn't do this to myself. I vowed I'd never reincarnate again, not after what happened in Egypt. The memory flashed through her awareness, then disappeared into darkness as if she'd turned off a light somewhere in her soul. She shivered with a foreboding sense of fear, somehow managing to free herself from the restrictive energies of a physical form. How on earth did I get myself into this predicament? she wondered.

"Perspectives," Rainbow said. "You tripped on your thought perspectives."

What am I doing here? she wondered, oblivious to the rainbow energies vibrating all around her. And why am I here? Earth is the last place I ever wanted to be. Is this a test or am I here to learn something? Calming herself so she could think clearly, she looked into her thoughts and saw double images. The fall must have blurred my vision, she thought. "Is there a higher reason or purpose for being here?" she quietly asked herself. There didn't seem to be anyone else to talk to.

Feeling a dense cloud surround her, she realized that she was about to be born. Being this close to what appeared to be her inevitable birth, with no memory of why she was here or what she was going to do with her life, or even of choosing this incarnation for herself, she became frantic.

"Now wait just a minute here," she said. "I have some serious doubts and second thoughts about this matter." Time was running out and she knew she'd have to find some answers soon if she was going to save herself from experiencing another lifetime on earth. It was an awful thought.

She felt as if she was precariously balanced between knowing and unknowing. One wrong move now and she was sure she'd be sentenced here for a long time, doomed to an unknown destiny. Feeling quite shaky, she tried to hold on to her thoughts, but couldn't tune into a clear picture. She sensed that her frame of mind was a little out of sync, maybe even warped a bit by the turn of events, but she couldn't seem to collect her energies and get centered. Images were wavering in and out of her mind, her thoughts were spinning and she felt dizzy and disoriented.

She knew the answers she was looking for were just out of reach, just beyond the grasp of her understanding. Focus, she told herself. Focus clearly into one thought at a time. A shadowy image of an old, bearded man floated into her mind but the image wouldn't stay in place; it kept fading away. As the image disappeared, she watched herself enter a parallel place somewhere between the earth and the universe—a duplicate dimension that was strangely familiar—and she heard an echo whisper her name in a sudden gust of wind that blew through her soul.

She knew she'd been here before—experienced this place before—but couldn't remember where or when. The déjà vu feelings seemed unreal, as if she'd seen and felt the images in a dream or read them in a book. The place was filled with shadowy spaces and shapes of past events and future experiences that loomed silently through her thoughts; the feelings and images were interwoven with fear in a timeless frame of energy.

She'd always thought herself to be a brave soul, fearless enough to find the truth within all her experiences. Concentrating her attention and summoning every bit of her courage, she looked into the shadows and knew that she'd chosen to find her spiritual knowledge from the past and place it in the present, but fear shrouded the rest of the memory in darkness.

As the recognition flowed through her awareness, Amanda sighed, practicing her breathing. I did it again, she thought. I slipped out of the vibration of my true spiritual nature for a split second in time. "It was those damn earth energies," she muttered, wondering if there was any possible way out of the incarnation she'd created for herself, even though it looked like it was probably too late to do anything about it right now. Maybe the opportunity will present itself later, she thought.

Resignedly accepting her imminent birth, she hovered on the ceiling and watched the activities. Her new mother seemed to be in a lot of pain and was concerned because it was taking such a long time. Amanda debated whether to tell her that she was late because she'd had second thoughts about reincarnating, but decided to keep it to herself. This was the first time she was meeting her mother in person and wanted to begin their relationship on a friendly note. Her mother didn't seem to be listening anyway. She was concentrating all her attention on giving birth and was breathing strangely.

Amanda looked at her father and smiled at him. He didn't look at all like the archaeologist she'd known in Africa. He was standing behind her mother, whispering words into her ear. "Pant, honey. Short, shallow breaths. That's it. Now blow. You're doing great. One more deep breath," he breathed with her, "and now PUSH."

Amanda was embarrassed at her entrance. Advanced souls were supposed to waft gently into their bodies, on currents of light and energy, with their awareness completely clear. She had landed very ungracefully on her derriere into her new lifetime on earth. She burst into tears.

"It's a girl," the doctor said, holding her upside down and slapping her. Waving her arms in every direction, she tried to slap him back. Maybe he knew I said a swear word, she thought. Feeling uncoordinated and out of balance, she took stock of the situation, noticing that only her pride was hurt and her sense of harmony was a little out of sync. She began to hiccup. Trying to regain her composure, she took a few deep breaths.

The doctor placed Amanda in her mother's arms. She snuggled into the warmth, feeling safe and secure. Her father put his arms around them both, kissing them, and laughing and crying at the same time. "It's so cute the way she was waving her arms and putting her hands into fists," he said to the doctor. "It looked like she was trying to punch you."

Amanda heard Rainbow laughing and wondered how she could be so happy about her birth. It's humiliating to be stuck in a physical body, she thought, wondering who else knew about her entrance into earth energies.

Red-faced and more embarrassed than before, she decided that there were a few announcements she just had to make about birth to her mother and to the doctor, and to anyone else who might be listening. Looking into the thoughts and images in her mind for words to clearly express herself, she tried to talk. "On earth, you have a silly idea that birth is a celebration. Birth is really a supremely complicated exercise in mental maneuvering and energy revibration."

The words seemed clear enough to Amanda but sounded like gurgles when she spoke them. "It's an intricate process of mind over matter. The real miracle of birth is that a soul has somehow managed to synchronize an innumerable number of circumstances and energies and opportunities into the appropriate vibrations. When a soul gets everything in the right place at the right time, *that's* something to celebrate."

Getting caught up in the feelings of joy around her, she smiled, realizing that she'd just accomplished something very magical. It *was* kind of awesome, she thought, and even though her birth was far from perfect, it was still something to be proud of. Then she remembered where she was. "And the concept that birth is a new beginning of life is silly, too! Who would ever believe a thing like that?"

She looked at her mother. "No matter how many times you're born, it's very shocking to transform spiritual energies into physical energies. Even though you went through labor, I did all the work."

Her mother smiled at her with pure happiness. It was the nicest smile Amanda had ever seen and she loved her immediately. "She's so beautiful," Beth said to Jim. "Look at her big blue eyes and blond hair. She looks like a bright ray of sunshine."

"She does have a special glow about her," Jim replied, smiling at Amanda. She reached for his finger and held it tightly in her hand. We're forming a daddy-daughter bond, he thought, feeling a powerful surge of energy and emotion flow between them. But there's more to it than that, he sensed, wondering what it was. "Her eyes sparkle with light, as if she knows a secret she'd share with us if she could talk."

The nurse agreed with both of them as she gently took Amanda from Beth. "Look at this," she said. "She has a little bump on her right arm. It looks like a mosquito bite."

Amanda shivered instinctively, without knowing why.

"Maybe she's cold," the nurse said, wrapping her securely in a soft blanket. "I'm going to give you a nice, warm bath," she crooned to Amanda, "and then let you rest for awhile. Birth is hard on babies too," she said, smiling at Beth and the doctor.

Amanda felt trapped in her new body; it was too small and confining. Worst of all, it appeared to be solid. Trying to rise through the dense layer of physical energy that surrounded her, she fell back into her body, landing with a soft thud. Then she remembered the gravity of the situation she was in. After several attempts at synchronizing her thoughts with her projected images, she began to move upward, slowly at first, then more rapidly as the energy vibrations became finer.

Thank goodness, she thought. It isn't as solid as it appears to be. She practiced rising through the levels of rainbow-colored energies until her flights were smooth and rhythmic, and she could flow through the vibrations easily.

Floating above her newly-acquired physical body, she watched the nurse put a diaper on her. How disgusting, she thought. There are some stinky things you never get used to. The nurse began humming a song as she dressed her in a little pink gown. Amanda floated gently into her body as the nurse picked her up and softly rubbed her back.

That feels nice, she thought, listening to the melody as the loving touch of the nurse soothed her soul. After all the commotion of birth, it's good to have a hug from an old friend, she thought, recognizing her from a lifetime in Atlantis where they'd studied practical applications of universal energies. The nurse laid her gently in a bassinet and smiled into her eyes, as if she remembered her.

Amanda smiled back at her, then closed her eyes and drifted into sleep, watching sketchy shapes of her new incarnation show themselves in the mindscape of her dream images. Looking at the misty scenes, she didn't know how the images would form into experiences but the way they kept weaving in and out, and around and through her thoughts gave her the feeling that she'd have to put the pieces into their proper places.

Rainbow appeared and smiled brilliantly. "Welcome to the world, Amanda. You made a wonderful entrance, with such a promising beginning." She laughed. "I couldn't tell which way you were going to land the way you kept fluttering around and changing your mind. It was so much like you. But now that you're in a physical body, you have to abide by physical laws."

Amanda slowly opened her eyes and looked through a window at Rainbow. I've only been here twenty minutes, she thought. Birth was bad enough and now she has to remind me about the rules. She reverberated unhappily in her energies.

"You're too young to swear; you're not even supposed to be able to think or talk. People will treat you like a baby and you'll have to get used to it. It's part of the illusion. And please don't play energy games with your mother. She doesn't have any idea that you're an advanced soul. When you learn how to walk, you'll forget you can fly. You have to use words to communicate instead of images. Matter is slower than thoughts."

Amanda threw up. "Anything else I have to deal with here?"

"You seem to be a little cranky and irritable," Rainbow said gently.

Who wouldn't be, Amanda thought, if they tripped through the light and saw that they'd been reincarnated. Feeling the slow vibrations of earth energy close in around you is enough to make even the most highly-evolved soul cranky and irritable. She took a deep, shuddering breath, not feeling at all like herself. "It's just that I feel so ... *physical,"* she said, searching for the right word.

"I know exactly how you feel," Rainbow said reassuringly. "Before you completely adjust to earth energies, remember that one of the reasons for your reincarnation is to understand your true spiritual nature by applying your knowledge into all your experiences."

I've read this somewhere before, Amanda thought, trying to envision where she'd seen the words. She felt so energy-depleted from birth that all she wanted to do was go to sleep and dream. "It would be helpful if I knew where my knowledge was and I could find it when I wake up," she managed to say. An image of a golden key flashed through her mind.

"Remember your promise to Lavender," Rainbow said.

Amanda's thoughts and images began to fade. Before the pictures in her mind disappeared into misty dream images and cloudy thoughts, she knew she had to put the golden key in a safe place. Looking around herself for somewhere to keep the key that would open her spiritual knowledge, she saw a rainbow shining through a misty ray of sunlight. There's supposed to be a treasure at the end of the rainbow, she thought. A rainbow will keep it safe.

Five

The School of Spirituality

The school campus was surrounded with a softly-curving arc of light that reflected a majestic sunset of oranges and purples pulsating into the universe. The buildings and trees were bathed in subdued rays of light and hues of color that vibrated a magical aura of knowledge. It was a spectacular arrangement of energy.

"Oh, how super," breathed Lavender, in awe. "It's so beautiful. It looks like a replica of an earth university, except it has more ..." She paused, trying to find just the right word to describe the feeling of the campus. "Ambiance." The school radiated a quiet, peaceful atmosphere, almost sacred. It was a picture-perfect combination of earth elements blended with universal energy.

"I'm glad you like it," Rainbow said. "You created it from an image in your mind."

It's a perfect place to study spirituality, Lavender thought proudly. "Really knowing how to use the power of my mind, expressing my thoughts and feelings, and transforming my ideas into energy, then watching their images shape into forms of matter and motions of experiences is one of the most fulfilling rewards of having knowledge," she said happily.

"You still have a lot to learn," Rainbow said. "The concept of creating your own reality is where most souls begin to limit the expression of their power. You'll be choosing most of your classes based on what you feel you need to learn and the things you'd like to know more about, but there are a few required courses you have to take in order to graduate."

"Do I *have* to take them now?" Lavender asked. Maybe I could take them some other time, she thought to herself. "I mean, are these classes absolutely necessary? I thought that in this dimension my free will was more expansive." Fringes of illusion crept into her half-formed picture of reality. The corners of her ambient image of school began to curl up around the edges.

"You agreed to take these courses when you said you wanted to study spirituality," Rainbow replied. "Acquiring knowledge calls for a dedicated effort. Understanding knowledge is what allows you to learn. By learning, you begin to evolve. Applying knowledge in your experiences is what really sets you free to master energy and attain enlightenment. However, you can always change your mind. That's what free will is all about." Rainbow looked at her with more than a little bit of concern.

"What are the required courses?" Lavender asked, somehow knowing she wasn't going to like the answer.

Rainbow smiled at her. "I think you'll like the classes. They're **Reality Awareness**, **Time and Space**, and **Energy and Matter**."

Lavender knew why she'd been procrastinating; she'd flunked those classes in varying degrees in several of her earthly lifetimes. She wondered how Amanda was doing in her new physical body and how she was adjusting to earth energies. She breathed a sigh of relief, knowing she'd almost been caught in that vibration. If she hadn't realized at the last possible moment that she was paralleling herself, she would have been stuck in that little body too, for an entire lifetime. She shuddered at the thought.

The required courses aren't so bad if you look at them from this perspective, she reasoned. It's better than reincarnating on earth again. Even though I have to repeat the classes until I get them right, at least I'll be studying them in a spiritual vibration of energy instead of in a physical vibration. It didn't occur to her that Amanda had signed up for the same classes by choosing to experience another life on earth and Rainbow didn't have the heart to tell her; she'd find that out for herself soon enough.

"There's no time like the present to begin my studies," she said brightly, smiling at Rainbow. "See ya later." She wasn't looking forward to the Time and Space class, but knew she'd chosen to learn more about synchronicity. Walking into the ivy-covered building through the triple-arched entryway, she carefully chose the center arch, thinking that it represented the present. She knew from past experience that Rainbow liked to give surprise tests when you weren't in class and especially when you weren't expecting them.

At first glance, the Time and Space classroom looked like any other classroom in every world that she'd ever been in before. There was nothing distinguishing about this one, except for the doodles drawn on the chalkboard. Taking a closer look, she saw that the doodles weren't really what they first appeared to be. The drawing was actually a detailed diagram showing circles and spirals revolving around and rippling through one another in an ever-changing pattern, highlighted with sparkles of energy that were superimposed on and within the intricate design.

The diagram appeared to be moving, continuously changing shape and flowing with energy, but there were a few empty spaces where the energy was still and silent. In several other places, there were open areas that vibrated into thin air and yet the air with filled with something almost tangible that she couldn't quite see or touch. She sensed that the energy was very special; there was a magical quality about it. Studying it for a moment, she saw that the energy shimmered with an ethereal light, as if it was awaiting form and expression.

Picking up a piece of chalk and adding her own unique touches to the diagram, she sketched images of words in the open areas. Then she drew parallel lines through some of the circles and spirals, connecting a few sparkles in the empty spaces, not realizing that the pattern reflected her future experiences and past-life memories. Looking at the diagram, she saw that the parallel lines she'd drawn weren't perfectly straight; they merged into points that vibrated together. I wonder what that means, she thought.

Deciding not to give it a second thought right now, she looked around the room carefully, trying to notice everything. It was almost completely empty. There wasn't even a clock on the wall. That's probably because time is simultaneous, she thought, and where would the hands of the clock point to if time is happening at the same time in every dimension and vibration of energy?

A closed book sitting silently on a shelf drew her attention. Next to the shelf was a window that was shut and there was dust on the windowsill. She opened the window, trying to clear the air that seemed suspended in motion. The dust scattered in the sudden breeze. She knew her thoughts were wandering, but was trying to kill time until the rest of the students appeared. I can't possibly be the only soul in the entire universe who ever misunderstood time vibrations or misplaced dimensions of space, she thought to herself.

Sitting down at the desk, she opened the top. Looking inside, she saw the energy-form of her pencil. She touched it lovingly, feeling its familiar shape. Her pencil was a treasured reminder of the joy she'd found in writing in several of her earth incarnations.

"Where the heck are the rest of the students?" she wondered aloud. The words sent echoing reverberations throughout the room. Beginning to feel a little out of place, she wondered, this time silently, if she was in the right place. The sign on the door had said Time and Space. Maybe I've got the timing wrong and I'm too early, she thought. But then there's always the possibility that I'm too late, she added as an afterthought slowly drifted into her mind.

Or even worse—maybe I'm in the wrong space at the right time, or the right space at the wrong time.

Just then Rainbow walked in and looked at her hopelessly. "Your perceptions form your reality," she said. "And you are in the wrong space at the wrong time. You've warped the placement of your energies with your linear thought perspectives and your vibrations are out of sync. You completely missed Orientation and the welcoming talk on Energy Revibration. While you were deciding which path to take to begin your studies, the sessions were held in the next building where there are no arches that might represent past, present, and future."

Lavender responded with the hiccups. Time and space, and getting them synchronized, could really throw you for a loop.

Rainbow smiled at her. "It's becoming obvious that you're planning to make this difficult for yourself. You create your own reality here and it's just as real as it is on earth, even though it appears to be an illusion. Your experiences here are subject to the same universal rules and vibrations of energy. As you think it to be, so you create it. Or so it seems," she added. "In other words, you have to think of something before it can exist for you," Rainbow reminded her. "Consider all the possibilities. At the very least, ponder the probabilities."

Back to the basics, Lavender thought. It really does appear that I'm the only student in this class.

"If you center your awareness without clarity while you simultaneously focus your energies and attention into only one direction at a time, you'll see your thoughts express themselves in what appears to be limiting images," Rainbow said, responding to Lavender's unspoken thought and at the same time returning to her misplacement of time/space energies, she continued, "and because you thought it was impossible to be in two places at once, that's exactly what you experienced."

"I forgot that for a moment."

"Lavender, it's important for you in your spiritual studies to understand how time and space really work," Rainbow said. "Time and Space, in relation to all aspects of Reality Awareness and Energy and Matter, are the cornerstone concepts that build the foundation for acquiring and applying knowledge. Images and experiences, formed from thoughts and shaped by feelings, are the essence of energy in motion, manifesting in mirrored realms of matter and awareness."

I know all that, Lavender thought, embarrassed about the review and wondering at the same time why Rainbow was telling her this;

she should be telling Amanda. Before every incarnation, a soul was given a refresher course in energy vibrations. One of the most important skills you learned, very early in your evolvement, was how to rearrange and change the motions of energy into matter, and how to center your awareness into all the vibrations and expressions of your experiences simultaneously. It was fundamental in finding your direction and in maneuvering through earth energies if you ever wanted to see the light again.

"If there's no time like the present, then where have you put your past and your future?" Rainbow's voice interrupted her thoughts.

"They're all the same," she replied absent-mindedly, wondering why some of her experiences seemed to disappear into nothingness at times.

"Then why did you say *there's no time like the present?*"

Rainbow can certainly be picky, Lavender thought. "Because," she answered, "this time, this space, this dimension, this vibration, is what I choose to be aware of **now**. This is where I've placed my awareness and my attention—where I've focused my energy and directed my thoughts."

"But the present now is timeless. Doesn't it incorporate the past and the future within itself?"

"Yes," Lavender responded. "But there's no time like the present because it's all really an illusion, isn't it? You've said so yourself."

"But if there's **no** time, then where is the present?" Rainbow asked, persistent in her efforts to help Lavender see things clearly. "Aren't you completely obliterating several spaces of energy and more than one vibration of time from your awareness with that thought? And what about the limits you're placing on the vibrations and expressions of your experiences? Isn't reality happening everywhere at once?"

Focusing her attention into the lecture, Lavender began to see what she thought Rainbow was saying. Trying to answer all the questions in one sentence, she responded, "The present seems to be happening separately here and now, even though it's perpetually created and simultaneously influencing my past and future, just as those vibrations are constantly caused and effected by my present perceptions of feelings and my current perspectives of thoughts." Just like the ripples and sparkles of energy, she thought, remembering the diagram of circles and spirals on the chalkboard.

She knew she was slipping on the explanation; it didn't sound complete. There was something about probable realities that she was missing and something else about duplicate dimensions and parallel places. And there were alternate avenues of expression and other movements of energy that she wasn't including. It'll just have to do for now, she thought, wishing she could fully open up her awareness and see everything all at once.

Looking at the closed book on the shelf, she wondered what the words inside said. A thought that words were parallels of their own pictures that reflected mirror images danced into her mind as an idea/image leaped into her thoughts. For some unknown reason, seemingly from out of a clear, blue sky, she began to formulate and translate her thought vibrations into words.

"This is just an idea," she said, opening up her thought and looking into the image, "but I think I'd like to expand my imagination and acquire knowledge by exploring how words create a world within a book." She could see that she was stumbling on her words; they seemed to be separating from their energies in two dimensions, becoming parallels simultaneously, each word/thought becoming a transparent image/expression of itself.

She felt around in the desk for her pencil. "I'd like to enhance my awareness of word/thoughts and image/expressions by drawing pictures of pages—creating words from the images in my mind. I want to completely understand the energy vibrations of words so I can see how word energies vibrate and expand to create experiences as they open up inner knowledge from thought/images." As she began to flow into her words, she could feel her pencil begin to vibrate in her hand. "It's so interesting that words, in an earthly dimension and vibration of energy, are used to communicate when thoughts and their images show a universal understanding and say so much more."

She smiled at an image that sparkled in her mind. "Thoughts are like rays of sunshine that whisper images and feelings into motion. Images are a mystical blend of magic and mystery that bring meaning and understanding together with imagination and knowledge. Words weave in and out of thoughts and feelings as they inspire and create images in the process of forming ever-changing and intricate expressions of energy."

Barely pausing for a breath, she continued. "Words are like lyrics of a song played in tune with thought/images that create a symphony of sound vibrations. Thoughts are like musical notes that dance on a page in rhythm and harmony with their images, ever so gently reaching and softly stretching into a brilliant crescendo of awareness as they form sparkling lights and expressions of energy above and between, and in and through the melody of the words themselves."

Sunlight streamed in through the open window, forming magical and myriad patterns in the dust particles that were floating through the air. The words, it seemed, had taken on a life of their own—their vibrations moving through matter in time and space, their images springing into action—coming alive with energy in the light of awareness.

She looked out the window, gathering her thoughts. She'd become so enchanted in her own special world created by words that she'd dropped her pencil in the flow of images. She sorted through the images looking for her pencil, at the same time trying to keep the energies of words combined with their thoughts as she picked up her pencil and held it tightly in her hand. Still and silent words echoed in her mind as she looked at the closed book again, sitting on the dusty shelf next to the window.

You have to set words free to express themselves, she remembered, knowing that words, as they were being formed from thoughts, were really secret symbols of knowledge interwoven with universal light energies swirling in a magical, mystical mindscape of motion before their images shaped themselves into the energy expression of a book. A thought began to whisper itself into her awareness. Writing a book would be a magical way to share knowledge.

The thought sounded like a gentle waterfall of words, flowing softly and harmoniously into images. As the thought began to take shape, forming itself into a portrait of pages in her mind, she felt a surge of energy soar through her soul. "I'm going to open up and explore and expand the earthly energy vibrations of words," Lavender said, smiling at Rainbow. "It's a matter of illumination—of knowing what your thought/images and experiences are really saying and showing you about your true spiritual nature."

Rainbow returned her smile. "Keep in mind that universal knowledge that is shaped into a solid vibration of matter on earth sometimes settles like dust into silent words, and thought/images sometimes show themselves without motion and form. Words that are misunderstood, and thought/images that aren't recognized in the magical world of imagination, tend to become suspended in space and their power seems to become inactive in time."

"Words are like treasures, buried under layers of dust," Lavender mused. "When you blow off the dust and open a book and read the words inside, the thoughts again become myriad and magical images of motion, awaiting only form and expression to turn into experiences that reveal truth and knowledge."

Imaging thoughts of dusty words was enough to make her nose start twitching. Her sneeze scattered the dust, clearing the air for fresh words and thoughts, allowing new images to form and take shape—to be molded into matter and sculpted into symbols that showed the mystery of knowledge and the mastery of truth, all mirrored within the reflection of the words.

"There's a wonderful library on campus, Lavender, that you'll really like," Rainbow said thoughtfully. "It's the Light Library and it's filled with books that emanate energy in rays of light; the vibrations of words show images of knowledge as they draw pictures in your mind." Moving to the open window, sunlight shimmered through her colors. "And the energy is always in motion, so there's no dust for you to sneeze at."

If I created this campus, then I also created the Light Library and how does Rainbow know about it before I realized it? Lavender wondered. Maybe my center of awareness and focus of attention isn't as clear as it could be. Maybe I need to look more deeply into my thoughts—to expand my outlook and open my insights.

A sparkle of light danced in Rainbow's eyes. "Now that you've decided to be a writer, would you like to have a computer?" she asked. "It might be very helpful with your writing and you wouldn't have to talk with a pencil in your hand to express your thought/images. You could create and form a world of words directly into the computer from the pictures in your mind."

Lavender clutched her pencil close to her heart. "I love my pencil," she said. "I've always been able to make my points with it. Besides, my pencil sharpener is special; it's shaped like a light bulb." She wasn't about to give up her pencil, not even for a cosmic computer.

"But you don't really need a pencil here," Rainbow said. "You've advanced into a new age. You gave up your chisel and stone when pens and paintbrushes were invented. Why are you refusing to give up your pencil now?"

"My pencil is how I express myself and I like the eraser," Lavender replied. "It saves me a lot of time and trouble and I can erase my words if I don't like the shape they're taking. Pens are like promises; they're too permanent and always leave long-lasting effects. Paintbrushes have their drawbacks; they aren't definitive enough and only create traces and sketchy images. But brushes are good for bringing feelings up to the surface," she added softly. "And the colors can do wonders for your vibrations."

Wandering out of the present, with a far-away look in her eyes, she continued. "In the early days of expressing the pictures in my mind, when I was learning about the concept of communication and I was beginning to understand the essence of written images, the chisel and stone were the only tools available to me."

She felt as if she was in first grade again and thought that Rainbow might assign a composition entitled: *What I Did in My Past Lives*. I wonder why they're called past lives when all vibrations of time are simultaneous, she thought to herself.

"They're called past lives because the energy seems to be vibrating in slow motion, out of rhythm and sync with present time," Rainbow said, waiting while Lavender adjusted her energies so she could hear the simultaneous sentence. "And at the same time, future lives appear to vibrate at a faster rate of energy."

In a smooth and synchronized movement, returning to the present time and to the pencil/eraser image, Rainbow said, "With a computer, you can push a button to erase your errors, just by highlighting them. You can supersede any kind of mistakes and they disappear, just like magic."

I don't believe that for a minute, Lavender thought. I wasn't born yesterday. "They disappear just like magic sounds like a fairy tale," she said. "Are you sure?"

Rainbow smiled. "It's really a matter of awareness. Your mistakes have to be corrected first through understanding and action. Then they do more than disappear; they reappear in a new form as self-knowledge. But it's just as magical as pushing a button and as easy as rearranging energy."

Or sharpening your pencil, Lavender thought, looking at Rainbow. "Okay, I'll use the computer to transform my thought/images into words, but I'll keep my pencil too," she said, wrapping her fingers around it. "By the way, what exactly are the requirements for graduation?"

"You have to unearth the mysteries of the universe, and you have to learn ..."

I'd better rearrange the school structure, Lavender thought quickly as she changed the picture in her mind. This is more than a place to study. This is an entire dimension in which to learn.

"... how to apply your knowledge in every vibration of energy and awareness," Rainbow said, as other students began to walk into the classroom that was reshaping itself into images of experiences.

Six

Earth Energies

Amanda was becoming more adjusted to her new physical body every day, but there was something missing—something separate and apart from her that she felt deep inside her soul. No one seemed to recognize that she was a highly-developed spiritual being; they treated her like a baby.

Her mother talked to her a lot and read her wonderful stories about magical things. If only she remembered her true nature, Amanda thought wistfully, we could have meaningful, mind-to-mind conversations, transferring thought/images and sharing our inner knowledge. Her mother was warm and loving, but Amanda couldn't seem to communicate with her on a spiritual level.

Her father could sense his inner knowing, but couldn't connect the realities and bridge the knowledge into truth. She'd see the recognition flicker in his eyes and watch as he closed off the images inside his mind before they formed into thoughts and opened up into spiritual awareness. It was like he turned off a light switch but it wasn't electric current; it was universal energy. He seemed to misunderstand the vibrations of inner knowledge and wasn't able to express his thought/images and feelings in a way that fit his ordered world and his view of reality. So he simply ignored them.

Amanda felt like a stranger in a world that was upside down and unreal. Not having another soul nearby in physical form to communicate with made her feel even more separate and alone. She knew she'd soon forget the spiritual side of truth as the physical side of illusion became her reality unless she could find a way to remember her true nature.

She saw that her own spiritual awareness was beginning to drift in and out of her mind between her dreams and her daily life, and felt as though she was becoming more forgetful and disconnected from her true nature every day. But when she was sleeping, she knew her awareness was awake and she'd travel into the universe and talk to Rainbow. Sometimes she'd watch her teach classes at the School of Spirituality. It helped her stay in touch with her spiritual nature and Rainbow had a very interesting student named Lavender.

Amanda would listen to their conversations and understood almost everything they said. Rainbow and Lavender talked a lot about the appearances and manifestations of energy through perceptions of thoughts. It seemed to Amanda that Lavender had an uncanny knack for misinterpreting Rainbow's explanations and more often than not, she misplaced her inner knowledge and warped her thought/images by looking at only one frame of awareness at a time which caused her to view things from a limited perspective.

Rainbow kept reminding her that expressions of energy were really a matter of perspective and of clearly seeing the things that were right in front of you, but Lavender couldn't seem to see the entire picture all at once and the predicaments she unknowingly created because of it were sometimes very serious, but some of the situations were a lot of fun.

Amanda could see that Lavender was in a spiritual dimension of energy surrounded by a vibrant, radiating frame of universal awareness but whenever she misplaced her image perceptions or misapplied her thought perspectives, she slipped into a parallel dimension of energy that was similar to an earthly vibration. She wondered why Lavender was having such a problem with it. Mastering the energies of your thoughts and experiences seemed to be easy. But Reality Awareness was a confusing class in any dimension. At least that's what Lavender said from time to time.

Amanda floated up to the classroom. Rainbow was sitting in the open window transforming herself into rays of light as she talked to her students about the earthly appearances of universal energy. "A great number of souls get stuck in the energies of creating their own reality without completely understanding their true reality and their real power in creating it."

Looking directly at Lavender, she continued. "Quite often, they don't see the multi-dimensional vibrations of energy; they lose sight of the many expressions and manifestations of their experiences by only seeing one side or one piece of the picture clearly. This shows them a lopsided and limited vision of their reality and restricts the perceptions of their thought/images and their full power. They misplace their area of attention and misunderstand the vibrations of time, space, matter, and motion in a universal frame of awareness. On earth, as well as in every other reality, they misread their image perceptions and trip on their thought perspectives."

That'll never happen to me, Lavender thought. I know all there is to know about creating your own reality.

Amanda felt irritated with Lavender's lofty and arrogant attitude.

If she really knew all there was to know, she wouldn't be taking a class in Reality Awareness, she thought, wondering why it was so easy for her to tune into Lavender's thoughts. It was like reading her mind.

Rainbow smiled. "The awareness of your image perceptions and the way you feel about them forms the basis of your reality while it simultaneously creates the foundation for your thought perspectives. Sometimes the earth reality is the ultimate test to see the truth within ourselves."

"Then knowing the truth about your spiritual nature is the answer to what life is really all about," Lavender said.

"Yes, partly," Rainbow replied. "What are your image perceptions of your spiritual nature?"

"The images are blurry; they appear to be colors, vibrating like a kaleidoscope of energy that's constantly in motion around me," Lavender said. "But some of the vibrations feel limiting." Like earth, she thought.

If Lavender would only listen to herself, she'd see her true nature, Amanda thought, realizing that she knew what the energy vibrations of the colors were; she just wasn't paying attention to her images and focusing her awareness into her inner knowledge. The truth was in her words, but she wasn't recognizing the images. It's a good thing she plans to enhance her understanding of word energies by writing books in a spiritual frame of knowledge, she thought to herself.

Lavender's words *like earth* caused Amanda to wake up crying. For a moment, she felt as if she was falling before she remembered where she was. The thought that she would soon forget her spiritual nature began to seem very real.

To keep her inner knowledge intact, she flowed energy through her thoughts and focused their images into a tangible expression. Then she'd make her thought/images disappear. It was the closest she could come to exercising her spiritual energies while she was locked up in a physical body pretending to be a baby. She liked playing with illusions of reality; manifesting thoughts into things was an interesting game and helped to pass the time.

What bothered her most about the pretense of being a baby was dependence on other people. She'd always been able to take care of herself and it was frustrating to wait for someone to feed her when she was hungry and she absolutely hated wearing a diaper. Even though Rainbow had asked her not to play energy games, there were just some things she had to do for herself. It was rude to demand food by crying, and she didn't like to bother her mother at two o'clock in the morning, so she materialized her own bottle most of the time.

But every now and then, she cooperated in the baby games and cried to wake her mother up. It worked every time. Her mother would come into the nursery, rubbing the sleep out of her eyes and mumble, "Hi sweetie. Hungry? Wanna bottle?" It became a nightly ritual. She'd coo and gurgle, her mother would change her diaper, pick her up and take her into the kitchen to warm the bottle.

One night she was halfway through her breakfast in bed before she remembered to wake her mother up, but this time she forgot to make the bottle disappear. Just like always, her mother came into the room and started to mumble, "Hi hungry, wanna bottle," when she saw the bottle in Amanda's crib. Her eyes seemed to grow larger and she looked wide awake now. Amanda smiled innocently at her and shrugged her shoulders, making little baby sounds as if to say, "Oops. How'd this happen?"

Beth started muttering to herself. "Must've gotten the bottle in my sleep. Must've been half dreaming or something while I was feeding her. But I never feed her in here," she reminded herself. "We always cuddle in the rocking chair while I'm feeding her. And Amanda couldn't have gotten the bottle for herself." She squinted her eyes at the thought, as if she was picturing it in her mind and considering that it might be a real possibility.

"Don't be absurd," she told herself. "Amanda is only two months old. She couldn't possibly get her own bottle or feed herself. And I'm probably changing her diapers in my sleep too. This is just postpartum depression that the doctor told me about when he said my hormones would go back to normal." But even logical, rational explanations couldn't quiet the doubts in her mind. She was becoming a little concerned, but decided to keep it to herself. It wasn't the first time things like this had happened.

A few months later, after the bottle games got boring, Amanda was ready for some real food. When she tried to communicate to her mother that she wanted spaghetti with meatballs and garlic bread, she got creamy rice cereal with mashed bananas and stale crackers instead. It was absolutely revolting and she would have almost sold her soul for a slice of pizza.

There's only one thing to do about this, she thought. I'll just have to take matters into my own hands and send out for pizza. It's a good thing I remember how to change energy into matter, otherwise I'd starve to death before I got out of diapers. That was another thing she'd have to take care of. She decided to talk to her mother about early potty training and hoped her mother would interpret the thought/images clearly.

But the most immediate thought on her mind was food. With all her power, she energized her thoughts and imaged a pepperoni pizza in her mind. The pizza appeared out of thin air a few minutes later and so did Rainbow. Just as she was about to take a bite, Rainbow took it out of her hands.

"Amanda," Rainbow said, "I asked you not to play energy games with your mother. And creating Italian food is going too far." She took a bite of the pizza. "This is really good pizza, Amanda, but rules are rules."

"Just one tiny bite," Amanda begged, her little tongue hanging out of her mouth. "I haven't had pizza for centuries and the smell of it is making my mouth water." Rainbow picked up a tissue from the dresser beside Amanda's crib and wiped her mouth.

"I want my pizza," Amanda screamed. "I manifested it from energy into matter and now you're eating it." She tried to bite Rainbow, she was so angry, but Rainbow disappeared, taking the pizza with her.

Just then her mother came into the room. "Poor little baby," she said. "You're drooling. I'll bet you're hungry. I'll make you a nice, warm bottle of milk and give you a piece of Melba toast."

"Don't *poor little baby* me," Amanda screamed. "I'm a full-grown soul, and I want my pizza. Pizza, pizza, I want my pizza," she wailed.

Beth looked at her strangely. In between Amanda's screams, she could have sworn that she just said her first word and it sounded like pizza. Picking her up and trying to comfort her, she gently rubbed her back as she walked into the kitchen with her to get her bottle.

Amanda saw Rainbow over her mother's shoulder. "Why'd you eat my pizza? Now I have to eat this crummy biscuit and it tastes terrible. And if I have to drink one more bottle of luke-warm milk, I'll puke. And what about my free will? You're not supposed to interfere with my free will. Free will is my birthright," she screamed at Rainbow.

"Yes, Amanda, it is. But you have to remember that of your own free will, you chose to be in a physical vibration of energy and now your free will is governed by physical laws."

"But we both know that the universal laws of energy supersede all the physical laws," Amanda began, determined to have her pizza and eat it too. "It's so ..." she groped for just the right word to express what she was feeling. "It's so damned unspiritual of you to place a limit like that on my free will."

"I understand how you feel," Rainbow said quietly. "But your physical reality is part of a test to help you see who you really are. The test requires that limits be placed on your awareness. Within the energies of the earth environment, you have to remember that you're a spiritual being and you have to learn how to be true to yourself."

Amanda wanted to say that knowing about your spiritual nature made it extremely difficult to relate to the energy vibration of a physical body, and that total awareness would make it impossible to flunk any test because you would already know the answers, but didn't want to say anything in defense of the lifetime on earth that she was apparently doomed to have. Then she began to realize that if you applied your spiritual awareness into all your experiences in the first place, you wouldn't have to reincarnate to discover what life was all about, so she didn't say anything at all.

"Every soul can recognize their energy essence by looking for the truth within themselves and by clearly seeing their own inner light that will guide them into their spiritual awareness and set them free to rediscover their true nature," Rainbow said as multi-dimensional echoes of light and sound reverberated through the kitchen.

Beth jumped and almost dropped Amanda at the suddenness of the thunderstorm that had seemed to come from out of nowhere. Amanda's sobs turned into hiccups. Beth thought the hiccups were caused from crying, but Amanda knew they were really caused by her spiritual energies becoming completely unsynchronized and separated.

Seven

The Secrets of Nature

"Happy birthday, Amanda. Make a wish and blow out all the candles. If you blow out all the candles, your wish will come true but you have to keep it a secret."

Amanda looked solemnly at her parents. She couldn't understand why they thought birthdays were special; she thought they were silly. The main purpose of life on earth was to remember your spiritual nature and the true signposts on a soul's journey were measured by knowledge, not by years.

Taking a deep breath, she blew out all four candles on her cake. Now I can have my wish, she thought, wanting her friend to be real. Her mother had said he wasn't real because she couldn't see him.

Amanda had found him soon after she'd planted her vegetable garden. Her mother was planting flowers and asked if she wanted her own garden. She'd said yes; the earth needed to grow natural foods. Beth smiled and agreed to let her grow broccoli in the backyard.

The next morning, just before sunrise, Amanda began her garden by placing a circle of stones around the area her mother had said she could have. With special care, she watered the earth to make it soft and muddy. Then she held the seeds gently in her hands and whispered to them before planting them at the first rays of light.

She seems to be communicating with them, Beth thought, noticing the tenderness with which Amanda planted the seeds.

Amanda went outside every morning at sunrise and sat very peacefully beside her garden, talking to the seeds inside the earth, encouraging them to grow.

She looks like she's meditating, Beth thought, wondering why Amanda didn't like playing with dolls or toys—preferring real, living things instead, like the caterpillar she'd found a few months ago.

She seemed fascinated with the way the caterpillar wove its cocoon and then completely changed its form. She named her

Morpy and set her free when she became a butterfly. She even made up a story about what Morpy had done inside her golden castle—something about free spirits emerging into the light from the sun. It was a charming, magical tale and she thought that Amanda had a wonderful imagination.

Closing her eyes, she tried to remember everything Amanda had told her. She smiled as the memory became clear in her mind. The caterpillar lived underneath a leaf in a tree in Africa. One day, after a thunderstorm, she talked to the color at the top of the rainbow. When the caterpillar learned a special secret, it began to "morpy" into a bright and beautiful butterfly, and became a free spirit when it remembered that it was really a free spirit all the time.

It had only been hiding inside its castle because it was afraid of a shadow. When the light from the sun, named Ra, showed her a golden key that could open up magical things, the caterpillar remembered how to be her real self. And then she flew home, somewhere over the rainbow. Or maybe Amanda had said that home was somewhere inside the rainbow.

A few days after Amanda planted the seeds, little green shoots began to push up through the ground. Seeing them, she jumped up with joy and ran excitedly into the house, pulling her mother outside to proudly show them to her. "Look, mommy. My garden is saying hi," she said.

"You must have a magic touch," Beth replied, wondering if broccoli really grew that fast and what Amanda had said to the seeds.

After seeing the first leaf, Amanda laid on the ground next to her garden, resting her chin in her hands, intently watching her garden grow as other leaves began to appear. As they unfolded, she saw tightly-curled buds begin to form inside the leaves.

A few hours later a small, white flower appeared and a bright sparkle of light started to glow in the center of the first broccoli bud as it began to open up. The light grew brighter, forming into an image of a little boy with blond hair and blue eyes, just like hers. Sunlight shimmered all around him.

"Hi," Amanda said. "Who are you?"

"Adam," the sparkle of light replied.

Amanda smiled, feeling a surge of happiness inside her heart.

"We've been friends forever and I want to help you remember the secrets of nature and inner light," Adam said, smiling at her.

They spent every day together, sharing stories and secrets about magical things. On rainy days, they ran through the rain, searching the sky for rainbows when the sun appeared. On sunny days, they climbed trees and listened to the leaves whisper about the earth and the universe, the stars and the sky, the sun and the rain, and the wind and the clouds.

"Why is the sky blue?" she asked.

"It's how universal energy blends into earthly energy. The color blue also reflects the communication between your spiritual side and your physical side."

Amanda put her hand over her mouth. "Secrets," she whispered. "Why is the sun yellow?"

"The color of sunshine is the color of knowledge, and the energy of the sun reflects light in many different ways."

All the plants in her garden were beginning to open up, reaching and growing and stretching for the light of the sun. Amanda felt the same way, knowing inside that she was opening up her true nature and that she was free to grow in the light from the sun.

Then a few days ago Beth overheard her talking to the broccoli and asked who she was talking to.

"My best friend in the whole world, Adam," Amanda replied, telling her about all the special things she'd discovered. "I know how flowers and plants grow; they have nature spirits inside them and I made friends with them too. I can hear trees when they talk, and I'm part of the sun just like everyone is. And a rainbow even showed me how to fly."

She felt so happy that she bubbled over with all her secrets about the energy of nature. With a dramatic flair, as if she was saving the best knowledge for last, she said, "And mommy, I'll tell you a very special secret the tree told me. The earth is in harmony with the universe."

"That's nice, Amanda. You have a wonderful imagination, but it's all pretend and your friend isn't real."

"He is too real. He's right here. Can't you see him?" She could see Adam clearly in the sunshine. He was sitting in the broccoli, as plain as day.

"Come in now and eat lunch, Amanda."

"No! I want to stay here with my friend."

"Amanda, it's time for lunch," Beth repeated.

"Can my friend eat lunch with us?"

"Amanda, I just told you. Your friend isn't real. He's a figment of your imagination. Real people don't live in vegetable gardens. They live in houses, like you and me."

Amanda knew that Adam was just as real as her mother was. "My friend **is** real," she insisted, knowing it was true and wondering who to believe—herself or her mother. She was beginning to think that maybe her mother wasn't real. Confusion and doubt clouded her clear blue eyes.

* * * *

Rainbow and Lavender watched Amanda struggle to determine the truth. "Can we do anything to help her?" Lavender asked.

"She has to learn what is real and what is an illusion all by herself," Rainbow replied. "It's time for her to make a choice."

"But she knows her friend is real, and she also knows her mother is real. How can she choose? She's beginning to open up her inner knowledge and freeing herself to be who she really is. Her mother is trying to stop her awareness from growing because she doesn't know the truth about imagination and she doesn't remember her spiritual nature."

"Her mother doesn't know what's real for Amanda because she doesn't see the same realms of reality that Amanda sees. Her mother chooses not to see those vibrations of energy in the same way that Amanda chooses to see them. They're not real to her mother, and her beliefs about reality and imagination must be respected," Rainbow said. "Every soul is free to believe whatever they choose to believe. It's a matter of perception and free will."

"But her mother is wrong," Lavender said, feeling very angry with Amanda's mother. "Amanda is in harmony with both worlds and she sees the truth in her imagination. It's not fair that her mother is forcing her to choose her perceptions when Amanda already knows what's real."

"That's your belief," Rainbow said ambiguously. "It doesn't mean her mother is wrong; it only means their beliefs are different and therefore, their experiences are different. Her mother is seeing what she believes is real. And Amanda isn't being forced to choose her mother's perceptions; it only looks that way to you. Amanda has agreed to make this choice and it is fair, even though it may not seem like it."

Lavender knew that Rainbow was right—that truth was how you saw it within yourself and experienced it in your life—but she felt a sense of despair deep inside her soul. "Why did Amanda agree to this?" she asked, becoming worried that Amanda would fail this lifetime.

"Because she wants to test the strength of her determination to remember her spiritual knowledge and to express her true nature in all her experiences. It's part of her search to remember who she really is, and to see if she's ready to harmonize the energies of her soul," Rainbow said. "But you already know that; look within yourself."

"But what if she chooses her mother's perceptions?" Lavender asked, feeling as if she was precariously balanced between the light of truth and the shadow of illusion. "What will happen to her? And what will happen to Adam? Will he still be real to her?"

"See for yourself," Rainbow replied.

Lavender unfolded a panorama of pictures that Amanda shared with Adam and understood their spiritual bond with one another. She saw them as poor slave farmers, working with the earth to grow crops, learning all about nature and finding happiness within themselves and harmony in the naturalness of life. Watching another image of them as world-famous horticulturists who applied the laws of nature to creating and growing new species of flowers and plants, she noticed how those images were intertwined with Amanda's love for her garden and Adam's respect for nature.

Viewing fragments of past and future images, she saw Adam as a shaman in Africa where he understood and applied the secrets of nature to all things in the physical and spiritual worlds. Since he'd mastered all forms of energy by learning how to interweave universal vibrations of energy into every aspect of life, his physical incarnations were complete; because he wanted to be with Amanda, he'd chosen to vibrate to the energies of her present reality.

Lavender noticed that the images were beginning to move and change, vibrating and becoming superimposed upon themselves, taking on new dimensions and forms. Amanda appeared to be silhouetted by a shadow and she wasn't sure if Amanda was really in the picture in the first place. There's something else about the images, she thought, something not quite right. Looking at them closely and trying to understand what it was, she saw that they were double images, separate from one another and they didn't seem to fit together perfectly or to be synchronized with themselves. They looked like parallel pictures, mirroring and reflecting images and experiences of each other, but they kept wavering, fading in and out of sunlight and shadow. She shook her head, trying to clear her vision.

Feeling torn with the dilemma Amanda was in, Lavender turned to Rainbow and asked, "How can Amanda make the choice between her inner knowing and her mother's perceptions, and prove that Adam is real, when she's just a little child who can't make her mother understand?"

"Amanda isn't a little child. You're only seeing the outer appearance; you know the inner image is truly the reality. She's an advanced soul standing on the edge of enlightenment," Rainbow said.

Lavender felt the images and vibrations of energy begin to circle around her. Everything began to get dark and she felt as if she was slowly falling into a shadowy space. She sensed that she was somehow lost in time, drifting through misty images in her mind.

"Amanda knows the truth inside." Rainbow's voice seemed to echo from everywhere at once. "And Lavender, you also have a choice to make."

"What choice?" Lavender asked, trying to focus her attention on a ray of light that was traveling from the center of a sunrise somewhere within herself.

"The same choice Amanda has to make," Rainbow replied. "You've chosen the same test between opening up the truth about your spiritual nature or living in the world of illusion. Do you want to remember who you really are or do you want to play with shadowy images?"

"Do I have to make my choice right now?"

"Sooner or later," Rainbow replied. "Whenever you decide to place yourself in the appropriate situation."

* * * *

Amanda smiled a very special, very secret smile, remembering what Adam had told her about the sun being a universal energy spirit who helped the nature spirits in plants and trees to be free. When they were free in the light, they could grow and flower and be true to themselves. He'd also said that the light from the sun helped people to remember who they really are, and when you can remember who you are, you're free to be yourself.

"My friend is real," she repeated. "And I'm a rainbow, free in the sky, and I'm part of the air and the sunshine and the rain." As if in agreement, the wind blew a cloud over Amanda's garden. Rays of sunshine shimmered through the soft mist, reflecting a rainbow centered between the earth and the universe.

Beth looked up at the sky, noticing the rainbow above the clouds that were gathering. The clouds had seemed to appear from out of nowhere in the clear, blue sky. The wind became stronger and the sound of thunder boomed ominously. Flashes of lightning lit up the gray clouds as large raindrops began to fall.

"Amanda, you're not a rainbow," she said firmly. "Come into the house right now and eat lunch. It looks like we're going to have a thunderstorm in a few minutes. We'll play with dolls this afternoon and you can pretend all you want with them."

Amanda sat down on the ground beside her garden and burst into tears. "There's no such thing as pretend. Everything is for real. If I can't play with my friend, I want a dog—not dolls. Dolls are stupid. They can't talk or play games or do anything. They just sit there and never change because they don't have any magic inside them. I want a dog."

She didn't give her mother a chance to answer. "Please let my friend eat lunch with us," she begged. "You'd really like him if you knew him and he's just as real as you are, mommy."

Seeing how upset Amanda was, Beth knelt down beside her and hugged her. "Amanda, your friend isn't real," she said gently. "I'll talk to your daddy later today and see if we can get you a nice little doggy. A puppy would be a special friend for you to play with."

"Really?" she asked.

"Yes," Beth replied. At least the dog would be real, not imaginary, she thought, and it might help Amanda let go of the fantasy that her friend was real.

Amanda looked at her mother with tears in her eyes. Even the thought of a puppy to play with couldn't cheer her up right now.

"Let's go into the house, Amanda. It's beginning to pour out here and we're both getting all wet."

"Okay, mommy," she said sadly, feeling as if her heart was breaking because now she'd have to tell her friend good-bye.

"That's a good girl, Amanda," Beth said, standing up and reaching for her hand. "Let's get out of the rain."

Sobbing, she pulled away from her mother's touch. Feeling cold and miserable inside her soul, she promised herself she'd never again tell anyone what she knew. The rainbow in the sky began to fade, going inside a misty cloud. Amanda watched her thoughts and images become cloudy as the light of knowledge grew shadowy and dim. But *somewhere* inside her soul, she knew the truth and she held on to her knowledge, determined to keep it safe.

Eight

Images of Illusion

After lunch, Amanda looked sadly through the window at the rain that fell gently. Listening to the raindrops tap on the window, she thought she heard a voice somewhere inside her mind whisper, calling her name.

Going outside and sitting quietly underneath the tree with her head on her knees, she listened to the raindrops patter softly on the leaves. Slowly the rain turned to mist and the sun emerged, but she didn't notice the rainbow that appeared momentarily in the sky.

"Look at this leaf, Amanda. What color is it?"

Amanda looked up at the tree. "Green," she said.

"No, it isn't green. It only *appears* to be green. The color is an illusion. The leaf is really yellow or red; sometimes the colors blend into orange."

"It's green!" Amanda stated emphatically.

"It looks green to you because that's how you see it now. The leaf is really playing a game called *Illusion.* The leaf helps you remember who you really are so you can see through the illusion into your inner nature. When the time is right, the leaf stops playing the game and returns to its true nature. Do you remember when the leaves changed color last year?"

"Yes," Amanda answered.

"That's when the leaves became real because they were being true to their inner nature. As they change color, they become very vibrant because they know the truth and they're finished playing the game for awhile.

Then, every spring, they play a new game of Illusion to see if anyone will discover what they're doing. It's such a fun game that they play it every year. While they're green, they're growing in the light and enjoying the illusion too."

Amanda looked over at her broccoli garden and saw the sparkle of light that formed Adam's energy essence. Slowly the light changed into the little boy image and he smiled. "The leaves are gathering awareness in the light and turning it into inner knowledge, reflecting the sunshine inward. The sun helps them play the game because the sun god, Ra, is very wise," Adam said.

"Egypt," Amanda said, choking on the word.

* * * *

Lavender felt an echo of energy and fear go through her. She waited silently, seeing if Amanda would say more.

Rainbow responded to Lavender's thought. "If she remembered the game of Illusion and all her spiritual knowledge, she'd be quite articulate about it. And she does remember Egypt, but doesn't really know yet that she remembers her experiences there because she isn't ready to put words to her thoughts and feelings, or to see through the shadowy images so she can understand the reasons for her reincarnation."

"I suppose that's why we have to learn how to talk all over again in every lifetime," Lavender said. "Part of the game is trying to say what we know but by the time we learn how to talk, we've forgotten how to communicate with our thought/images." Suddenly she saw what the tree had been saying to Amanda. "The leaf is really a synonym for soul." She smiled to herself, pleased that she'd read the image in her mind and knew the corresponding word for it.

"Remembering and recognizing inner images can be very illuminating, but is saying what we know the reality of knowing or the illusion of truth?" Rainbow asked, wondering if Lavender really knew the truth about illusion or if she was playing with words.

"When we know the reality of our spiritual nature, we know that true knowledge doesn't require words," Lavender answered. "Words inspire our inner images that show us our truth. The perceptions of our images shape our thoughts and feelings, and create the illusions in our physical reality. Part of the game of life on earth is trying to remember what we've always known by looking into our thoughts and images that we see in our imagination and in our dreams."

"That's only half the answer," Rainbow said.

"Words can help us open up the thought/images and feelings that reveal our inner knowledge and show us who we really are. The game is to decipher what the words truly mean by watching our images and by understanding our thoughts and feelings. As we play with our interpretations, in the form of our experiences, we turn our experiences into learning and translate our words into knowledge. When souls remember their inner nature, they see through the outer illusions of their experiences and understand themselves on both a physical and a spiritual level."

Rainbow smiled, recognizing that Lavender understood the

meanings of words and their multi-dimensional vibrations that went beyond thought/images and feelings into true knowing. She watched the *Scroll of Knowledge* begin to open up in Lavender's not-yet-remembered images of Egypt.

* * * *

"When you see a new leaf in the spring," Adam said, "it's really the same leaf that has returned in a new form. If you look at what the leaf does, you'll see that the end is part of the beginning. It's like a continuous circle that spirals around itself and returns to where it came from. When the leaf returns as a new bud, it's a bit different because it went through a process of inner growth and change, but in essence it's the same leaf."

"Where does the leaf go when it changes color and falls off the tree?" Amanda asked, "And how can it grow when it isn't there anymore?"

"The leaf returns to its true nature and becomes more real than ever before. Like knowledge, it only appears to go away and that's the illusion. The essence of the leaf—the real part—goes inside itself."

Amanda looked at Adam, knowing that he was getting ready to leave. Tears filled her eyes.

"When I leave, I'll change my energy vibrations and metamorphose my form as I return into myself," Adam said softly, answering her unspoken question. "The next time you see me, I'll be expressing myself differently, but I'll still be who I really am."

"Butterfly." Amanda pointed to the caterpillar on the leaf. "I'm the butterfly. Can we play the game now?"

* * * *

"She remembers that she's really a free spirit, and she knows that all she's done is to change form." Lavender lit up into sparkles of energy that radiated rainbow colors all around her. "But if she understands the illusion, why does she want to play the game?" she asked Rainbow.

"You tell me," Rainbow replied.

Nine

The Mystery of Magic

Amanda watched Adam's sparkle of light glow brightly just before it floated up through the leaves of the tree and disappeared through the clouds into the universe. "Good-bye, my real friend," she whispered. She was still sitting under the tree sobbing when her father came home from work.

"Amanda, honey, what's wrong?" he asked. "You look like you've just lost your best friend."

"Oh, daddy, I did lose my best friend today," Amanda replied, looking at the sunshine sparkling through the leaves of the tree. Deep in her heart she knew that Adam wasn't really lost; he'd only changed form for awhile, but she felt as though she'd lost him.

"What happened?" he asked, sitting down next to her and putting his arm around her.

"Mommy said my friend wasn't real because she couldn't see him and now I don't have anyone to talk to or play with."

"Amanda, I'm so sorry your friend went away," he said. "I have a surprise for you that I think you'll really like." Muffled noises came from inside his raincoat and a small lump moved around. A furry little head popped up out of his coat and barked happily as a puppy licked his face, then jumped into her lap and joyously licked her face too.

"Hi puppy," she said, laughing and hugging and kissing the puppy.

"He whispered in my ear that he wanted a little girl just like you to play with. Then he jumped into my coat and came home with me, just like magic. What do you think about that?"

Before she could answer, Beth came outside and saw the puppy in Amanda's lap. "Where did he come from?" she asked, with an astonished look on her face.

"Beth, I can explain," Jim said, smiling. "I didn't have time to call to let you know I was bringing home a special friend from the office. My secretary's dog had puppies two months ago and she brought them in today to try to find homes for them. Before I knew it, this little guy adopted me. He followed me everywhere I went in the office and slept on my desk all afternoon. Can we keep him, please?"

Beth started to laugh. She laughed so hard she almost fell into the broccoli garden. Suddenly she became very serious. "How did you know Amanda wanted a puppy?"

"It's magic, mommy, and magic is real," Amanda said. "I tried to tell you that, but you wouldn't believe me."

"I had no idea she wanted a puppy," he said. "I just couldn't resist this little guy. As I was getting ready to come home, he jumped on my briefcase and barked at me; he wasn't going to let me leave without him." Laughing, he reached over and petted the dog. "Right, little guy?" The dog barked in agreement, licking his hand. "Besides, her birthday is next week and I thought a puppy would be a special present for her."

"Jim, I tried to call you but you were in a meeting all afternoon. Amanda said she wanted a dog and I called to ask you if we could get one for her."

"Are you telling me that you and Amanda talked about getting a dog today, and somehow ..." he paused for a moment, trying to figure it out in his mind. "Somehow I knew this, and that's why I brought the dog home?" He looked puzzled, then started to laugh. "Or the puppy knew it and that's why he adopted me?"

She took a deep breath, wondering how *imaginary* Amanda's world really was. The implications were just too much for her to think about right now. "Yes," she said, not sure what question she was answering.

"Maybe I tuned into Amanda's feelings," he said softly. "And I sensed that she wanted a puppy. She told me that her best friend, the one you can't see, went away today." He looked at Amanda with the puppy nestled in her arms. "What are you going to name him?"

"Magic," she replied.

Beth smiled. Get a grip on reality, she told herself. "I'm glad you have a real friend now," she said to Amanda. "He sure is cute. He looks like a little ball of fur. Can I hold him?"

"Okay, mommy." Magic looked at her and growled. "I don't think he likes you," Amanda said.

"What kind of dog is it?" she asked, wondering what she could have possibly done to this dog to make him not like her.

"It's a Pomeranian and they're normally very gentle and good-natured," Jim replied, trying to be serious but laughing instead. He wondered how he'd *really* known that Amanda wanted a puppy. Maybe it is magic, he thought to himself.

Ten

Shadowy Spaces

Lavender was deeply troubled by Amanda's choice to turn off her inner knowing. It appeared that she was playing with illusions and had traded in her truth for a puppy named Magic. When she'd gone against what she knew was real, and promised herself she'd never again tell anyone what she knew, it had struck a chord deep inside her soul. She recalled Rainbow's words, *Amanda knows the truth inside*. Lavender knew she also held the truth within herself, and that she'd also turned off her spiritual knowledge but couldn't remember why. It bothered her more than words could say. The shadowy images had haunted her awareness for centuries; clear answers eluded her recognition.

"I wish I could remember everything I used to know. I wish I could remember who I was before," she whispered to herself, wanting to see through the shadows inside her soul—to look at her experiences clearly in the light. Images of Egypt began to surface and she felt spiritual pain and fear. Deadly fear. Her throat began to hurt.

An image of an old, bearded man—a philosopher—came into a misty focus and half-remembered experiences echoed silently through her mind as they spun the shadowy images that wove through her thoughts and feelings. Suddenly she knew that she'd suffered for sharing secret knowledge and that was when and why she'd turned off her spiritual knowing. But somewhere inside her soul, she also knew she'd kept the knowledge safe and had written the mystical teachings in a scroll.

Knowing how valuable the knowledge was, she began to write. *From the pictures in your mind come words* ... The reed pen she held in her hand dissolved into a pencil and her images blurred. Shutting out her feelings of fear and the shadowy images, she closed her eyes and began to dream about a lavender sphere of light and a butterfly, about being free to fly in the universal energies of light. A golden key shimmering in the center of a sunrise drifted through the colors of a rainbow somewhere inside her dream.

Eleven

When You Wish Upon a Star

It wasn't anything Beth could put her finger on. Something was wrong with Amanda and she didn't know exactly what it was. She'd become quiet and withdrawn. She seemed lonely, even with her new puppy. She stayed in the house most of the time looking through books, even though she was too young to read. She said she wanted to be a writer when she grew up and whispered that words showed pictures. She found a pencil and wrote a book, with markings that looked like hieroglyphics. On the cover, she sketched a butterfly inside a rainbow, then rolled the pages up, tying them together with a lavender ribbon.

Maybe she's playing school, Beth thought, or maybe she's upset because I'm going back to work. Amanda had seemed to accept the news rather well and said she liked the teachers at the day care center when they went to visit. But still, there's something wrong. I can feel it. I wish I knew what it was.

She walked into Amanda's room and sat down next to her on the floor. "Hi sweetie. What'cha doing?" she asked quietly, noticing that Magic was sleeping on the bed.

"I'm watching Magic dream," Amanda answered. "His eyes move because he sees pictures in his mind. He's in a special place inside himself where his dreams are real."

"Maybe dogs dream just like people do," Beth said.

Magic woke up and stretched. Opening his eyes sleepily, he looked at Beth and yawned. She reached over to pet him, but he quickly jumped off the bed.

I wonder why he doesn't like me, she thought, watching him leave the room. Looking at Amanda, she asked, "How have you been feeling lately?"

"I feel fine, mommy."

"Do you miss your friend—the one in the broccoli?"

Amanda looked at her suspiciously. "You know he wasn't real," she replied guardedly. Her mother mustn't find out that she could still see him sometimes. Every once in awhile when the sun was especially sparkly and bright, she'd see him smiling at her through the leaves of the tree. "I have Magic now to play with. He's my special friend."

Beth nodded. Changing the subject, she said, "Summer is almost over and you'll be going to pre-school next week. I'm sure it'll be fun for you and there's lots of interesting things to do and learn. Are you happy about going to school?"

Amanda shrugged her shoulders indifferently.

"We'll both have new things to do. I'll miss being with you, but I'll pick you up at five o'clock every day. Then we'll come home and you can tell me about all the things you do at school."

"Are the leaves going to change color soon?" Amanda asked.

"Yes, they are."

"Then it's okay for me to go to school because the leaves will stop playing the game when they fall off the tree."

"What game do they play?"

"It's just a game, mommy," Amanda said, wanting to add that it was really a magical game about appearances, but she didn't think her mother would understand.

"Amanda, you don't seem like yourself. Are you sure you feel okay?"

"My throat hurts when I swallow."

"Sounds like you might have a sore throat; maybe you're coming down with a cold." She's never been sick a day in her life, Beth thought, wondering how she stayed so healthy.

"What's a cold?"

"A cold is when your throat hurts, and you cough and sneeze. Your eyes water and your nose runs. You feel *icky* for a few days before you get all better."

"Oh, I know what a cold is now," Amanda said, seeing through the words into what her mother was describing. "It's when your feelings hurt and they cry because you keep them locked up inside and you don't look at them or let them talk." Seeing the confused look on her mother's face, she explained, "Feelings are afraid of the dark and they want to tell you what hurts. When you look at your feelings and let them talk, then they get all better."

"Is there something your feelings want to talk about?" Beth asked, putting her arms around Amanda.

She rested her head on her mother's shoulder. "No, mommy. My feelings don't want to talk. They're too scared to tell secrets."

"That's certainly an interesting way to look at a cold," Beth said. Only Amanda would see it from that perspective, she thought. "You're quite a philosopher, aren't you?"

"What's a phosphor?" Amanda asked. It was such a big word, she couldn't say it, but she liked the sound of it.

Beth smiled. "A phosphor, the way you said it, is a light source that glows in the dark. It's also another name for a planet in the universe. Venus, the morning star."

Amanda looked at her in surprise. "Do you know about stars?" she asked. Maybe she knows about the universe too, she thought. It was almost more than she dared hope for; only Adam had talked about stars and light energies.

"I took a few astronomy courses in college. It's a science of the stars. Do you like stars?"

Amanda wondered if she could trust her mother with a special secret. "I lived on a star before I was born."

"What star did you live on? And what did you look like?" Beth asked, glad that Amanda's imagination was beginning to show itself again.

"I was a sparkle of light and I lived in a bubble. It was a pretty color, like the one at the top of a rainbow." She smiled at her mother. "I'll draw you a picture of my star," she said, getting up and walking over to the little desk in her room. Picking up a piece of paper, she drew a picture of her star and all the surrounding stars. "This star is mine," she said, pointing to it.

"It looks like you lived in the constellation of Orion, just above and to the left of the center star of the belt," Beth said, amazed at the detail in her picture. She went to the bookcase in the hallway and got her astronomy book. Bringing it into Amanda's room, she double-checked her picture with one of the star maps. Amanda's picture was identical to the star map in the astronomy book.

That particular star is barely visible without a telescope, even on a clear night, Beth thought, wondering how Amanda would know that star even existed. She couldn't possibly know about it, unless she'd really lived there. No, she said to herself, shaking her head as if to shake the thought out of her mind. Amanda probably saw the star map in my book, she thought, looking for a reasonable answer. But even if she had seen the picture, how could she copy it so well from memory? I wonder if she's somehow reading the books or absorbing knowledge in some way? Or what if she has a photographic memory? Or maybe she really did live on that star before she was born. But that's absurd, she told herself, noticing that she'd returned to the same answer.

"When the stars come out tonight, I'll show you my star." Amanda's voice interrupted her thoughts.

"I'd like that," Beth said. Get a grip on reality, she told herself.

"When I was a little girl, about your age, I used to make a wish on the first star I saw at night. Would you like to make a wish on your star tonight?"

"Yes," Amanda said, very seriously.

"What will you wish for?"

"It's a secret," Amanda replied. I wish I could remember everything I used to know. I wish I could remember who I was before I lived on my star, she thought. "Can I make two wishes?" she asked.

"You can make as many wishes as you'd like, and they'll all come true if you believe they will."

Amanda thought it was curious that her mother believed in wishes, but didn't believe in magic, because wishes were filled with magic. "What does that big word mean?" she asked. "Phlossfer. I can't say that word."

Beth smiled. "A *philosopher* is someone who is very wise. They look into their thoughts and they have a lot of knowledge. They talk and write about everything they know. They share their knowledge because they want to help people learn more about themselves so they can understand their experiences and see how the world they live in really works."

Amanda was quiet for a few minutes, appearing to ponder something very important. "Okay, I'll have a cold for awhile," she said, wondering what it would be like to feel icky.

"Honey, you don't decide to have a cold. You just get a cold for lots of different reasons."

"That's silly. Then a cold has you, instead of you having a cold."

Beth laughed. "Amanda, you have a wonderful way of playing with words," she said.

Twelve

Echoes of Energy

Beth watched the doctor as he read the notes the nurse had written. Jim stared out the window at the hospital adjacent to the medical center they were in, seemingly lost in his thoughts. Amanda was busy inspecting the books on the bookcase. She opened one and sneezed.

"You say she has laryngitis and has been having trouble swallowing for the past week?" the doctor asked. "And this started with a sore throat, followed by a cold?"

Beth nodded.

The doctor turned to Amanda. "Can you open your mouth for me and say aaahh?"

Amanda shook her head no, backing away from him. She covered her mouth with her hands, looking fearfully at the tongue depressor he held in his hand.

"I only want to put this stick in your mouth to hold down your tongue," he explained, "so I can look at your throat."

"No," she said through clenched teeth in a raspy little voice that was barely above a whisper. She glared at the doctor.

"This won't hurt; I just want to look at your throat," he said gently.

Amanda climbed into her father's lap, still covering her mouth with her hands. Jim put his arms around her, beginning to feel a vague sense of anxiety. "She seems to be terrified of you putting that tongue depressor in her mouth," he said.

With the help of the nurse, the doctor examined Amanda's throat. When he was done, the nurse put several Band-Aids on his fingers before leaving the room.

"It appears that Amanda might have to have her tonsils removed," he said, rubbing his fingers gently. "Her tonsils are enlarged and inflamed, and she has a severe throat infection which is causing her laryngitis and the pain she feels on swallowing. I'd like to have a throat specialist take a look at her."

Jim and Beth exchanged worried glances. "Is it really that

serious?" Jim asked. "Couldn't you just give her penicillin or some other medicine to clear up the infection?"

Beth remembered what Amanda had said about a cold. *It's when your feelings hurt and they cry because you keep them locked up inside and you don't look at them or let them talk.* She wondered if there was a connection between the laryngitis and something Amanda was keeping locked up in her feelings that she refused to talk about. Maybe that's why she has a sore throat and it's painful for her to talk now, she thought, considering the possibility. Don't be absurd, she told herself. The laryngitis is obviously caused from her throat infection.

"Before we begin any type of treatment, we'll need to get a complete medical history on her. Then we'd start with a program of antibiotics," the doctor said, "but the infection is quite severe. After the throat specialist examines her and the culture we took comes back from the lab, we'll have a better indication of whether a tonsillectomy is necessary." He paused for a moment. "Has she had throat surgery before, or any kind of dental work?" he asked.

"No," Beth replied.

Jim felt a sense of helplessness sweep over him, as if something was about to happen that he had no control over. A misty image of a bloody knife appeared in his mind and he rubbed his eyes, trying to erase the image. "I feel shaky," he said, "as if I'm going to pass out. I'd like to get some fresh air."

"I saw something unusual," the doctor said, opening the window in his office. "There's a jagged scar across her tongue."

* * * *

"What's going on?" Lavender asked Rainbow. "Why is Amanda sick, and why does the doctor think taking her tonsils out will clear up her laryngitis and cure her sore throat?" Earth doctors are balmy in the head, she thought. Some were even downright bloody dangerous. Most of them had never heard of healing with universal light energy and harmonious sound vibrations, yet they'd studied for years to become a healer.

Suddenly she felt an overwhelming sense of fear. "What's the scar all about?" she asked quietly, finding it difficult to voice the question. Her throat felt sore and she tried to swallow, noticing that it was very painful.

"It's a soul scar," Rainbow wanted to say, but she was having trouble talking too. She borrowed Lavender's pencil and began to write, explaining the reasons for Amanda's laryngitis and why her throat hurt. It was important for Lavender to see the truth.

"Echoes of experiences are surfacing because Amanda wants to remember who she was. She's responding to past-life energies from Egypt. Her sore throat is symbolic of the physical and spiritual pain you endured. Her laryngitis is a result of the dying promise you made to yourself, and is compounded by the recent choice she made to keep her knowledge secret. But she knows deep inside her soul that she wants to share the knowledge.

"She's trying to open up the memories you agreed to face to evolve your soul. She wants to help you remember your spiritual knowledge so she can apply the knowledge in her earth experiences and express her true nature. She needs your cooperation to do that. Your spiritual pain has to be accepted and understood before it can be healed. You can help her by overcoming your fear. When you bring the past experiences into the light, you can see what really happened and why it happened to you, Lavender. The truth will set you free. Will you look at your experiences in Egypt now?"

Bravely trying to overcome her fear, Lavender looked at the shadowy images in her memory. In a flash of light, she saw the *Scroll of Knowledge* she'd written because she could no longer speak and knew that it contained the mystical teachings she'd learned in that lifetime. Remembering that she'd been persecuted and put to death for sharing secret knowledge, she promised herself she'd never again reveal her knowledge. Her last thought was that the scroll would be destroyed. The images began to blur and fade into darkness. The next thing she remembered was waking up in a lavender sphere of light.

Lavender looked at Rainbow for a long moment. Her eyes revealed the horror of what she'd experienced in Egypt. "It's too awful to see," she said, closing her eyes. Her voice was raspy and her breathing was ragged. "And I refuse to talk about it," she whispered, clutching her throat in severe pain.

"You're feeling the pain because you're not accepting the experiences and allowing yourself to understand them," Rainbow finally managed to say. "There are missing pieces in your memory and you're not seeing the entire picture. The truth is inside the shadows you've surrounded your soul with. You're suffering needlessly because of your fear and holding yourself back from evolving. Bring your experiences into the light and let your feelings speak, so you can understand them and heal your soul."

"No," Lavender said, turning off the memories.

Rainbow handed Lavender her pencil. "You'll be needing this, so you can write. Your words will reveal the images of your memories and show you the truth as you remember who you were before." She smiled at her. "I respect your choice to reopen your spiritual knowledge through the energy vibrations of words."

* * * *

"NO!" Amanda screamed as loud as she could, putting her hands over her mouth again. "Don't let them do it daddy," she said, her voice trembling with fear. "You were there before, but you couldn't stop them. I won't be able to talk and all my friends will be gone. I wrote down everything I knew, but the words were lost." She burst into tears, burying her face in her father's chest.

"What's she talking about?" Beth asked, frightened by Amanda's response.

Jim shrugged his shoulders. "I don't know," he replied. A look of anguish crossed his face as he saw the image of a bloody knife again. "I'm not going to let you take my daughter's tonsils out," he said to the doctor, hugging Amanda closer to him as if he was protecting her. What he was protecting her from, he didn't know. He could see that his wife and the doctor couldn't understand his reaction. For that matter, he couldn't understand it either. "I just know she'll get better by herself," he said.

"Her sore throat may be an emotional reaction to a consciously-forgotten experience in her life," the doctor said, looking at Jim. "Surgery may not be necessary, and we certainly wouldn't proceed without your consent. I'd like to start her on antibiotics to clear up the infection and I'd like to have the throat specialist see her today."

"We'd like to talk about this before we decide anything," Beth said. The doctor nodded and left the room. She leaned over and softly stroked Amanda's hair, trying to comfort her.

Amanda was sobbing as she turned to look at her mother; Beth saw the pain and fear in her eyes. She sensed that the pain was more than physical and wished she could do something to help her ease the pain. "Are you okay, sweetie?" she asked, gently wiping Amanda's tears away.

Amanda took her hands away from her mouth. "I'm scared they're going to hurt me like they did before."

"We won't let them hurt you, Amanda. You're safe and there's nothing to be afraid of. We just want you to get better," she said, putting her arms around both of them. "Jim, you seem to be just as upset as Amanda is about the thought of surgery."

"I don't know what came over me," he said. "Some strange, intense feeling grabbed me inside." He shuddered. "Maybe it was a nightmare I had a long time ago where I saw something horrible happen with throat surgery and I couldn't or didn't do anything to try to prevent it. That's the only way I can explain it," he said.

"Maybe you and Amanda had the same nightmare," Beth said

softly.

Just then a nurse knocked quietly on the door and entered the room. "You probably don't remember me," she said, smiling. "I'm Carrie. I was one of the nurses at your daughter's birth. I remember Amanda because she and I had a nice conversation while I was bathing and dressing her."

Amanda looked at her and smiled. Climbing off her father's lap, she walked over to her. "I remember you," she said, looking into her eyes. "You rubbed my back and hummed a song to me."

Carrie nodded, offering her a grape-flavored lollipop.

"How can Amanda remember that?" Beth asked.

"I sing to all the babies when they're born. It helps them adjust to their new environment," Carrie said. "Babies are very aware of everything that occurs around them. After they learn how to talk, they can relate their early impressions and images, and tell about their feelings and experiences both before and after birth, all the way up through their pre-verbal years."

Beth pondered the explanation for a moment, then smiled. "It does make sense," she said.

"I'm working in Pediatrics now and the doctor said that Amanda might be coming to visit us. If it's all right with you, I can show her the children's wing. Then if she decides to spend a few days with us, she'll feel more comfortable. We even have an indoor garden with a skylight."

Amanda placed her hand in Carrie's hand. "It's okay," she said, looking at her mother and father. "Carrie is my friend from a long time ago."

"After you've talked to the doctor again and the throat specialist, they'll walk you over to the children's wing. We'll be in the garden," Carrie said.

Thirteen

Universal Light Energy

Amanda took her shoes off and sat comfortably on the soft, green grass. The warmth of the sun felt soothing. "The flowers are pretty and they smell so nice," she said, gently touching the petals. "Flowers have a special energy inside them," she added, sharing one of her secrets.

Carrie smiled, understanding the secret. "This garden is very special because the flowers are in harmony with their true nature," she said, sitting down next to her. "I'd like to help you get better, but you have to want to get better inside. You have to let the pain talk about what's hurting you."

"I can't do that," Amanda whispered. "I'm afraid to look at it because it's so awful."

"When you're ready to heal yourself, you'll be able to face your fear," Carrie said. "Do you like rainbows?"

"I love rainbows."

"Then close your eyes and see a rainbow," Carrie said.

Amanda closed her eyes and saw a rainbow smiling at her.

"Imagine that you're inside that rainbow and you're floating upward through the colors into the white light above the rainbow. Feel the white light all around you and breathe it inside every part of your body, your mind, and your soul. It's the nicest feeling in the world and you feel really, truly at home within yourself."

Amanda floated slowly through the colors inside the rainbow, flowing into the energies of red and orange, then yellow. A bright ray of sunlight shimmered, illuminating a golden key. Flowing into the color green, she began vibrating in harmony with the rhythm of energy gently pulsing through her, like a heartbeat.

Entering the color blue and blending into the sky, she felt a soothing warmth bathe and cleanse her throat. Softly floating on a cloud through the color indigo, she saw misty images of almost-forgotten spiritual knowledge weave through her mind. On a gentle current of air, rising through the color violet, she felt in tune with her soul.

Somewhere over the rainbow, the universal light was a warm mist of pure white, loving energy, surrounding her softly as she breathed in the harmony of its energy. She opened her eyes and smiled. "I like the white light," she said.

"Your soul is the essence of universal light energy," Carrie replied. "When you center white light around you and breathe it inside you, you can feel the energy of your soul as it vibrates in your body."

Amanda took another deep breath, breathing in the light. She was quiet for a moment, remembering. "I want to help people learn all about the light when I grow up," she said. "But I have to make my voice better first."

"There's a song I'd like to sing to you," Carrie said. "It's from a very wonderful movie about a little girl who wanted to go home and she didn't know that she was really home all the time. She just needed to wake up from her dream to know that home was inside her heart. The song is *Over the Rainbow*. I hummed the melody to you when you were born. As I sing the song, I'll change the words to help you be in tune with your feelings."

Somewhere, over the rainbow, way up high.
There's a place that you know of, once in a time near by.

Somewhere, over the rainbow, skies are blue.
All your dreams that you choose to dream really do come true.

Somewhere, over the rainbow, souls are free.
When you're home in your thoughts, your heart can be so happy.

Someday, you'll wish upon your star
and wake up where the clouds are far behind you.

Where truth is clear and light is bright,
that's where you'll find you.

Amanda smiled. "The song makes me feel happy inside."

Carrie nodded. "You sing it now, Amanda. Change the words so they say what's inside your heart."

Amanda began to sing softly, feeling the music in her words and seeing magical images in her mind.

Somewhere, over the rainbow, clouds are clear.
There's a place that I dreamed of, once in a time now here.

When I wish upon my star, I'll wake
up with a rainbow all around me.

Where truth is clear and light is bright,
that's where I'll find me.

Amanda laughed and her eyes sparkled with joy. "My throat doesn't hurt anymore," she said. "But my soul isn't all better yet."

"Just remember to go inside the rainbow, Amanda. The rainbow will show you how to be all better," Carrie said, hugging her.

"Hi mommy and daddy," Amanda said in a clear voice as they walked into the garden. "Carrie helped me remember white light and she sang me a song called *Over the Rainbow*, and my throat doesn't hurt anymore."

Her parents and the doctor looked at Amanda in amazement. The laryngitis was completely gone. The throat specialist smiled at her. She smiled back at him; a very special, very secret smile.

"Just twenty minutes ago, we had a sick little girl on our hands and now she seems to be all better," the doctor said. "Amanda, this is Dr. Adam Deva. He's a throat specialist and he'd like to look at your throat. Would that be all right?" He smiled at his colleague. "She won't let you near her mouth and she'll bite your hands," he said quietly, so only Adam could hear.

Amanda opened her mouth wide so the throat specialist could look inside. "She's perfectly healthy," he said. "Her throat isn't infected and I don't see any signs of inflammation or swollen tonsils." He winked at her. "I'll bet you like broccoli," he said.

"How'd this happen?" the doctor asked, looking at Adam. "I've never seen a case like this before and quite frankly, I'm at a loss to explain it. I don't understand how her laryngitis could disappear so quickly and how the infection could simply vanish without a trace." He shook his head, bewildered. "And why didn't she bite you? It's as if she completely trusted you not to hurt her."

"You'll have to ask Amanda how her voice cleared up. She probably didn't bite me because of something in my nature," Adam replied.

Amanda and Carrie looked at one another and smiled. "My voice is better," Amanda said, "because I believe in rainbows."

Fourteen

Somewhere in Nowhere

Lavender was seemingly lost in a shadow, drifting through the universe in search of her soul. In flashes of illumination, she watched Amanda flutter in and out of her mind. It appeared that she was playing a game of Illusion with intermittent reaches of recognition.

Lavender decided to return to school to pick up her studies where she'd left off. Trying to balance herself in the middle of nowhere, she jumped into what she thought was the present. She landed in an image of a tree. The scenery was strangely familiar, then she saw Amanda's broccoli garden and realized she'd overshot her mark.

At least I'm close, she thought. It's only a near-miss from the campus at school. She fell out of the tree, landing ungracefully in a crumpled heap of energy on the ground.

"Hi, Lavender," Rainbow said, helping her up.

"Can I come back to school?" Lavender asked, trying to pull herself together. "I'd like to continue my spiritual studies and it's obvious I need help by the way I just warped time and space." Not to mention what I did with dropping out of my dimension and losing my grip on gravity like that, she thought, rubbing a sore spot.

"Yes," Rainbow replied. "Your sense of timing and synchronicity leaves a lot to be desired." She couldn't help but smile at Lavender. "And it's more than a near-miss. You hit the vibrations of earth, two years in the past according to linear time and your awareness seems to be stuck in that space of energy. In terms of simultaneous time, you haven't missed anything, and you did accomplish a lot, but you don't know that yet."

Lavender started to hiccup. "Will you take into consideration that I landed in my last clear thought/image before I left school?" she asked. "When Amanda turned off her inner knowing, the world started spinning around me and I lost my balance and fell into a shadowy space." Watching images surface in her mind, she shivered. "I had a terrible nightmare. I went to Africa and I got sick, then I went to Egypt to look for a hidden treasure and shadows kept surrounding me, and Amanda was trying to talk except there wasn't any sound, just words that she rolled up in a piece of paper."

Rainbow nodded. "I'm glad you decided to return. When you slipped into the shadows of your soul, you entered a time/space lapse of light awareness. You've been in soul shock and misting for what appears to be an eternity. You may feel dizzy and disoriented for awhile before you're able to revibrate your energies to the present and return to an atmosphere of knowledge."

"I feel like a caterpillar in a cocoon," Lavender said.

"Amanda has made a lot of changes in your absence and they're not all what they appear to be. You might be tempted to play energy games to stretch your awareness, but don't get caught up in the illusion."

"I'm really a butterfly," Lavender reminded herself.

Fifteen

The Freedom of Flight

Lavender readjusted her energies to school and hung around the campus for awhile before she looked in on Amanda. It appeared that she was going around in circles, looking for herself, and was becoming too earth-oriented at too young of an age. It seems I've come back just in time to help her, she thought, still a bit dizzy from her recent return.

Hoping that Rainbow wouldn't find out what she was up to, she decided to make an appearance to remind Amanda that she was really a free spirit. Amassing her knowledge of energy, and rearranging her vibrations, she materialized out of thin air in Amanda's room.

Magic wagged his tail and danced around on his hind legs. Barking happily at Lavender, he tried to jump up so she could pet him. What an adorable little dog, she thought, forgetting for a moment that Amanda had gotten a puppy for her fourth birthday.

"Shhsh, Magic," Amanda said, wondering why he was behaving as if he was welcoming a long-lost friend. He only acted like this when he saw Adam in the leaves of the tree. Magic jumped into her lap and looked up at the ceiling.

"Hi, Amanda. I'm up here."

Amanda heard someone talking in her mind and looked around her room. No one was there. "Where is here?" she asked.

"Look higher than yourself."

Amanda looked directly above herself and saw a shimmering sphere of lavender light. "Who are you?" she asked.

Lavender knew it was against the rules to tell Amanda exactly who she was. In the universal plan, she had to find that out for herself. "I'm a special friend," she replied. "I'm sort of like your friend in the broccoli."

"My mom said he wasn't real, so you're not real either and you'd better go away."

Knowing that she was only supposed to appear when Amanda was ready to see her, Lavender floated down to the window and expanded her energy vibrations, radiating and reflecting sparkles of rainbow-colored rays of sunlight. Then she floated back up to the ceiling.

"You're just a figment of my imagination," Amanda said.

The words reflected her mother's belief and Lavender was tempted to show Amanda's mother a thing or two about what was real, but decided that the best thing to do would be to help Amanda remember. "You know inside that your friend is real, no matter what anyone else tells you," she said.

"How do you know that?" Amanda asked, surprised that the light on the ceiling knew about Adam and agreed that he was real. She had vowed to keep him secret so that no one would say she was wrong when she knew she was right. But lately, she was beginning to have her doubts.

"I know lots of secret things," Lavender replied.

Amanda liked the light and the way it made rainbows in the sunshine. "Can you teach me how to do that?" she asked.

"When you see the light within yourself, and you know in your heart and mind, and in your soul, that you're a free spirit, you can be free to be who you are. You can be yourself."

"Adam told me that too," Amanda said.

"Would you like to learn how to fly?" Lavender asked. It was important to let Amanda rediscover how to synchronize and focus energy; she'd just temporarily forgotten. It's okay to help her with hints and remind her of things she's already accomplished, Lavender reasoned uncomfortably to herself. She was interfering and she knew it. If Rainbow found out, she'd be in trouble.

Amanda smiled brightly. "I already know how to fly. I used to play with rainbows in the sky," she said. "And a rainbow taught me how to fly." She began radiating light energy from within her body and rose up to meet her new friend on the ceiling.

Lavender knew she wasn't supposed to take Amanda over the rainbow because of her choice to experience the lower vibrations of earth, but wanted to help her remember her spiritual side. And if Rainbow had shown Amanda the light within herself and taught her how to flow her energies through the vibrations of rainbow colors, then she could certainly take her a few steps further above the rainbow. Besides, above and over were almost the same thing. It was only a matter of the energy expressions of the words. But she knew there was a big difference between the experiences of the words.

Taking Amanda by the hand, she gave her a guided tour of the universe, showing her the star where she'd lived before she was born. Inside her soul, she was hoping Amanda would remember her pre-birth promise.

An ethereal mist wove softly through Amanda's thoughts and feelings as it echoed through a whisper of dream images. "I made a wish on this star once," she said. "But when it started to come true, I got scared."

"What did you wish for?"

"I don't remember." Amanda thought for a moment, then asked, "Is your name Lavender?"

"Yes," Lavender replied, smiling.

Amanda put her arms around Lavender and hugged her. "You're a very special part of my rainbow," she said. "I know you're real and magical at the same time."

Lavender vibrated happily. Amanda remembered her, but she sensed that there was something out of sync, something more to remember.

"My friend, Adam, lives in the universe now. Can we visit him?"

"He's in a higher realm of awareness than we are," Lavender replied. "His vibrations are centered in a lighter dimension of energy and we can't get there from here."

"Oh," Amanda said, disappointed.

Lavender wanted to tell her so many things about her spiritual nature, but knew Amanda wasn't ready to understand them. And she wasn't sure she understood them either. "I have to go back to school now," she said, showing Amanda the School of Spirituality before taking her down to earth on a gentle current of air.

Amanda waved good-bye as she watched Lavender disappear into a misty cloud. She looks like a rainbow, she thought.

Amanda hung around on the ceiling for awhile and practiced flying through the house before deciding to expand her horizons and explore even further. She zoomed out of the window into the sky, then used the roof as her launching pad. She practiced flying higher into the universe, through the clouds into the clear light of knowledge.

Liking her new-found freedom, she wanted to teach her mother how to fly. Floating into the kitchen where she was making dinner, she said, "Hi mom, I'm up here on the ceiling. Look at me. I can fly." Beth didn't look up or seem to hear her, so she floated down to the window and radiated rainbow colors at her. "And guess what else happened today," she said happily. "I explored the universe and I have a new friend who wants to show you a thing or two." It seemed that Beth couldn't see her, no matter how much she vibrated, so she floated back up to the ceiling and watched her make dinner.

When her father came home from work and stretched out in his favorite chair to relax, she floated lightly onto his shoulder and offered to take him on a trip to Africa to show him sights of who he'd been before. He nodded his head just before he dozed off to sleep. Amanda interpreted the nod as a yes and began to flow past-life images from her mind into his thoughts, projecting them to her mother at the same time.

As she expanded the wave of energy, an image she hadn't seen before appeared. Her father was placing a cool cloth on her forehead and showing her a map to find a hidden treasure. He said their next dig site was near an entrance to a temple in Egypt, then the image turned dark and she lost the connection with him in a swirling echo of energy that separated his thoughts from hers.

As the sound of someone's voice slowly roused Jim from sleep, he watched dream images weave through his mind and wondered why parts of this dream recurred and seemed to interconnect with earlier dreams he'd had where Amanda's face was superimposed on that of an old, bearded man. I drew a map, he thought, because I promised myself I'd help Amanda find something in Egypt. But then she caught malaria in a jungle in Africa. He stretched, thinking that the dream was curious because recently he'd begun to take an interest in archaeology and wanted to go to Egypt.

When Amanda heard her mother calling them to dinner, she rearranged her energy vibrations. Drifting back into her body, she began to shiver and her head felt hot. An image of her father standing next to a pyramid spun through her mind and she thought she was in Egypt; it took her a moment to realize she'd been showing him images of Africa.

After they sat down to dinner, Amanda listened to her father tell her mother about some of the people at the office, about how they liked to play a game called *Kick the Scapegoat in the Asterisk.* He said he'd had just about enough of watching it and didn't want to be in the office when the shoe hit the fan.

Amanda smiled into the vegetables. He's ready to be real, she thought, and his next sentence confirmed it. Waving his fork in the air like a flag of freedom, he announced that he was thinking about quitting his job and going to Egypt on an archaeological expedition.

"You must be dreaming!" Beth exclaimed. "Ever since you saw that TV documentary on pyramids a few weeks ago, you've been mumbling in your sleep about sphinxes and secret hiding places. Now you tell me you want to go to Egypt on some sort of a dig to look for hidden treasure. Why not go to Africa and look for medicine men? Maybe they've found a cure for malaria by now."

Amanda was impressed with her mother's ability to read the images she'd projected to her, but couldn't understand where the image of malaria had come from. "Can I go to Africa with you, daddy? We used to live there before, remember? And mommy, the medicine men are called shamans and they know everything there is to know about natural healing. They work in harmony with the energies of the earth and the universe."

Beth looked like she was turning purple and red at the same time. "Now I've heard it all!" she yelled, trying to speak calmly. "When I was making dinner, I could have sworn there was a little rainbow sitting on the windowsill talking to me and offering to teach me how to fly and I thought I was crazy, and now Amanda tells me about shamans and I've never heard the word before, and you want to go to Egypt for a few weeks, and Amanda wants to go to Africa because you both lived there before, and I think you're both ... you're both ..."

She stopped talking in mid-sentence, as if she'd either run out of breath or words to say what she was thinking. She took a deep breath. "I don't really know what I think! What's happening here? Are we all out of our minds?"

Amanda said yes, she hoped so and was excused from dinner and sent to bed. Jim said he'd return to the office and never mention Egypt again, not even in his sleep. Beth, wondering how Amanda would know about shamans, went to look up the word in the encyclopedia.

Just before she went to sleep, Amanda thought that it had been a wonderful day because she'd seen realness in the world around her. She knew that her mother thought exactly the opposite. Smiling, she floated up to the ceiling to look for Lavender.

Sixteen

Reverberating Repercussions

Lavender found a note from Rainbow on her desk when she returned to school after showing Amanda the universe. She opened it slowly, noticing it was written in pencil. Maybe it's not as bad as I think it is, she thought. Maybe Rainbow isn't going to throw the book at me and I can erase some of this.

She looked at the words on the paper. *You've set enormous echoes of energy into motion and caused serious reverberations that will bring multi-dimensional repercussions into effect. There was another part to your pre-birth promise and by showing Amanda her star, you've shown her too much too soon.*

As if in a far-away dream in another place, she heard the sound of thunder roll through the clouds as lightning flashed across the universe, illuminating a shadowy image of an old, bearded man standing silently inside a doorway, holding a scroll in his hands. Mystical knowledge echoed through her mind as the wind whispered her name in a sudden quiet, calling to her through the reaches of time. The philosopher began to move toward her, offering her the scroll. She shivered with a deadly fear and the image disappeared into darkness.

Shaking, she looked at the paper in her hands. It was only a piece of paper, a note from Rainbow, nothing more. Pushing the fear out of her mind, she began reading the note again through the tears in her eyes.

The words turned into chiseled images, etched into granite. ***You have stretched and superseded Cosmic Commandment #9: Thou shalt not interfere with, nor attempt to escalate or unduly influence, any soul's self-discovery of their true spiritual nature.***

The words turned into penciled inscriptions again. *In the universal plan, through their own choice and timing, a soul must discover and pursue their individual path that will lead them into their knowledge. Lavender, you know better than to do what you did. There are spiritual safeguards to opening up awareness. Amanda wasn't ready to see that memory of Egypt yet, and neither were you.*

"I was only trying to lift a few limits. I wanted to remind Amanda that she was a free spirit and I wanted to help her see the light within herself so she can remember who she really is. I know I'm not supposed to rush her search for her soul, but it seemed to me that she'd already begun to look and was a little lost, so I tried to point her in the right direction. Besides, there are light teachers on earth who are trying to do what I did and they're thought of very highly," she said to herself, trying to account for her actions. "I didn't mean to scare her," she whispered silently.

She continued reading the note. *As a soul journeys through many experiences in every lifetime, that soul must find their way, directed by their inner light. When they truly see the light within themselves, they've found the path that leads them home—the path into knowing their true spiritual nature.*

Lavender was beginning to get the picture. The purpose of the light teachers who had reincarnated on earth was to help people who were ready to see the light. When a soul chose to become aware of their true nature, and wanted to remember their spiritual knowledge, the teachers could then guide them toward their individual truth. It was one way of looking for the light within yourself.

She began to feel very philosophical about the entire incident. One of the secrets of soul searching was that you didn't need a teacher to help you rediscover your truth. You could find it all by yourself just by looking within your feelings and experiences to see the reflections of your inner images. And the most powerful way was to simply open up your mind and look inside your imagination and dreams.

Lavender was puzzled about one thing though. She thought she was Amanda's inner light, and part of her purpose in studying spirituality was to share knowledge with her.

There was a P.S. on the note. *I've done the same thing myself when I've tried to help you learn by showing you the light.*

Seventeen

The Sun and the Shadow

Lavender wandered around the campus, wondering about the essence of inner light. How could a soul recognize it unless they knew it was there and knew where to look for it? If no one told them about it or showed them how to find the light within themselves, then how on earth could they possibly become aware of it?

She thought about the P.S. on the note that Rainbow had written her. Part of the reason a soul was connected with their spiritual side was to enable them to remember who they really are, and one of her assignments in the Reality Awareness class was to help Amanda rediscover her true spiritual nature. After she recognized that she was truly a spiritual being and she remembered her inner knowledge, the next step was applying that knowledge in all her experiences so she could completely understand herself and evolve her soul into higher levels of awareness.

If only she could see the light within herself, Lavender thought, it would be reflected in all her thoughts and she wouldn't get stuck between physical awareness and spiritual understanding. She was so wrapped up in her thoughts about showing Amanda the light that she didn't notice the sun was disappearing into a misty cloud. As the wind moved gently through the leaves of the trees, the interplay of sunlight and shadow formed intricate patterns on the buildings, bathing the winding sidewalks in a hazy light.

A thought sparkled into a bright ray of sunlight inside her mind. While the energy of light reflected knowledge, the essence of light originated within a person's soul. The light was always there; it was just a matter of remembering it and seeing it clearly from an unclouded perspective. As universal light illuminated every aspect of a soul's awareness, all the shadows disappeared, allowing a soul to evolve into higher realms of light.

"Did you finally see the light?" Rainbow asked.

"Yes," Lavender replied. "I think you have to look for something before you really see it, even if you're surrounded with it every day."

"Like the light from the sun," Rainbow suggested. "It's always there and yet most souls don't see it clearly."

"Or they only see shadows in the sunlight," Lavender replied, not yet seeing or recognizing the hazy image of school she was experiencing at this very moment. Her thoughts were centered on the time that Amanda saw the butterfly's shadow when the sun was shining through the leaves of a tree.

"Why does it bother you that Amanda chose to play the game of Illusion?" Rainbow asked.

"Because even when she knew the truth about the butterfly, she chose the shadow side. She was so close to remembering her true spiritual nature and knowing who she is. She could just as easily have chosen to fly into the light and be free," Lavender replied, remembering the scene as if it had happened only yesterday. Amanda and Adam were talking about how the leaves in the tree turned real. Pointing to the caterpillar, she said, "I'm the butterfly." Then she'd asked to play the game.

Adam showed her its shadow on the opposite side of the leaf and said that the shadow appeared to be an illusion of the real butterfly because when you look at the butterfly in the light, the shadow disappears. Amanda had wavered between the real butterfly and its shadow before she chose to play the illusion of shadow.

"Do you think playing with shadows could have anything to do with Amanda choosing to experience the vibrations of earth in order to see the light within herself?" Rainbow asked. "Maybe the earth is really a shadow of the universe in the sunshine. And maybe Amanda doesn't recognize that a real rainbow is only visible in the shadow side of sunshine," she said.

"Then maybe the shadow is real; not an illusion," Lavender replied, confused. Maybe if Amanda could truly see the light within herself, there wouldn't be any shadows, she thought silently.

"Appearances can often be deceiving," Rainbow said. "Like shadow and sunlight. It's important to look at both sides so you can see the whole picture. Have you ever considered the possibility that reality and illusion are mirror images of one another, and they only seem to be opposites because they aren't yet in harmony with themselves?"

Looking through the double images of Rainbow's words, Lavender said thoughtfully, "Maybe Amanda really is being true to her nature by looking at her shadow in the light from the sun. And maybe she is learning how to see through the illusion of shadow into the real light within herself."

"And maybe the sun and the shadow are the same thing, viewed from separate thought perspectives and parallel image perceptions," Rainbow said. Appearing to change the subject, she added, "There's a seminar coming up at the university I'd like for you to attend."

Rainbow is so multi-dimensional, Lavender thought. In addition to teaching at the School of Spirituality, she also lectures at the University of Understanding from time to time. "What's the seminar about?" she asked.

"It's a sunrise seminar on **The Spiritual Perspectives of Living in a Physical Body** and since you seem to need some help in this area, it might be a good idea for you to be there." Rainbow tried to hide her smile behind a cloud and wondered if Lavender could see through it.

Lavender was just about to ask if she could bring Amanda to the seminar, but the look on Rainbow's face changed her mind. She had the distinct feeling that Rainbow was hiding something. I'll bet it has to do with the P.S. on the note, she thought, wondering if she could shine some light on Amanda without Rainbow finding out.

Eighteen

The Edge of Enlightenment

Amanda was hanging on a precarious ledge between being too wise for her tender years and pretending to be too innocent with all she seemed to know. Beth couldn't decide which one. If she'd asked Amanda, she would have said that the ledge was the balance between the earth and the universe; between physical awareness and spiritual knowing.

Lavender thought she must have missed something important and wondered what had happened with Amanda while she'd been wandering around in her thoughts, wondering how to show her the light. If Amanda knew she was balanced between the imagination of knowing and the insight of understanding, then she must have discovered the light all by herself.

If I could just keep my images from wavering, I'd be able to center my awareness and see what Amanda experienced, Lavender thought, but the images kept going around in her mind, like ripples in a pond. Deciding to take an alternate route into what had occurred, she recalled what Rainbow had said about straight and spiral time in the Time/Space class.

"Time, when viewed as a continuum, is perceived as a straight line with past, present, and future occupying isolated and unrelated areas of separate space. When viewed as a spiral, time is perceived as parallel circles with past, present, and future occupying the same space in interrelated vibrations of energy and matter."

Straightening out her thoughts, Lavender looked into the past images she hadn't seen while she was wrapped up in her thoughts about sunlight and shadow.

"Mommy, where do babies come from?"

"What makes you ask a question like that, Amanda?"

"Because Gary said he was going to be born in six months and he promised to be my little brother. I wondered how he was going to get here. That's why I asked."

Beth was flabbergasted, but didn't have time to say anything; the phone was ringing. It was the doctor, calling to confirm the pregnancy, saying she was already three months along. She slowly hung up the phone and looked at Amanda. "How did you know I was going to have a baby even before I knew for sure myself?" she asked.

Amanda smiled at her. "I just told you. Gary told me."

"Who's Gary?"

"Don't you remember Gary?"

"Amanda, just tell me how you knew and don't play games with me. I want the truth," Beth said, her voice a mixture of irritation and curiosity.

"Before I was born, Gary was my friend but he was a girl. You used to know him when he was your Aunt Sarah."

Beth looked startled. "Aunt Sarah died ten years ago, and she was always a little crazy. She believed in spirits. You never knew her."

"I've known her almost forever."

"But how on earth ...?"

"It wasn't on earth. It was in the universe. And mommy, it's time you knew where babies really come from."

Beth sat down, wondering what Amanda was going to say. She'd planned to tell her about the facts of life when she was old enough to understand. She almost began to laugh at their role reversals, but didn't see anything funny in the situation. She was beginning to feel a little hysterical. "Okay, Amanda," she said quietly. "Where do babies come from?"

"In a physical way, they grow in a special place in their mother's stomach—just like you were going to tell me—but in a spiritual way, their soul grows in the universal essence of light. When they choose to be born, their soul travels through energy vibrations of awareness, knowledge and light. It's like floating through time and space in a rainbow. When they arrive on earth, they're usually greeted by someone who slaps them. It's very shocking. That's what Gary says."

"When did he tell you this?"

"Last night, when he decided to be my brother again." Amanda gently patted her mother's stomach and said, "Hi in there. Can you hear me, Gary?"

Beth started to smile, wondering how she'd really known about the pregnancy. "Is that what happened to you when you were born?"

"I don't remember. It sounds like a silly story to me and I thought I dreamed it, but Gary said it was real and promised to tell me about the time we were Indians. And honest mom, that's the whole truth."

"Amanda, I just don't know what to do with you, or what to think."

For the first time, Lavender agreed with Amanda's mother, amazed that Amanda thought she was remembering a dream instead of recognizing her spiritual awareness. Amanda's thought perspectives sent her mind spinning. It appeared that she was wavering on the edge between knowing and unknowing, and her apparent acceptance of the physical world and its unreal reality called for drastic measures. She just had to wake up from her dream and see the light within herself before she became hopelessly lost in earth energies.

"Amanda," Lavender said, "Come and explore the sunrise with me. I'll introduce you to Ra, the sun god, and you'll experience the dawning of the light within you."

Just before dawn, Lavender appeared at the university and found a shadowy space to hide, hoping no one would notice Amanda and if they did, that they would think she was supposed to be there.

"Hi, Lavender. Hi, Amanda," Rainbow said. "It's nice that Lavender brought you with her to the seminar. Why don't you both sit right up front so you can get a clearer view?"

Lavender knew she'd get the cosmic consequences for this one, and wondered how Rainbow had seen them through the crowd of souls who had gathered for the seminar. Everyone was radiating rays of light; it looked like the sunrise had begun and they were all part of it.

Rainbow began her lecture by saying, "The sun is the energy of light and forms the essence of universal awareness. The vibrations of sunlight are the same as the vibrations of knowledge. Universal light energy is the key to ..."

"Lavender," Amanda whispered, "I have to go now. Thank you for bringing me here. It was a wonderful dream, but I have to wake up. It's almost time for breakfast."

At that moment, Lavender watched a light begin to dawn somewhere inside her soul. It looked like sunshine radiating through the reflection of a rainbow and she realized that when Amanda was ready to remember her true spiritual nature, she'd be able to clearly see through the shadows into the light. If she chose to experience her inner knowledge in a dream, that would just have to be the way it is for now.

Rainbow smiled at her, wondering when Lavender was really going to wake up and see the light.

Lavender watched the early morning sun rise over the edge of both the earth and the universe. Rays of light shimmered through the ethereal mist, splashing sunlight and shadow on the earth. She heard Amanda say, "Good morning, mommy. What's for breakfast?"

"Amanda, you're all red; you look as if you've spent the night in the sun. How on earth could you have gotten sunburned in your sleep?"

"I had the most wonderful dream about ..."

"Never mind," Beth said quickly. "Don't answer that. By this time, I should know better than to ask you. I can just imagine what you'll say."

Amanda looked through the window at the sunrise and smiled at the reflection of a rainbow in the mist.

Nineteen

The Matter of Energy

"What goes up, must come down."

The things people on earth have to contend with, Lavender thought. As if it isn't enough to have the burden of a body, you have to put up with things like gravity. She sympathized with Amanda as the science teacher's voice droned on.

"Everything is relative."

Now **that** was a joke, she thought, but noticed Amanda was taking it way too seriously. Lavender didn't like gravity, and *Everything is relative* was an incomplete sentence.

Amanda raised her hand. "Everything is relative to what?"

"Energy and motion," the teacher replied.

Lavender knew she had to do something fast, before Amanda started to believe the science teacher. His perspectives were certainly limited and he wasn't telling the whole truth about energy, even in its restricted form on earth. She projected words into the teacher's mouth.

"Energy is always in motion. It's most often seen as a vibration of thought and it's lighter than air. It's here, there, and everywhere at the same time, waiting around ever so patiently for someone to acknowledge it and pay it the proper respect. Scientists think they discover new forms of energy every once in awhile; what they're really discovering is something that already exists that they're just now becoming aware of.

"Scientists are notorious for locking energy into limiting expressions, rather than opening it up to reveal all of its harmonious and unlimited applications. When they find an expression of energy that appears to be unusual or extraordinary, they tend to isolate it and label the visible vibrations with restricting properties and qualities, never recognizing all of its potentials or realizing its many unseen manifestations. They misunderstand energy by squishing it into forms that aren't properly fitting and by squelching its true nature so that energy can't fully express itself as it really is."

The teacher shook his head. Where had those thoughts come

from? he wondered. Looking down at his notes, he continued, "Newton discovered gravity and light rays, and Einstein continued Newton's work by exploring mass and light with the equation of $E = mc^2$."

"Now wait just a minute here," Lavender said. "You've got it all wrong. Newton-Einstein made a terrible mistake. And he wasn't two people; he was one soul that flunked two lifetimes because he didn't completely understand energy."

She turned to Newton-Einstein sitting in the seat beside her. It was their third semester of Energy and Matter class together, and Lavender felt she just had to tell him how badly he'd misdirected energy by forgetting to include that everything is relative to energy in all of its forms and to all of its many multi-dimensional vibrations of time, space, matter, and motion. She tried to begin gently. She was angrier than she'd ever been before but didn't want to start out on the wrong foot, especially with someone who had so much power with what people believed about energy.

"You crazy old soul," she screamed. He was quite startled and jumped a few light years in his chair. "You think you can float around on a cloud forever, like you had all the time in the world, when people—**real** people—still believe what you said about energy. You know that *what goes up* continues to rise, yet you said it *must come down.* You should be hung for calling that energy gravity." She felt like punching a hole in his cloud with the point of her pencil, just to prove that his theory was full of holes.

"Well," he began softly. "That took a lot of mass and motion for you to bring it to my attention."

Always the scientist, Lavender thought.

"It just sort of happened, that's all," he continued. "I was under the influence of earth energies when I originally noticed this energy floating around and decided to call it gravity."

"That's a lousy excuse. I'll bet when the apple fell on your head, it knocked the spiritual sense right out of you."

"Well, I was going to say something like that but you said it for me. You mustn't put words in my mouth." He looked annoyed.

If you'd told the whole truth about energy, no one would have to speak for you, she thought. "Instead of saying *What goes up, must come down*, you could have said *As Above, So Below*, except someone already discovered that concept before you were born. And when you said *Everything is relative*, you could have completed the sentence and said *Everything is relative to every expression of energy in synchronous motion with thought.*

"And furthermore," Lavender said, barely pausing for a breath, "why do you preface your sentences with *Well?*"

Before he could answer, she said, "Well holds water. The water comes up. Energy is up. There, I proved my point," she said, stabbing her pencil in the air. In a voice dripping with sarcasm, she continued. "Well is a deep subject, but you probably think it's a black hole or a time warp."

Newton-Einstein looked at her very seriously from behind his brand new, horn-rimmed glasses that he'd manifested out of thin air while she'd been talking.

He looks scholarly in those glasses, she thought. He's probably practicing his appearance for his next lifetime.

"*Well holds water* is an awkward sentence," he said. "If you were really a writer, you'd know that and wouldn't make such a silly mistake. And you'd also get your past, present, and future tenses straight, instead of mixing them."

He's certainly all wound up, she thought.

"And you'd stop rephrasing your words repetitively, and you'd clarify the triplicate parallelity of your images, as well as ..."

Lavender interrupted him. "**That's only your perception**," she yelled. "It's all the same stuff, but being a scientist, you stereotype things and make relatively unqualified judgments about them."

Her computer started to flash big, red, neon eights on the screen. She was about to add that until he knew all the answers, he shouldn't be critical, but didn't have time to say it; he was already talking.

"*Well* is a good way to start a sentence when you want time to gather your thoughts before you form the words."

Time! What does he know about time? Next to nothing, Lavender thought. He's almost always late for the Time and Space class.

Looking directly at her, he paused for a few minutes and somehow managed to stretch it into several eons.

Lavender was impressed with his grasp of time, but was determined not to show it. She was tempted to ask him how he'd pulled time that far out in space when she remembered how it was done. It was a spiral illusion with transparent images, accomplished by stretching the circular motion of time through the energies of space, matter, and motion. She'd been so angry for a moment that she was seeing red and had forgotten. She almost smiled at him, but glared instead.

"You're a wonder," Rainbow said to Lavender. "Are you going to include **your perceptions** of time and transparent energies in the thesis for your master's degree?"

Lavender thought she heard someone say she was wandering, but didn't listen to or pay attention to the thought.

"Well, now, the apple was my only major mistake in that life ..."

He said *well* on purpose this time, Lavender thought. He must have stretched his thoughts too far out in space and when they bounced back, they came loose from their images. She was glad she hadn't smiled at him. He doesn't understand energy in motion as well as it appears that he does. It's obvious that he's still playing at being a scientist by believing the theory of action and reaction. She didn't recognize that it was the universal Law of Balance in earth-energy form because it had been placed in a scientific perspective.

"... and," he continued, "I did discover that the colors of the rainbow are found in sunlight. I just forgot to mention that the vibrations of energy from sunlight form the essence of universal knowledge."

"You **forgot**!?!" Lavender yelled. "You leave out the most important part, and you say you **forgot**!?!" She was enraged. "Before Amanda's mind got messed up with earth energies, she knew that she was part of the rainbow but because you **forgot** to say what you knew about the universal vibrations and expressions of energy, she's still looking for the light. When she was born, even her mother could see that she was a ray of sunshine.

"And when she tried to transform herself into a butterfly, vis-`a-vis a free spirit, it didn't work because people on earth believe it's impossible to metamorphose into their true form because you **forgot** to tell them about **all** the applications and expressions of energy," Lavender continued, conveniently forgetting that Amanda had chosen to see her reflection in the shadow of sunlight and to play the game of Illusion even after she knew the truth about the butterfly. "You ought to be ashamed of yourself. A spiritual scientist should know better."

"Lavender, sometimes you amaze me with your insights," Rainbow said, but she wasn't heard above the shouting.

Lavender took a deep breath, trying to calm herself. She was so angry at Newton-Einstein that she didn't see what she'd just said. If she'd looked clearly at her words and understood their images by relating them to herself, she would have raised her awareness into the universal vibrations of her soul and passed the Energy and Matter class with flying colors. But she was too busy blaming him for the limits that Amanda had accepted to see that his mistakes and the matter with energy were only relative to her thought perspectives and image perceptions.

She flew into a raging fury. "And you had the nerve to call yourself *Sir* when you were Newton," she screamed at him. Probably fell susceptible to visions of grandeur, she thought contemptuously, feeling very judgmental and smug that he'd set his soul evolvement back.

Her computer lit up again, flashing big, red, neon eights all over the screen, but she didn't pay attention to the warning. If the computer hadn't been plugged into universal energy, she would have unplugged it. The eights were beginning to get on her nerves.

"Well," she said. "Don't you have anything to say for yourself?" she asked, noticing that he'd become very quiet. He seemed to be spacing out and his thought-forms were circling around his frame of reference; some were escaping his attention. She caught the closest one and looked at the image. It was a reflection of Newton's error.

When he recognized his mistake, he decided to correct it and to make things clearer by returning as Einstein to explain that *Everything is relative*. As if that wasn't enough, he then expounded quantum theories of time and space, though she suspected that he hadn't completely understood them.

She turned the thought-form over and looked at the mirror image. He was scheduled to return to earth for a final exam, where he'd use the energies of gravity and relativity to pull scientific and spiritual thought together by discovering ***Metamorpheus Light Synergy***.

Sounds like Greek to me, she thought, as she asked him very nicely to explain the high points.

Newton-Einstein smiled at their momentary truce. "The theory involves the energy of knowledge as it rises in accordance with light shining through a soul's awareness. The light rises both between and higher than the images of dreams."

In English, please, Lavender thought.

"It means literally to transcend dreams by changing your awareness of dream images through being above and spiritually separate from matter in cooperative action with energy. It's like a parallel light of knowledge."

She thought it was a wonderful theory. It sounded as though light reflected through a rainbow would manifest into matter and then mirror the higher aspects of matter that were being transformed through light. She smiled at him, thinking that this theory—as soon as he discovered it—would set everyone on earth free to be themselves. They'd be able to rise above physical energy into spiritual energy.

She wanted to ask him how you could be separate simultaneously in dream images and cooperate with two parallel forms of energy at the same time and in the same space, but didn't have time to comprehend the finer vibrations. She wanted to tell Amanda about it immediately so she could remember her true nature.

"Now, Lavender ..." Rainbow began, "Wait a minute here. This is a very complex concept. You might want to take your time to completely understand it by going inside the parallel images of light and through the mirror reflections of matter as you go into the center of dream images." She vibrated rays of light into Lavender's thoughts, trying to get her attention. "Don't jump out of your mind; you wouldn't want to trip on physical thought perspectives by thinking that you could really be spiritually separate from yourself. Take into consideration that Newton-Einstein might be relating this theory in its earth-energy form and forgetting to include all the universal aspects and expressions of it."

But Lavender wasn't listening. She didn't have time to wait for him to go through the slow motions of birth and grow to adulthood so he could discover that life is really a dream. In a flash of sparkling colors, she slipped into Amanda's mind and shared the theory with her, hoping it would raise her thoughts.

Amanda was looking through an open window watching a butterfly in the breeze. She brightened up immediately and said to the science teacher, "Now I understand what energy is relative to."

Lavender was feeling calmer, and her computer quieted to a loud hum, vibrating at a corresponding rate of energy, when she remembered what Newton-Einstein had said about her writing. She got angry again and the sound waves on her computer began to beep.

How dare he tell me how to be a writer! she thought. He doesn't understand the concept of the written word. Just because he wrote one scientific book on principles, and believed in the magic power of imagination, doesn't make him an authority on writing. Even a beginning scribe knows that words are formed from thought/images drawn from knowledge. I wrote a very knowledgeable scroll on the esoteric power of images and the mystical properties of thought when I lived in Egypt.

Shadowy images flashed into her mind. Inside the images, she sensed that spiritual awareness and understanding were hanging in the balance. A feeling of fear surrounded her and she quickly turned off the images.

"Oh, and one more thing, or should I say two more things," she began, determined to have one more jab at Newton-Einstein. The eights flashed on her computer screen again, this time with a resounding signal that sounded like a foghorn.

"Before your next lifetime, you'll have to learn how to count and how to tell time correctly. When you reincarnate, people will tell you that one and one equals two, and that time is a straight line. You'll have to know that their illusionary images are their reality, not yours.

"If you say that one and one are really one and the same in a shared, synchronous movement, or if you ask them if they've ever seen a clock that stretched itself in a straight line, and you show them a clock so they can see that time is circular and returns to itself, don't insist that they're not making any sense. It makes them crazy. Believe me; I've been there before. If you go along with their illusions of reality and play at being a scientist, you won't remember how to circulate through time and spiral through space, or how to synchronize energy into motion and matter, and you'll fail your next lifetime."

"Lavender, you haven't learned how to count or tell time either," Rainbow said. "You still see Amanda as your physical side—your parallel self. And more often than not, you look at time in a linear way. I wish you'd recognize your own words."

Learning how to count was equivalent to equalizing karma, and he'd learn his lessons in time, Lavender thought. She almost offered to let him borrow her abacus for his next lifetime, but remembered that she'd flunked abundance and generosity in the early part of her evolvement by buying into greed and selfishness instead of giving and sharing, and had to pay for it by being poor in another lifetime. She wasn't going to take any chances on experiencing that again and decided to keep her abacus. He'd probably prefer a solar-powered calculator anyway, she thought.

Glancing over at him, she saw that he seemed absent-minded and lost in his thoughts. She lightened up a bit, starting to feel guilty for losing her temper and yelling at him. After all, he really was doing the best he could, even though it didn't seem like it. There was something she wanted to say to him, but couldn't think of what it was. Looking into her own thoughts, she felt she'd accomplished something. Amanda knew about *Metamorpheus Light Synergy.* I hope she understands it and doesn't think it's just a dream.

She vaguely heard Rainbow say that she was in some sort of trouble, and had stepped out of line this time, but the words sounded as if they were coming from far away. She felt deflated, like all the air had been knocked out of her. It takes an awful lot of energy to be angry, she thought.

"Lavender, your spiritual perspectives have been slipping and you're getting too far out in your frame of mind and dangerously close to dropping out of your dimension into earth energies," Rainbow said. "Unless you correct your thoughts, you'll have to deal with the cosmic consequences of them."

"Sounds like a space shift," she mumbled, feeling dragged down by her emotions. She took several deep breaths until she began to feel light-headed from the vibrations of etheric energy.

"Lavender, you're not really listening and I know you're not paying attention." Rainbow motioned toward her computer.

Number eight, in big red letters, flashed on the screen. Lavender looked up from her thoughts. ***Cosmic Commandment #8: Thou shalt not judge another soul for their actions, nor criticize their ideas or intentions.***

She immediately apologized to Newton-Einstein, but it was too late; she'd broken a commandment. The granite boulder with the cosmic commandments inscribed on them landed heavily on her desk and smashed her Alpha/Omega computer. Her printout on universal energy was ground to bits as the dust settled around her.

Lavender didn't know whether to laugh or cry. "It's all relative, I suppose," she muttered, looking at the dust and debris as it settled on the floor. There's one bright spot in all of this, she thought glumly. I still have my pencil. She barely noticed that the eraser was missing. And I learned that like attracts like, she thought. At the same time, I learned that opposites attract. And I almost understand the matter with energy. She looked over at Newton-Einstein and saw the astonished look on his face. His computer was crushed too, and he was holding a broken clock with the inner springs dangling in slow motion in the air.

Rainbow looked at her students. "That concludes today's segment on energy in motion, and how much it really matters, relative to individual thought perspectives." She smiled at Lavender and Newton-Einstein. "We also saw how eruptions of energy manifest by looking at their equivalent in scientific and spiritual energy storms.

"Before the next class, please review and revise energy in motion as it inherently shows itself in your thoughts and manifests in the multi-dimensional vibrations of your experiences." The other students gathered their notes and left the classroom. Lavender helped Newton-Einstein put his clock back together and offered him her abacus. He reached into space and gave her a new eraser for her pencil.

Twenty

The Direction of Destiny

"How'd the interview go?"

"I got the job," Amanda answered.

Her mother hugged her. "I knew you would. You're all grown up now and it doesn't seem like you're eighteen. The time just flew by."

Gary looked at his sister. "Now you get to go out into the real world, and you get to find out what life is *really* all about. You might even see how unreal all of it is," he said ominously.

"Ignore him," Beth said, smiling at him. "He's too young to know what life is really all about. He wants to be an Indian and conduct peaceful pow-wows when he grows up. Tell me about your job, Amanda."

"The corporation is a high-technology firm that researches ways to use light energy. They develop practical applications for solar energy by turning the light into power. There's a huge lab where they conduct energy experiments. I'll be a secretary for the assistant supervisor of a department called ISIS—Inter-Solar Infrared Spectrum."

"It sounds illuminating. Maybe now you'll begin to see the light within yourself," Gary said, smiling at the spiritual symbolism in her job. "Is that going to be your career for life?" he asked. "Or do you plan to find yourself and pursue your destiny? Amanda, is this what you *really* had in mind when you decided to reincarnate so you could share vibrations of universal light energy?"

Amanda laughed. "You're a little crazy, Gary. Do you really believe all that stuff about living before and searching for your soul's true purpose?"

Gary nodded. "It's the spiritual truth," he replied solemnly.

She looked thoughtfully at her brother. "I don't know why, but I'd like to save enough money and go to Africa in a few years. I'm not sure what I want to do there and I can't explain my feeling," she said. "It's just something I'd like to do."

Gary smiled again. Amanda knew more than she thought she did about her destiny. Even though she didn't realize it yet, she was beginning to open up the awareness of her true nature and to travel a path that would lead her into remembering her spiritual knowledge. "Maybe you want to go to Africa so you can meet one of those medicine men you called shamans when you were a little girl," he said.

Beth rolled her eyes up to the ceiling, recalling the incident in her mind. "Gary, you couldn't possibly know about that and Amanda was too young to remember it."

"I'll bet if we wait till daddy comes home from work, he'd remember it," Gary said. "Even though he doesn't talk about it, he still wants to go to Egypt and dig up the treasure he hid for Amanda."

"I think that somehow the two of you planned to drive me out of my mind, but fortunately I've always been able to keep my grip on reality even though I did have a few doubts from time to time." Beth smiled, remembering how absurd some of her thoughts had been.

"We were just trying to help you open up your inner knowing," Gary said. "Amanda got lost in earth energies and forgot who she is and what life is really all about, so I decided to come along to remind you both about your spiritual nature." He looked at his mother. "You wouldn't listen to me when I was your Aunt Sarah."

"Is that your destiny, Gary—to help me remember my spiritual nature and to show Amanda the way through these earth energies called life?"

"I just want you to see your real self. My purpose in this life is to help bring back the ways of the Indians in respecting the earth and its natural resources. Amanda already knows the way to see the truth about herself, but she doesn't recognize it anymore."

"I know, Gary. You've told me before," Amanda said.

"It's worth repeating," he replied. "Rainbow is your higher self, the higher vibration of your soul that holds the key to your spiritual knowledge and the memories of your past lives. And Lavender ..."

"... is my favorite color," Amanda said, finishing the sentence for him.

"She's more than that. Lavender is the energy expression of your spiritual side and is just as real as you are. They're both more than they appear to be, and you'll discover that when you wake up from your dream. You know the truth about your spiritual nature without really knowing that you know because one of your favorite things to do is to walk through the rain and look for rainbows. And," he added, looking directly into Amanda's eyes, "a rainbow is only visible in the sunshine—when the light of the universe shines through the mist."

As if the conversation had turned too serious for him, he grinned in the annoying eleven-year-old way he had before saying something that he knew would irritate Amanda. "Hey mom, do you remember when Amanda took off all her clothes and ran naked through the rain, and you and daddy had to chase after her? Remember what you told the neighbors?"

"Gary! That happened before you were born. Amanda was only two years old. How do you know about it?"

Not answering the question, he replied, "I liked your explanation because it was so real. You told the neighbors that Amanda was just being natural and that she thought she was a rainbow." He turned to Amanda. "Rainbow thought you were adorable and Lavender laughed so hard that she almost fell through her duplicate dimension."

"Mom," Amanda said pleadingly. "Can't we do something about him? Maybe trade him in for a myopic goldfish or something? How does he know about things that I don't even remember?"

Beth shrugged her shoulders. "You used to do the same thing to me, Amanda—telling me things you had no earthly way of knowing. You said you dreamed it all, and some of your dreams really did seem to be out of this world." She smiled. "But you came to your senses by the time you were seven."

"Just about the time I was born," Gary said.

"Why don't you go outside and pretend you're an Indian," Amanda said.

"I don't have to pretend," he replied.

Amanda smiled. She almost believed he really was an Indian. On a deep, inner level, she admired his spiritual sureness about who he was. She wondered if what he'd said about rainbows was true, and if lavender really was more than her favorite color.

Twenty-One

The Real World

Amanda was wandering through a rainbow as she watched herself floating through the colors. "I want to find myself," she said. "I want to know who I am and what my life is all about. I want to know what's real."

She heard the sound of thunder echoing through the clouds. If I could wake up from this dream, she thought, feeling comfortably drowsy and half-asleep in her dream world, maybe I'd know if the rainbow is real or if it's just a misty dream image in my mind. Opening her eyes, she looked at the clock. It was too early to get up and get ready for work so she lay in bed, listening to the rain tap softly on the window as it gently lulled her back to sleep. Closing her eyes, she thought she heard a rainbow whisper in the wind, calling her name.

She woke to the sound of an alarm clock. Looking out the window, she saw that it was bright and sunny. A rainbow shimmered through the mist in the early morning light. The conversation yesterday with Mom and Gary must have inspired my dream, she thought.

A fragment from another dream about walking through the rain appeared in her mind—or maybe it was a fragment from the same dream—a dream about a doorway and talking to the color lavender inside the rainbow. She pushed the images to the back of her mind, not wanting to be late on her first day of work.

But the image of the rainbow stayed on her mind. "Gary, wake up. I need to talk to you," Amanda said softly, touching his shoulder. "I have to go to work now and I want to know how to know what's real."

He yawned loudly. "You just know, that's all," he said, turning over and going back to sleep.

What kind of an answer is that? she wondered, thinking that it couldn't possibly be that easy. Her little brother could be so complacent at times, she wasn't sure if he did know what was real. I'll find out for myself, she thought. She walked outside, determined to explore the real world and to discover what life was really all about.

* * * *

Lavender watched Amanda wander through etheric energies in her dream. She couldn't clearly see through the cloud that surrounded her and felt as if she was lost somewhere in a foggy mist. Lately she'd been feeling separate and disconnected from herself, and was having trouble concentrating on her spiritual studies. For some unknown reason, the knowledge seemed to be slipping away. Through the mist in her mind, she vaguely heard Rainbow say, "It looks like Amanda is taking a U-turn outside of herself; she appears to be going in the wrong direction."

"Looking after your parallel self is so challenging when they insist on being so physical about everything," Lavender muttered.

On the surface, everything appeared normal. The only problem was that Amanda was beginning to wonder what was real. It was **that** question again; the one that seemed to come up in every lifetime and Lavender still didn't have the answer. She knew she'd flunk the Reality Awareness class unless she could somehow find the realness in the experiences that Amanda was beginning to create for herself.

Looking through the window, she saw that it was raining. The day was dismal and gray, and matched her feelings. Why does Amanda want to have those experiences in the first place? she wondered irritably. Can't she see they aren't real? Lavender sighed, knowing she'd have to help her find herself in the real world.

This is probably going to be difficult. Amanda can be so determined about some things and once she makes up her mind, it's almost impossible to change it, she thought to herself, feeling sure that Amanda would become hopelessly lost in earth energies unless she could turn her around in the right direction.

She's going around in circles and doesn't even know it, Lavender thought, watching her move through the foggy mist in her mind. Until she finds the center of the circle and sees herself, she'll just keep going around and around, returning to the same place over and over again until she finds the center of the circle. Lavender didn't seem to realize how circular her own thought was.

She felt as if she was coming down with a mind cold; her thoughts and images were foggy from the etheric vibrations of energy. I must have caught it when I was wandering through a cloud in the earth's atmosphere, she thought. Mind colds are awful when you're in spiritual form and have no way to express yourself out of them. I can't even get a good sneeze into motion; everything feels clogged up inside of me.

She started to sniffle, feeling sorry for herself. Mind colds were a bad sign. Free spirits were supposed to know better. You weren't supposed to be negative or make mistakes; you were supposed to be in a higher level of awareness and above all that sort of stuff. Most importantly, you were supposed to be able to see things clearly; you weren't supposed to scatter and separate your thoughts. You were supposed to be able to synchronize all your energy vibrations and keep yourself together. She sighed again, sinking deeper into the cloud she was floating around on.

She began to feel dizzy as she watched Amanda go around herself in circles. Everything seemed to be so unreal. She couldn't seem to recognize that if she wanted to find herself and know what was real, all she had to do was look within herself and see inside her thoughts and experiences. It seemed to be an easy enough thing to do, but then she noticed that her thoughts were beginning to look like foggy ghosts moving through misty illusions of reality.

Lavender felt as if she was coming apart at the seams. Everything *seemed* to be this or *seemed* to be that. With everything *seeming* to be something else, life *seemed* to be something it wasn't, and her thoughts *seemed* to be illusionary images that floated through realms of reality that were misty and unrecognizable. No wonder Amanda *seemed* to be going around in circles and couldn't *seem* to find herself or see what was real.

Just then Rainbow seemed to weave into her thoughts, carrying a thread that unraveled the truth to the tapestry of life. "Lavender," she said, "Pull yourself together. Why don't we take a walk through the rain? It might help you center your thoughts so you can see yourself more clearly and find out why you feel separate from yourself."

She's probably going to tell me I'm flunking Reality Awareness, Lavender thought miserably, because it's raining here at school and it's sunny on earth and I'm not sure what's real. It was bothering her more than words could say and was at the heart of her thoughts. She didn't **know** what was real.

"Let's just walk through the clouds," Rainbow suggested. "I have something I'd like to show you."

Lavender sensed that her mind cold was getting worse; she felt foggier by the minute and was losing her thought/images in cloudy perspectives and misty perceptions. I wonder if she's going to show me the silver lining in the cloud, Lavender thought, then answered her own question. That would be too obvious. Rainbow's style is to let me learn for myself.

Rainbow showed her the future images of Amanda's present

thoughts and actions. It looked as though she'd become completely caught up in playing the game of Illusion and was hopelessly lost in earth energies. I just knew it, Lavender thought to herself.

It appeared that Amanda had thought that looking for herself in the real world and trying to discover what life is really all about was an interesting and exciting adventure that soon became a difficult challenge. She wasn't sure if she could find the realness in the first place, or even if she'd recognize it if she saw it in the second place, because she didn't know exactly what she was looking for.

Working at her new job, meeting new people, and making her own way in the world had seemed to be a lot of fun to begin with, but then it all turned dreary. Something was missing. Deep inside, she didn't feel real and knew that she wasn't being true to herself. Feeling lost, she began to despair of ever finding realness. She was drifting, with no clear sense of direction.

This is awful, Lavender thought. Truly nauseating. She believes that her earth experiences are real. She got sidetracked by listening to what other people said was real, instead of listening to herself. If she'd look below the surface of her experiences, she'd see through their outer appearances and recognize the thoughts and feelings inside them and understand why they were happening. Then she'd know what was real and she'd be able to change her experiences to reflect the realness.

Lavender was taking notes on Amanda's experiences, knowing she'd have to write a report, when the lines blurred together and she began to see double images. Her words seemed to repeat themselves, showing one interpretation that had two meanings or was she seeing one image that had two understandings? She couldn't be sure. Amanda's thoughts were cloudy and she couldn't read them clearly. She knew that Amanda wanted to be real and express her true nature, but she wasn't sure exactly how to do that and couldn't seem to find herself in the first place or even in the second place.

Lavender felt her pencil begin to slip through her fingers. She tightened her grip on it, even though her hold on the words seemed to be stuck in a shadow. I'll never get this report done unless I get clear on it and see what I'm really saying, she thought to herself through the mist in her mind. She knew she was writing the same thing twice, but couldn't seem to find a fresh approach to her words and their thought/images.

Between the pithy puns and the wobbly words, she wasn't sure if she was a free spirit searching for truth or a spirited seeker of knowledge. Mind colds could do strange things to a soul, warping their thought perspectives and throwing their image perceptions off balance. Just then she sneezed with such velocity that she blew herself backwards into her original thoughts and their misty images. Rainbow handed her a Kleenex.

"My energy vibrations hurt and I feel bad all over," she said. "I'd like to feel better about myself," she added, sniffling partly from the pictures she'd seen and partly from her mind cold.

"Review the thoughts and feelings that preceded Amanda's experiences," Rainbow suggested.

Lavender looked inside her mind. Her thoughts of feeling separate and disconnected from herself, and the miserable thought that she was flunking Reality Awareness, combined with Amanda's actions of searching for herself in what *seemed* to be the real world and her despairing thought about not finding realness were the precipitating thoughts and feelings that had caused and created the current catastrophe. Lavender felt as though she'd been hit with the boomerang of her negative thoughts and it hurt. But it certainly cleared her senses, or so it seemed.

She felt responsible for Amanda's failure to find herself. It's not very spiritual to make mistakes, she thought. Or was that what everyone else thought? I think it can be helpful to make mistakes when you look inside them and learn from them, she told herself. Mistakes can be good for your soul when you turn them around; then they become interesting and enlightening insights and experiences that help you understand yourself.

A cloudy afterthought appeared in her mind. It wasn't all my fault. It was those damn earth energies; they could really bring you down. And Amanda is partly to blame too. I tried to tell her, but she wouldn't pay attention to me. Maybe if she'd changed her frame of mind and the way she looked at things in the beginning, this wouldn't have happened. And even after she started off the wrong way, if she'd listened to herself and looked twice, and clearly seen and read her inner images and feelings, she could have rearranged her thoughts and reshaped her experiences.

But I shouldn't have indulged in negative thinking in the first place. There's absolutely no excuse for it and I know better. Why should Amanda have to suffer when I'm the one who had the thought about flunking Reality Awareness? Amanda is searching for spiritual truth, trying to find herself—to see and know what's real—and I'm supposed to help her. If I hadn't felt so foggy from my mind cold, I would have seen what was really happening, she thought, watching the images circle in her mind.

But on second thought, I'm not being completely honest with myself. Somewhere in my mind, I was aware of all of this before it occurred; I just wasn't listening to myself. There's always a positive way to look at things, and I could have redirected my energy and focused spiritual thoughts and feelings into Amanda's awareness. It *seems* I've made a terrible mistake.

Lavender was so wrapped up in feeling guilty, and in blaming herself and earth energies for what she perceived to be the negative expressions of Amanda's experiences, that she failed to see what her *seeming* mistake really offered Amanda. Drifting through the cloudy images of her thoughts, she didn't hear Amanda say, "There **has** to be a way to see through the surface appearance of my experiences."

Amanda watched words run across an image of pages somewhere in her mind. *Maybe all my experiences are reflections of my thoughts and feelings, interwoven into a tapestry of truth and knowledge that shows me a picture of my soul.* Smiling to herself, she said, "If I look at life in a positive way, maybe I'll see that my experiences are really showing me a wonderful way to know myself better, and if I rearrange my thoughts and the way I look at things, I'm sure I'll see the truth within myself and I'll know what's real."

Twenty-Two

A Spiritual Shadow

"Maybe I'm not being true to myself—to my spiritual nature. Maybe I'm not real," Lavender whispered to herself. The thought seemed to come from a shadowy, voiceless past and the image was so frightening that she ran away from it instead of taking a U-turn into herself.

Lavender saw a misty dream image of her shadowy thought enter Amanda's awareness and send her spinning into a duplicate dimension of energy. It looked as though she was lost without herself in a parallel place in a world where she didn't understand what was real and couldn't seem to see the truth within herself. She felt separate from her soul as she journeyed through her earth experiences in search of herself.

Watching her dream, she saw her experiences fragmenting into images that circled the earth and the universe, repeating in echoes of energy that blew through the winds of time. The images showed a quest for truth and a spiritual search for answers to questions that had haunted her for ages, following her from lifetime through lifetime, like a dark, menacing shadow that obscured the light of her knowledge.

Rainbow wanted to tell her that the shadow originated in Egypt, when she turned off her soul memories and her spiritual knowledge, but knew that Lavender wasn't ready to read the scroll yet, or to clearly see through the shadows into the light. She remained silent as she watched Lavender's images flow through her thoughts.

Doubts and questions revolved in Lavender's mind. How do you know what's real? How can you be true to yourself in your earth experiences and in your spiritual awareness simultaneously when it seems that they're two separate worlds? How do you **know** which world is real when it seems that what you feel and think appears to be unreal, and what other people say appears to be real? I've searched high and low trying to find myself, but I haven't found the answers to who I am or what is real.

"Look through the shadows into the light, Lavender, and you'll see the truth within yourself," Rainbow said.

"I want to know who I really am. I want to **know** what's **real**," she said to herself. She thought she heard an echo of a voice say, "I want to remember my spiritual knowledge," but it sounded more like a whisper of wind.

Walking through the rain and listening to her thoughts, she came upon a door that was locked. Looking at the door, she thought about giving up the search for her spiritual knowledge but changed her mind. She knew, somewhere deep inside of her, that there was a way to open the door and if she wanted to find herself and know the truth about her soul, she'd be able to unlock the door that opened into a **real** world of **knowing**.

Somehow she knew that Amanda had seen the door in a foggy, misty dream, but didn't seem to know that she'd seen it and didn't know it was real. She was still going around in circles, looking for the door into her dream. Or maybe she was looking for her dream that showed her the doorway Lavender had found.

Somewhere inside herself, she saw a golden key shimmering in the center of a sunrise. Reaching within herself, she held the key in her hand for a moment and felt a magical power surge through her. She sensed that she was standing on the threshold of discovering the truth about her soul and finding her spiritual knowledge.

Turning the key in the lock, she felt her energies expanding into realms of awareness within herself. She had the strangest feeling for a moment, as if she was someone else. An old, bearded man stood inside a shadow in the open doorway, holding a scroll in his hands. She recognized him as the philosopher she'd seen in her images from time to time.

As she stood outside the doorway, she suddenly felt very afraid to enter. The philosopher was trying to speak, but she couldn't hear him above the gust of wind that blew through her soul. Reaching toward her, he offered her the scroll but she refused it. Tears welled up in her eyes as she watched Amanda walk through the open doorway and accept the scroll. Then the image disappeared into a misty light.

Lavender blinked her eyes and looked through the window. It wasn't raining anymore. The sunlight sparkled into a rainbow as it shone brightly through the clearing mist, reflecting a brilliant sunrise that showed a path leading into a world of knowledge and enlightenment.

Twenty-Three

Clearing Clouds

Rainbow looked at Lavender's and Amanda's dream images as she surrounded the energy vibrations of time and space in a simultaneous frame of separate awareness and parallel perceptions. "You found the key to open the door into your spiritual knowledge when Amanda said she wanted to understand her true nature," she said.

Lavender started to remind her that Amanda hadn't dreamed that part of her dream yet, but knew somewhere in her mind that she had, even if she didn't understand how it had already occurred. Maybe Amanda has to experience it before I can understand it, and I have to understand it so Amanda can experience it, she thought to herself. Somehow, that felt right.

Rainbow smiled at Lavender's thought. "Did you know that you used Amanda's key to open the door?"

Lavender looked at Rainbow in amazement. How could I use Amanda's key when she doesn't remember it yet? she wondered, knowing she already knew the answer to that question. It had something to do with becoming and being real in a frame of awareness that appeared to occur as a time-release process, when it actually happened all at once. It was still confusing to her and she was glad that Rainbow was separating the images into parallel pieces so she could understand them before she put the picture together.

"There are myriad and mystical thoughts always in motion that weave together to form images and perceptions of reality. Thoughts and feelings are the threads at the center of all experiences. The energy expressions of all experiences are directed by thought perspectives and image perceptions, and are put into motion through feelings."

Rainbow began to flow upward through spiraling vibrations of energy as she reviewed Lavender's and Amanda's earlier thoughts and experiences. "When you redirected your thought perspectives toward finding the truth by wanting to remember your knowledge, your feelings created the experiences that led you to the beginning of real understanding in your spiritual studies. When Amanda changed her image perceptions and her feelings in her search to know what's real, she created the way to see the truth within herself. Both of you influenced each other's thoughts and your seemingly separate experiences were reflections of each other's feelings."

Lavender didn't want to interrupt Rainbow, but it was beginning to seem as if she and Amanda had changed places. It appeared that Amanda had thought and experienced her feelings, and Amanda's feelings had influenced her thoughts and their energy expressions, and vice versa or something like that. At least that's what her notes read when she looked at them later.

"Thoughts and feelings are very closely interwoven with their corresponding experiences. Images and energy expressions are perfectly synchronized with thoughts. When thoughts and feelings are put into motion through the act of thinking the thought or feeling the emotion, the energy of matter begins to form in space and time, and the images of thoughts begin to express themselves as visible vibrations of energy. This is one of the ways that inner knowledge makes itself known and shows the truth."

Lavender loved listening to Rainbow talk about thoughts and images, and wished that Amanda could hear this lecture on creating your own reality. She knew it would help her to see through the illusions of her earth experiences and to understand the realness in her thoughts.

Rainbow's words sounded like gentle raindrops tapping softly on a window. Lavender began to feel as if she was dreaming, floating upward through the colors of a rainbow, feeling lighter and lighter, then soaring, free in spirit and form, somewhere over the rainbow.

Rainbow seemed to ramble on and on in a circular motion, looking at Lavender's and Amanda's shared experiences from several separate thought perspectives and image perceptions simultaneously. "You and Amanda are more in harmony than you realize. That's why you were able to use her key to open the door into your knowledge. Before you were born, you created a parallel pattern of energy that held within itself the power to transform its essence into vibrations of universal energy."

Lavender wondered why Rainbow was viewing Amanda as a parallel vibration of energy when the word *parallel* was supposed to be something that was simultaneously separate from itself, destined never to merge. Then she saw that Rainbow was talking about similarities while she was looking at both the physical and spiritual side of reality as she reviewed two seemingly separate lessons.

One lesson was about thoughts and feelings; the other lesson was about being in harmony with the essence of yourself and recognizing your true nature. Lavender saw that she was expressing two images at the same time. One image was about experiencing life; the other image was about understanding life. She watched separate and simultaneous images begin to merge as the picture of her soul and the tapestry of life began to come together in threads of awareness, woven by her thought perspectives.

Rainbow shimmered as sunlight sparkled through the energy vibrations of her colors. Her words had spun together, weaving higher meanings in each vibration of energy as they spiraled upward through levels of insight and awareness, and cleared the mist over the rainbow.

Lavender wished she'd paid closer attention to everything Rainbow had said because she felt that she was simultaneously opening a window into her spiritual knowledge and remembering her true nature, and that a new world was waking up inside of her and she was beginning to see herself as she really was, and she wasn't quite sure what had transpired to bring about those feelings. When it sounded as if Rainbow was rambling, she'd begun to wander in her thoughts.

Rainbow was now talking about vibrations of knowledge and living in the energies of simultaneous worlds. It seemed that she'd heard this lecture before at the sunrise seminar at the university, and she'd seen it just a moment ago in her mind. It was curious how you could lose track of time like that when you were wandering around in your thoughts, or when you felt as if you were somewhere inside the middle of a dream.

Returning to the swing of current events, Lavender picked up where she thought she'd left off. "I got lost in earth energies, just like Amanda, didn't I?" she asked. "That's why everything was so foggy and it's where I caught my cloudy mind cold. I was wandering through time and space in a duplicate dimension of energy before I saw the door. I was dreaming, but I thought I was awake. I found the key to knowledge while I was looking for the way to find myself and to know what's real."

"At the same time you were doing that," Rainbow said, "Amanda was walking through the rain looking for rainbows while she was wandering around in your thoughts looking for herself. The doorway into her dream is shrouded in a misty image and she's not really sure if she's seen it yet. That's why she seems to be going around in circles. She thinks she's dreaming about rainbows; she doesn't know how real they are." Rainbow looked at Lavender as if she was waiting for her to say something.

Lavender wondered who the philosopher was that had offered her the scroll. She felt that he was connected with her in a spiritual way, and that the scroll opened up into knowledge, but she didn't know who he really was. Her throat began to hurt, and she wasn't sure if she'd seen that image at all; it seemed more like a shadowy thought. She decided not to mention it to Rainbow.

She looked at the summary of her report. It was fairly clear and she thought she'd captured the high points of Amanda's experiences, even though she knew she still had a lot to learn about Reality Awareness.

One paragraph stood out above the rest; it seemed to be superimposed on the paper. "Amanda and I were traveling together from different thought perspectives for the same purpose. Even though we're worlds apart, it seemed that we merged for a time and then somehow changed places. I was in her world while she was simultaneously in mine. We're following a parallel path and searching for the same thing—she called it truth and I called it knowledge—and we've both taken the beginning steps on our journey home to rediscover our true spiritual nature and to remember who we really are."

Twenty-Four

A Portrait of Pages

"This picture is so beautiful," Lavender said, looking at the open book. "I can see the thoughts in the images and touch the feelings that formed the words." She ran her fingers lightly over the lines of the picture. "There are so many intricate vibrations and interweaves of energy flowing through the paragraphs and floating through the pages." Looking at Rainbow, she smiled. "The reflection of universal light looks like symbols shaped from words. It must have taken a lot of thought for the artist to paint the picture—to form the colors and images into expressions of energy."

"It's a still-life portrait," Rainbow said. "It's an illusion of reality." Seeing the look on Lavender's face, she continued softly. "It's a novel idea/image, but it's motionless; the energy isn't moving. The picture looks like silent words that once upon a time created a magical, mystical world have now solidified into a book."

Lavender wondered why Rainbow's viewpoint about the picture was disillusioning. Maybe she woke up on the wrong side of the universe this morning and her perceptions are out of sync, she thought. Even a rainbow can have a cloudy day every now and then. "This is a timeless treasure," she said, unaware that Rainbow was looking at the picture from an altogether higher perspective that clearly revealed aspects of her own soul.

"The picture is a parallel image captured in a time/space sequence of energy and held bondage within its frame," Rainbow said. "The picture shows esoteric images and portrays the essence of the artist's feelings and thought perspectives when that soul created their world with words. The pages hold an energy vibration of knowledge and the picture looks like a mosaic from a much larger masterpiece."

"If that's how you feel about it, then that's how you perceive it," Lavender said. "I think the artist leaves the images open for individual interpretation to show you a magical world within yourself because I can see and sense what the words symbolize. If you open up your imagination and look between the paragraphs and beyond the pages, you'll see that the energy is in motion because the words inspire feelings and images that you can't literally *see* in the picture, but you can read them within your own thoughts and feelings."

She touched the open book again. "The images are real, even if they appear to be illusions, because I can *feel* the energy inside the words. The words dance on the pages, in harmony with their images as they open up into expressions of experiences. The images soar into thoughts and form the essence of knowing within my mind. The thought/images give me a wonderful feeling about the transcendent nature of the artist. It looks as though the creator of this picture painted their soul into the images, and the pages literally vibrate with energy," she said, hugging the book to her heart.

Rainbow smiled at Lavender's perception of the picture. "It sounds as though you have some artistic ability yourself," she said.

Lavender glowed at Rainbow's compliment. "I do consider myself to be an artist, sculpting thoughts and shaping their forms into the energy expressions of experiences by creating word/images drawn from feelings that reveal inner knowledge. My pencil is my paintbrush and words draw the pictures of my imagination." Looking into her thoughts, she said, "I'd like to completely open up and explore my creative abilities."

"Then you might be interested in the **Art Appreciation** workshop," Rainbow suggested. "It begins today in the here and now, and the hands-on approach to applying what you learn would offer you a wonderful opportunity to look into the creative aspects of Reality Awareness in a higher vibration of knowledge." She looked at the book that Lavender held in her hands. "One of the projects could help you recognize more of your spiritual nature," she added.

"It sounds super, but maybe I should wait until Amanda is ready to move forward in her life," Lavender said. "Her frame of mind and focus of awareness still seems to be too physically centered and earth-oriented right now, and I'm not sure if this is the right time for me to do my own thing and to let her go her own way, even though the class sounds perfect for me. Maybe I should hang around for awhile to keep an eye on her so she doesn't get stuck somewhere or lost in the unreal world again." She wavered, unsure about attending the workshop.

But on second thought, maybe I'm standing in my own way. Revving up her energies, she said, "I'd love to expand my horizons and explore higher vibrations of reality." Answering Rainbow's unspoken question, she continued, "I know I have to respect Amanda's free will and her choice to create and explore her own experiences. What's she going to be doing while I'm learning how to express myself in creative forms of energy?"

"She's registered for classes in opening up her imagination to help her see inside her experiences. She wants to learn how to reframe her thoughts and feelings in a positive manner, and how to connect them with energy to create what she wants in life."

"That sounds like she's going to play with reality and illusion." A vision of Amanda as a beautiful butterfly floated past her eyes and soared somewhere over the rainbow into the universe, free in flight. Lavender felt lighter than air, as if she was flowing into Amanda's imagery and becoming part of it. An insight sparkled in her mind. "She's going to do more than rearrange and change energy; she's going to learn how to master it, isn't she?"

"That's the plan she has in mind, but first she needs to learn how to know the difference between reality and illusion, and how to synchronize her thoughts and feelings into a flowing movement of creative energy so she can shape her experiences into powerful and positive expressions of her true nature."

Lavender was so pleased that Amanda had raised her thoughts and was ready to explore being a free spirit. "When did this happen?" she asked, wondering how she could have missed something this important.

"It occurred while you were wandering through your cloudy mind cold and you'd misplaced your sense of awareness and focus of attention," Rainbow answered. "You didn't see her begin to act on her feelings about looking at life in a clearer way. In her thoughts, she knew that she'd created and was responsible for her own experiences. Within her words was the desire to explore her spiritual awareness and open herself up to knowing the truth about who she really is. She's ready to accept her power in finding herself and in learning all about **real**-life pictures."

Lavender looked at the still-life portrait she held in her hands. Leafing through the pages to a picture of a green, grassy meadow with a few trees, she saw a small, quiet pond that sparkled in the sunshine, reflecting an image of a rainbow. Looking at the tranquil nature scene that the words inspired, she surrounded one of the trees with a soft glow of energy. The tree moved as if it were being caressed by a gentle breeze. She tried it again, focusing her thoughts more directly this time. The tree shimmered in the wind.

Smiling to herself, as though she'd just remembered a special secret, she imagined a flower in the picture—a yellow rosebud. Closing her eyes, she created every detail of the rosebud in her mind, then held the image in her thoughts for a few minutes—seeing an early-morning dewdrop gently nourish the bud, watching the petals begin to slowly uncurl and open up in the warmth and light of the sunshine. Gently touching the rose and feeling the velvety softness of the petals, she breathed in its delicate fragrance.

Then she let her thought/image go, picturing the rose in the center of the meadow. When she opened her eyes and looked at the picture in the book, the rose was there—right where she'd imagined it to be. And even as she watched the rosebud, it began to magically open up by itself, petal by petal, reaching for the light, unfolding in a natural rhythm of harmony with the earth and the universe, as if it had a mind of its own once it was created and imbued with energy.

This is fun, she thought. And it's so easy to do that even a baby could do it. The pictures in my mind become real through my thoughts and spring into action from my feelings, just like magic. Looking through the pages at the words in the book and watching their images move in the mindscape of her imagination, she knew—with absolute certainty—that she could change or create anything in her awareness that she wanted to change or create, just by her thoughts and feelings.

Sparkling with light in her newly-remembered knowledge, she felt a surge of power rush through her as she began to focus her attention and direct her thoughts into expressions of energy. Looking into the mirror-like surface of the pond, she saw Amanda reflected in the image. Watching the image begin to ripple and move, she thought to herself, Real-life pictures are so much better than still-life pictures, knowing that even though Amanda's thought perspectives were different from hers, the images were woven into the same masterpiece.

Reading the thought/images in Amanda's mind, she watched herself being drawn into the picture. The dual-image portrait of the experiences they created and chose to have reflected their parallel search for truth and knowledge. Deciding to explore the images even further, she expanded the frame of the picture to open up a broader area of their experiences. As she widened the frame, it became deeper and showed higher dimensions of energy at the same time.

The images became superimposed upon one another, each image influencing and interacting with the thoughts and feelings that had originally created and shared in shaping it. She saw that all the images of their experiences were connected through vibrations of thought, and that each image was synchronized in a perfect rhythm of movement with all the other images in the picture.

It looked as if there were threads of energy that wove in and out, and between and through the picture as they unraveled and wove together, curling and connecting to create and form a new picture while the original picture was in the process of shaping itself. The energy was in perpetual motion, in an ever-changing process of creation and expression, renewing and reshaping itself in every moment.

Then she noticed that the picture was moving in tune with her here and now thoughts and feelings, and with Amanda's thoughts and feelings—the images vibrating with their individual perceptions and perspectives of each other's thoughts, opening up and expanding into all their past/present/future experiences at once. She saw how each of their actions caused reactions, and how Amanda's thoughts and feelings were interwoven with the expressions of her experiences, and how her own thoughts and feelings were intricately intertwined with Amanda's. And even as she watched the images of their experiences flow through the motions of matter in time and space, she saw that every experience was somehow influenced by an even higher vibration of energy that she couldn't clearly see.

The picture appeared to be breathing. The images and their interconnected experiences were alive with energy, vibrating and pulsating in a flowing movement, forming waves of energy that went everywhere at once, spiraling into infinity. Her mindscape became so vast that she couldn't see where it began or where it ended. The energy of the images flowed over the edges of the picture frame, spilling into a universal awareness that went beyond her realm of understanding. The power she held in her hands was so awesome that she became frightened.

"Rainbow," she called, through a rush of wind that surrounded her and echoed through her soul. "What's happening to the images in the picture—to me? I can influence energy and shape it through my merest wisp of thought, feeling, and belief. I can make it do whatever I want it to do, but it's out of my control and it scares me."

"Lavender, look at me. It only appears to be out of your control because you don't completely understand your full power or how to focus and direct it. The energy frightened you because you aren't yet ready to master the energy of the universe. There are so many things you need to know about the true art of creating your own reality. I tried to tell you this in your first semester of classes but you chose to lock yourself into limits, rather than freeing yourself to open up your awareness and expand into the energies of your soul." Rainbow's cryptic words went right into the heart of the matter.

Lavender remembered her lofty attitude and winced at her earlier arrogance. She wished she'd been more open to learning instead of thinking she already knew how to create her own reality. But then she was in good company; a lot of other highly-advanced souls thought they knew all the answers too. Rainbow's lecture on lopsided limits resonated in her mind.

"Many souls limit their true power by misunderstanding the concept of reality creation by thinking it applies only to their level of spiritual awareness and to their experiences in a physical vibration of energy. That's just one aspect of it. The creation of reality vibrates in every dimension of energy at once. A soul must experience and understand *all* the vibrations as they evolve into higher realms of light."

"Will you teach me how energy manifests in all of its multi-dimensional vibrations and tell me how it shows itself in all of its physical, spiritual, and universal forms?" Lavender asked, wanting to learn everything there was to know about reality creation, especially in this higher dimension, so she'd be able to see into and through her thought/images and understand their energy expressions on all levels of awareness.

Rainbow looked directly at her; it seemed as though she was looking right through her into a mirrored image that reflected universal light into a transparent form. "The clue to creating your own reality and understanding all your multi-dimensional experiences in every vibration of awareness is to clearly see all the energy expressions of your experiences, without any clouds to fog your view or mist your mind.

"I can teach you only what you're ready to learn by showing you the beginning steps through earthly and spiritual vibrations of energy. You must walk the steps yourself and learn about the power of universal energy through your own experiences. If you choose to pursue spiritual knowledge, you'll see the real meaning within your experiences and you'll know the way to enlightenment.

"I'll explain how all forms of energy manifest, and describe the manner in which the vibrations are expressed in every area of awareness," Rainbow said, "if you'll promise to respect what you don't yet understand by learning the true art of creating your own reality, and this includes accepting responsibility for all your experiences."

"I promise, and may you strike me down with lightning if I don't keep my word." Lavender smiled at her imagery, then immediately regretted her thought. She tried to erase it, but the eraser on her pencil wasn't working. Then she realized that every word, thought, feeling, idea, and image that a soul thought about or saw in their mind, manifested in multi-dimensional realms of reality and it didn't make any difference if a soul was aware of the many forms and expressions of the energy. All thoughts mattered.

Knowledge isn't anything to be played with. There's too much power involved and if it's misunderstood or misapplied, the energy repercussions could be far-reaching, maybe even mind-blowing. She took a deep breath. It's no wonder I got so scared when I saw the picture come to life, she thought, still shaking from the experience. "Okay, Rainbow, I'll be serious," she said respectfully. She settled comfortably in her chair, ready to listen to the long lecture on reality creation, knowing that one of her tests would be how Amanda applied the knowledge she acquired. She paid rapt attention to Rainbow's every word.

"The power of the universe is within every soul. Learning the true art of creating your own reality requires a sincere desire to understand and use your awareness of energy wisely. The knowledge is known to only those souls who have attained a heightened level of awareness. It seems to be secret and is hidden within the light for two reasons: The first is to ensure that the power is used wisely. The second is to ensure that the power is properly balanced. Universal energy flows from the essence of your soul through your mind and into your thoughts as it manifests into the physical form of experiences.

"Every soul inherently knows how to change energy into matter. It's their spiritual birthright. They have the power to shape any reality and form any experience they choose. If a soul isn't ready to engage their power in a proper manner, the complete knowledge of energy cannot be fully comprehended. This is a universal safeguard. A soul stands on the edges of enlightenment until they have evolved themselves in such a way that they can step into the center of awareness.

"Multi-dimensional vibrations of energy are simultaneously influencing and interacting with each other on more levels than a soul can see and understand until that soul has mastered their own energy vibrations. One of the purposes of experiencing life on earth is to understand universal energy in all of its forms, both seen and unseen.

"Mastering energy is a gentle art, even though it's very powerful. If you watch how nature interacts with every form and expression of life, you'll see how to live in harmony with all things, and this will show you how to master both earthly and universal energy. As a soul learns how to master the physical and spiritual energy expressions of their experiences, they're able to understand and master the power of the universe.

"In the journey of life, especially in a soul's journey through their earth experiences, they paint the mosaics of a masterpiece that reveals all the energy vibrations of their soul. Life, in all of its multi-dimensional vibrations, is energy in motion. Energy is focused and directed by free will; it becomes a visible vibration in the form of experiences. Feelings are the beginnings of the energy expressions of thoughts, and energy is expressed in accordance with thought/images in direct relationship and proportion to the feelings and beliefs that originate the creation of a soul's reality. Images and experiences change with choices and are influenced by every innuendo of feeling and every nuance of thought.

"You have within yourself everything you need to create a masterpiece of life. The artistic materials are your imagination, the world of your inner images—and your energy essence, the stuff that souls are made of. The most important thought to keep in mind is that the reality of your experiences is created inside; the illusion of your experiences is reflected outside.

"As you express your energy, you create your reality. As you begin to appreciate the art of creation, you begin to understand your soul. Are there any questions before we begin?" Rainbow handed Lavender a finely-woven paintbrush and a palette of seven colors. "I'd like you to paint a picture that symbolizes your soul."

Lavender was so surprised that the lecture was over. She thought it was going to cover every aspect of reality creation. It seemed that there were a lot of theories that Rainbow had left out, like alternate avenues of expression and probable presents and possible futures, and how to create the past in the present to shape and support future realities, and ways to change the future to reflect whatever you want the present/past to be. And she barely said one word about balances and had only breathed a few syllables about beliefs.

Rainbow smiled. "The principles of how energy creates and changes your reality are nice to know if you want to float around on a cloud forever, but if you dare to think even one thought, or see one image, or dream one dream, then you've chosen to experience learning about life. If you want to acquire knowledge and attain enlightenment, you must experience all the energies of your soul in all of its multi-dimensional expressions and forms. Put the principles into practice by putting your thoughts into motion. Then you'll see for yourself and really know how energy colors itself into visible vibrations of thoughts."

Lavender sat quietly for several minutes, wondering what picture to paint that would best symbolize her soul. The first thing to do is to be clear in my thought/images of what I want to create so I can understand why I want to create it and experience it, she thought. Getting in touch with her inner essence, she said to herself,

"I'll feel more like myself if I change the brush into a pencil and the colors into words." As her pencil appeared in her hand, she heard music flow into her mind and listened to a reworded verse from Amanda's favorite song. *Somewhere, over the rainbow, clouds are clear. There's a place that I dreamed of once in a time now here.*

The words inspired thought/images in her mind and she felt as if she was inside a rainbow, floating gently through the vibrations of the colors. I could paint a portrait of pages that shows a butterfly soaring somewhere over a rainbow into the light of the universe, she mused. The thought/image opened up a realm of possibilities and a higher vibration of energy and awareness began to unfold before her eyes. I could create a world with words, shaping secret symbols of knowledge into the energy expressions of experiences. It would be a wonderful way to share universal light.

Reveling in her higher thought/images, she barely noticed the furtive thought that crept into her mind and wedged itself into a corner of her awareness as it called for her attention. I could paint a cloudy image of a caterpillar and watch it slowly weave its chrysalis before it emerges as a butterfly, she thought, watching the image wend its way through her mind. Then I wouldn't have to interweave myriad and mystical vibrations of energy and knowledge into magical forms of matter.

Drifting in her thoughts of how to paint her picture with words, she didn't recognize a parallel thought of how circular and intricate a chrysalis was, and didn't look at the image of what occurred *inside* as the caterpillar changed into a butterfly. Ignoring her better judgment and her promise to be respectful, she listened to her less-developed thoughts and their scatter-brained images.

She raised her hand, waving her pencil around in a flashy motion, hoping Rainbow would notice how quickly she'd rearranged energy. Her pencil felt sticky, as if strands from a chrysalis were clinging to it. "I have a question about reality creation. On earth, thought takes such a long time to form into matter. How is Amanda going to connect the image of a thought into the experience that it ultimately creates?"

"She'll know the answer to that question when you see time in its proper vibration and place matter in its proper space," Rainbow said. She looked at the pencil that Lavender held in her hand. "Why did you change the brush into a pencil?" she asked.

"My pencil paints the picture of who I am as it reveals the essence of my soul," Lavender replied. "The words I draw with my pencil color the images of my soul into expressions of energy. Life is like an open book and experiences are paragraphs and pages, sometimes chapters, that show an eternal process of learning all about yourself and acquiring knowledge."

Rainbow smiled. "Only a writer would look at life phrased in a metaphor. What kind of picture are you going to paint with your pencil?"

"In the nature of individuality, there are probably millions of ways to symbolize your soul," Lavender said. "Your image would depend on how you see yourself. It's obvious that you view yourself as a rainbow. And I see Amanda as a bright, beautiful butterfly that metamorphoses into a free spirit." The image shimmered into sunlight in her mind and raised her thoughts. Watching an idea take shape and begin to form in her awareness, she saw an image of the masterpiece that would symbolize her true nature.

"I'll paint a picture of my soul inside the images of words to show you who I really am, and I'll dedicate the book to you, Rainbow," Lavender said, glowing and reverberating with the energy and enthusiasm of her idea. "In the process of reading and revising the pages, and exploring and experiencing the energies of my soul, I'll learn the true art of creating my reality while I help Amanda learn the difference between reality and illusion. I'll think my thoughts, dream my dreams, and see my images and feelings form into the expressions of my experiences."

"Watch how your words come to life," Rainbow said. "And pay special attention to the way your thought/images and feelings manifest as you create and experience all the mosaics that come together to form your masterpiece picture in all of its multidimensional vibrations and expressions. As you paint the portrait of your soul with the energies of words, Amanda will read and really experience every page and paragraph in the chapters of her life."

Lavender poised her pencil in her hand, ready to begin painting her picture. The sound of thunder echoed in the clouds and lightning flashed across the universe. That was too close for comfort, she thought. Then she remembered her earlier words, *strike me down with lightning*, and realized she'd broken her promise to respect the knowledge of energy by playing with power and creating her flashy pencil just to prove that she understood energy manifestation.

A bolt of lightning zapped through her pencil and splintered it into shooting sparks. Looking at the wisps of smoke curling around her fingers where her pencil used to be, she couldn't honestly say she was shocked. The experience reflected the reality of her previous thought in motion. Then she saw that the lightning had illuminated an interwoven thought that began to emerge, and knew that she wanted the real-life masterpiece picture of her soul to reflect a three-dimensional image of a free spirit.

Illusions being what they were, she knew she couldn't write any words without a pencil. Using the same power that had just splintered her pencil, she rearranged, refocused, and redirected her thoughts to create a new pencil. As the pencil began to form in perfect proportions to the image in her mind, she reviewed her experience, seeing it as a valuable lesson.

If I were a philosopher, she mused, I'd say you don't have to be an artist to paint a masterpiece picture of your soul. All you have to do is have the presence of mind to be in your thoughts. It sounded like a mystical concept and she saw images of words that were foreign and familiar to her at the same time. *From the pictures in your mind come words ...*

Opening up her imagination, she began to sketch words from the pictures she saw in her mind, forming and shaping her idea/images and insights into expressions of energy that showed her thoughts in motion. She watched her experiences print out in double-spaced lines of awareness, just like a manuscript before it was typeset into single-spaced pages of knowledge and bound into a book.

The images she was writing began to take on deeper dimensions of meanings, colored by her inner perceptions and higher thought perspectives. It almost looked like she and Amanda were the manuscript and when the pages turned into a book, the words showed a picture of Rainbow.

Twenty-Five

Insights Into Imagination

Amanda read the brochure on mind-enrichment classes that were being offered at the community college. One class description caught her attention:

Insights Into Imagination ... *Open up the positive power of your mind and explore your inner images. Lighten up your life as you learn how to look inside your imagination and see into your thoughts. Become more aware of yourself and your experiences as you uncover and understand what your subconscious mind is saying to you and showing you. Find out how you form your feelings and create your reality. Watch the world within you and around you open up as you discover your dreams. Experience the energies of the pictures in your mind as you put your thoughts and feelings into motion.*

It sounded like a wonderful way to open a window into herself. She smiled at the teacher as she entered the classroom.

"Hi, I'm Renee," the teacher said. "Just make yourself comfortable and have a seat anywhere."

Looking around the room, she saw that the chairs were placed in a semi-circle and large cushions were scattered on the floor. Wishing she had a friend to talk to, she noticed an empty chair next to a dark-haired girl with glasses. Sitting down and smiling, she said, "This class sounds like it's going to be very interesting."

"I think so too. I'm Judy," she said. "My sister took this class a few months ago and thought it was great. She said it helped her open up her imagination and develop a deeper awareness of her experiences. I'm attending the class because I'm not sure what I want to do with my life and I feel as though I'm drifting, trying to find where I belong. My sister believes in the metaphysical side of life and suggested that the class might help me find some answers within myself."

"I'm Amanda, and I'm here for the same reasons," she said, feeling a comfortable rapport with Judy. "I'd like to get some positive perspectives on my experiences, and I know there has to be more to life than meets the eye. I feel lost too, and I'm trying to find out who I really am. My brother is into spiritual stuff and I'd like to discover if there's any truth to some of the things he says." A picture of Gary as an Indian popped into her mind and she smiled at the image. "I don't think he's as crazy as I first thought he was."

Judy smiled. "It's so interesting to meet someone who feels the same way I do. I don't believe in coincidence; maybe we were meant to talk to one another," she said.

"Sort of like kindred spirits," Amanda agreed.

Renee began the class by saying, "I'd like to welcome all of you to the Insights Into Imagination class. Your imagination is the world of your inner images. Looking at the images inside your mind will show you sights into yourself and will open up a very special world within you. Your subconscious speaks in symbols and pictures instead of words. One of the goals of this class is to help you see within yourself to show you how you translate your subconscious images into clear, conscious thoughts.

"By looking into yourself, you'll understand how you transform your thoughts and their related images into all your experiences, and you'll see how you create your reality. As you watch your thoughts become visible in your life, you'll learn how to read them and interpret your images to see what your mind is saying and showing you, and you'll discover what you're really saying to yourself.

"Your thoughts and the way you see them pictured in your mind walk hand-in-hand with your imagination. The power of your mind pictures can change your life in any way that you choose. You create your experiences from the inside out, beginning with your feelings and what you see in your mind."

She smiled at her students. "I'll let you in on a little secret. Your thoughts are more real than you imagine them to be right now. Before something becomes real, it appears to be unreal because you see and feel the pictures of your experiences in your imagination before you see them expressed in your life. But I'm getting ahead of myself. We have twelve weeks of class, so I'll begin at the beginning."

* * * *

Lavender wondered what Amanda was doing with energy and how she planned to go about mastering it. Deciding to look in on her, she floated into the classroom and transformed herself into a sparkle of light on the ceiling. Just then, Amanda looked up and winked at her.

I don't think she really saw me, Lavender thought. She probably has an eyelash caught in her eye. The scene radiated feelings of déjà vu. I've done this before, she reminisced, when I was trying to show Amanda that she was a free spirit. There was something else about the feeling—another experience that was similar. Then the image flashed into her mind. In her first semester at school, Amanda had floated into the classroom to listen to the lectures. Lavender wondered why she was just now remembering it and why she hadn't noticed her presence in the classroom then.

She listened to Renee talk about opening a channel of communication between conscious and subconscious thoughts. "Your subconscious is your sixth sense. The way your subconscious talks to you is through the pictures you see with your mind's eye and in the thoughts you hear with your feelings. The way you communicate with your subconscious is through the pictures you form from your words, thoughts, feelings, and experiences. Even the words you read and hear inspire images in your mind."

Lavender thought the class sounded super. An image of an open window and a butterfly floating through a gentle breeze appeared in her mind. She realized she must have been daydreaming and had missed part of the lecture because Renee was now talking about mind movies and opening up awareness through imagery exercises.

"Reveries can help you open up and explore your imagination. By looking within your subconscious mind, you'll become more aware of your inner images to see how they're connected with your conscious thoughts, feelings, and experiences.

"A reverie is the same thing as a daydream. You've probably been taught that daydreaming in school isn't allowed, but it's okay to open up your imagination in this class. You'll be looking into your thoughts and feelings, and watching their images form and move in your mind. It's a wonderful way to learn more about yourself."

Dimming the lights in the room, she said, "If you want to, you can stretch out on the cushions on the floor, or you can wiggle around in your chair and get comfortable. Take a deep breath and begin to allow your body to relax. Just feel natural and peaceful within yourself. Continue to relax by breathing deeply. Center your thoughts into your feelings and be in tune with your natural body rhythms. Feel the muscles in your body relaxing as your mind begins to open up and become more aware. Close your eyes and relax even more. Feel comfortable and natural, peaceful and relaxed."

Renee's voice drifted into a smooth monotone. "Just continue to relax as you listen to your thoughts. Use your imagination and picture yourself with your mind's eye. Be in harmony with your inner nature as you see and feel a picture of who you are. Allow an image to form, and watch the image begin to move in the gentle flow of your imagination."

Lavender saw herself floating into Amanda's thoughts, watching their images reflected in her mind.

* * * *

Amanda felt completely relaxed and perfectly in tune with herself. Watching the images that her thoughts drew in her mind, she saw herself in a picture of an open meadow with a few trees. The green grass felt like velvet under her feet and the sun felt warm on her face. The sky was a vibrant azure blue with a few puffy white clouds, and sunshine sparkled on a quiet, tranquil pond. Looking into the still pond, she saw an image of herself reflected on the mirror-like surface of the water.

A soft breeze moved through the trees and seemed to flow through the entire picture. The interplay of sun and shadow on the leaves formed ever-changing patterns and she noticed a butterfly perched on one of the leaves. Sunlight shimmered on its wings as the butterfly opened them and began to float on gentle currents of air.

Watching the butterfly floating through the air, she began to feel as if she was the butterfly, free and natural. Looking up, she saw a rainbow sparkling in the sunshine over the clouds that had turned misty. Looking at the meadow below her, she saw a yellow rose just beginning to open up. That's curious, she thought. I didn't notice the rose when I first saw the meadow.

Flying higher in the air, the breeze became stronger and she began to feel frightened by the surge of wind. Stepping out of the picture, she watched the images continue to move in her mind. The wind became even stronger, blowing in all directions at once. The sound of thunder echoed through the clouds as flashes of lightning lit up the sky. The butterfly seemed to be caught in the center of a powerful thunderstorm. Concerned that it might become hurt, she wanted to help the butterfly but then saw that the butterfly began to move in harmony with the vortex of wind, spiraling higher and higher into the sky. She watched the butterfly soar through the clouds and go inside the rainbow, landing on a golden key.

She heard Renee's voice softly say, "Slowly and gradually, begin to bring your images into your conscious mind. Be in touch with your feelings and in harmony with yourself. Continue to be fully aware of your inner images, and your thoughts and feelings about them, as you flow the images into your conscious awareness. Continue to feel very relaxed and comfortable, opening your eyes when you feel ready to."

She waited a few minutes before speaking softly again. "Whenever you do a reverie, or any kind of imagery, give yourself time to connect your subconscious experiences with your conscious awareness of them. Think quietly about your reverie. Be introspective and allow yourself to integrate what you've seen and felt. In this way, you'll remember more of what you experience." Turning the lights back on, she said, "While the images are clear in your mind, write them down. This will help you gain additional insights."

After everyone was done writing, Renee said, "If anyone wants to, they can share what they experienced in their reverie."

One student spoke up. "I didn't see anything, but I somehow sensed the images and I was very aware of my feelings about them."

"There's no right or wrong way to do things," Renee said. "Whatever you experience in your reverie, and the way you experience it, is appropriate for you. It's quite common to feel or sense images before you see them. Sometimes your mind's eye has to redevelop its sense of sight. It's just as important to be in touch with your feelings. It sounds as if you're opening your inner sense of feeling before you open your inner sense of seeing. Keep in mind that you already know how to see subconscious images; you watch them every night in your dreams."

Another student raised her hand and said, "I felt that I was making up the images I saw. How do you know if they're real?"

Renee smiled as she answered the question. "Trust your feelings with everything you see and experience. At first you may think that you're making up what you see because you're not used to using your imagination and it might be a little out of shape. As you continue to consciously communicate with your subconscious mind, pay attention to how you feel about your thoughts and images. Your feelings will teach you how to trust yourself. That's how you know what's real."

"I think my imagination was so happy to be set free that it went a little out of its mind," Amanda said, describing her imagery.

"It sounds as if your reverie was showing you a way to explore higher aspects of yourself," Renee said.

"But what about that part when I became frightened?" Amanda asked.

"Maybe there's something you're afraid to see. Look inside your images and listen to your feelings; see what they symbolize and what they're saying to you," Renee suggested.

"I'll give it some thought," Amanda said.

"Any other questions or comments about reveries?" Renee asked.

"You mentioned earlier that reveries are like dreams. What's the difference between them?"

"They're quite similar, except reveries seem to be more consciously directed and occur while you're awake in a relaxed state, and dreams occur at night during sleep. They both bridge the gap between your subconscious and your conscious minds, bringing them together.

"Dreams are like in-depth reveries. While they may appear to be fragmented images residing in another realm of your awareness, if you look clearly into them, you'll see that they reflect a detailed and descriptive mindscape in motion. Dreams open up a real world of knowing that isn't apparent on the surface, and they reveal insights and answers into all your experiences. Some people even say that you dream your life before you experience it, and that life is just a dream."

She smiled and her eyes sparkled with light. "Dreams can help you get in touch with the real you, and will show you a magical, mystical world within yourself. They can open a doorway into your true spiritual nature."

Amanda saw a knowing quality in Renee's eyes that she couldn't quite understand. She's in touch with who she is, Amanda thought. She didn't know how she knew that; she just knew it was right.

* * * *

Lavender was so excited that Amanda had seen the energy essence of Renee's soul. She wanted to tell her that Renee was a light teacher from the universe, but Rainbow put her hand over her mouth before she could blurt out that a person's eyes showed a reflection of their soul.

"Amanda already knows that," Rainbow said. "She just has to connect what she knows with her conscious thoughts. Let her look within herself to open up and understand her inner sense of knowing. She's finding her own way into knowledge."

* * * *

"During the week, I'd like for you to continue to open up your subconscious mind," Renee said. "Look inside your imagination and discover more about the world within you. Watch your thoughts and images, and get in touch with your feelings. Give yourself some time every day to relax and enjoy a reverie.

"Also begin to explore and experience your dreams. Practice remembering them and interpret them the best you can to gain a level of understanding about them. Keep a journal and write down everything that occurs in your dreams. Next week we'll talk about the power of words and what they really say, but I have a feeling you'll find out for yourself as you read your inner images."

As everyone stood up and began to leave the room, Judy turned to Amanda and asked, "Would you like to go for coffee?"

"Yes," Amanda replied, watching a window begin to open up inside herself.

Twenty-Six

Nearly-Remembered Knowledge

Walking to her car, Amanda paused to look up at the clear, moon-lit sky. The stars sparkled in the universe. Smiling, she looked for her star in the constellation of Orion, thinking about how she'd forgotten it until just now. The star twinkled with light and she tried to remember the wish she made when she was a child.

Driving to the restaurant where she and Judy had agreed to meet for coffee, she began to look inside her images to see what they were really saying. "Just open up your imagination," she told herself, "and let your images show you the truth." Sounds easy enough, she thought. "Okay, subconscious, show me your stuff," she said.

A misty image of a door inside the lavender color at the top of a rainbow appeared in her mind and she instantly had a sense of knowing without clearly knowing what she knew. It was a frustrating feeling, not being able to remember.

"Focus on the image," she said to herself. "Go step by step, slowly. You talk to yourself all the time; now be quiet and listen to your thoughts. Let your image talk to you." She took a deep breath, centering her attention on the image in her mind. "There's something that I promised to remember; it's somehow connected with my star and with the reverie I had in class."

"But what?" she asked herself, experiencing again the frustrating feeling of not being able to remember, yet knowing at the same time that she knew, but the answer remained hidden as if it was a deep, dark secret. "It's probably something that I'm reluctant to see because I thought the butterfly was going to get hurt in the thunderstorm before it landed on a key inside the rainbow."

I wonder what the key opens, she thought. Probably opens the door, she answered herself. That makes sense. But why is the door locked? And what's inside? Another dream? And do I want to unlock the door and walk into a dream without knowing where I'm going or why? Or without having the foggiest idea of what I'm going to do when I get there?

C'mon, get real. People don't walk through dream doorways with keys they find in rainbows. But on second thought, maybe that's where I'll find my answers and my wish could come true. Besides, it might be fun to travel through the rainbow and see what the door opens into—to see what's inside. But once I'm inside the dream, what if I want to wake up but I'm lost or stuck somewhere and I can't find the way home?

A rainbow began to sparkle inside her mind, but she didn't have time to think about it or to look into the image. She parked her car next to Judy's and they walked into the restaurant together.

* * * *

"You're absolutely beaming," Lavender said to Rainbow. "What are you so happy about?" she asked.

"Amanda is beginning to remember her pre-birth promise about who she really is." Rainbow beamed brighter, emanating light rays all over the place. "She wants to see the truth about herself."

A misty light began to dawn in Lavender's awareness. Amanda had found the door into a secret place she'd hidden deep inside herself and she'd seen the key. She shivered as a feeling of fear swept through her, knowing that it was only a matter of time before Amanda was going to open the door and walk through it.

* * * *

"I thought the class was super," Amanda said. "It's just what I need to help me open myself up."

"I enjoyed the class too," Judy replied. "I like that Renee encourages people to look within themselves."

"I thought it was interesting that she asked us to see a picture of who we really are in the reverie we did," Amanda said. "To begin with, I saw an image of myself the way I am now but when I got involved in the picture and tuned into my feelings, I somehow magically turned into a butterfly." She smiled. "I wonder if your subconscious always speaks in symbols. Learning how to read your thoughts and images is like learning a new language."

"I thought your imagery was very clear," Judy said.

"I felt as though I was watching the images happen while I was participating in a three-dimensional movie at the same time. It was more than just a reverie; it was more like real life," Amanda said. "And there was something else about it. I felt that I'd seen or experienced the images before." A picture of an open book flashed through her mind. "What did you see in your reverie?"

"At first, everything was gray and nebulous—not formed into

any image, as if I wasn't sure what to see. Then a ray of sunlight began shining on a path, but the light was hazy. When I tried to see where the path would lead, I saw an oasis shimmering in heat waves in the distance. I thought it was a mirage but when I stepped into the sunshine, I sensed that I'd travel this path in the future."

Judy took her glasses off and squinted her eyes, trying to focus the images clearly in her mind—to bring them closer into view. "I think I was beginning to see my purpose in life, even though I don't have any idea what it is right now," she said.

"Maybe if you go into your reverie again and take a few more steps on the path, you'll discover what it is," Amanda said. She paused thoughtfully for a moment. "Doesn't it seem that even though our reveries were different, they were showing us the same thing—showing us a way into finding ourselves?" she asked.

Judy nodded, putting on her glasses. "Maybe the images are showing us a way into finding our higher selves. My sister told me that when you're ready to see who you really are, you become aware of your higher self and your higher self shows you the truth."

"Do you think we saw our higher selves tonight?"

"If we did," Judy said, "then I didn't recognize mine."

"And I probably fell over mine, without even knowing it."

Judy laughed. "How can you fall over a rainbow? Wouldn't you just fall through the colors?"

Amanda suddenly remembered that Gary had told her several years ago that a rainbow was her higher self. "Why do you think my higher self is symbolized as a rainbow?" she asked.

"I don't know; maybe it was something in your imagery or a feeling that I sensed about you. My sister, Patti, tells me I'm psychic and that I'm always saying things that are perceptive." Judy smiled. "Maybe my higher self is a ray of sunshine and I tripped through the light without seeing it."

Amanda laughed. "I can picture you walking through a ray of sunshine and coming out on the other side with a sunburn. When I was a little girl, I dreamed I went to visit the sun and when I woke up I was sunburned."

"You're joking," Judy said.

"No, I'm not," Amanda replied. "It really happened."

"I suppose anything is possible," Judy said, smiling, but not believing her.

"In the dream, I discovered that everyone is part of the sun, and that sunrises are symbolic of a magical, mystical moment when universal light begins to dawn in the center of your awareness."

Judy looked at her in surprise. She'd always felt that sunrises were special, and Amanda's words had struck a chord of recognition within her.

Amanda felt confused. She hadn't remembered that part of her dream until just now—until she'd spoken the words. Yet she knew that part of her dream hadn't been in her dream. So how would I know about that part of my dream if I didn't dream it? she wondered. Then she remembered she'd been there with a friend named Lavender and that a rainbow had said hi to her before the sunrise. Maybe Lavender dreamed that part, she thought, smiling at how crazy the idea was.

"I wonder if my higher self really is a rainbow," Amanda said. "I've always loved walking through the rain and looking for rainbows. But in my reverie, it appeared that my higher self is a butterfly."

"The butterfly flew through the clouds into the rainbow," Judy said. "I think your butterfly imagery really shows that you're a free spirit."

"I like that," Amanda said, laughing. "I'm a free spirit. I wish I knew how to fly."

Judy smiled, feeling as though Amanda was an old friend. "I feel I've known you before," she said, "but I can't remember where we've met."

Amanda smiled back at her. "I feel the same way," she replied. "It seems as if we're picking up our friendship where we left it off before."

An image of a pyramid flashed through Judy's mind. "Maybe we were friends in a past life."

"Maybe we were," Amanda said, half-seriously. "Do you believe in reincarnation?"

"My sister believes in it, and I think it's an interesting philosophy," Judy answered. "Patti has told me about some experiences she remembered from one of her past lives. She said that knowing about them helped her to understand why some of her present experiences are occurring."

"I don't remember any past lives," Amanda said, "but that doesn't mean they didn't happen."

"If neither one of us really believes in reincarnation, then why did we just talk about maybe knowing each other in a past life?" Judy asked.

Amanda shrugged her shoulders and smiled. "Maybe because it's true," she said. Foggy, blurred images appeared in her mind and she felt as if she was wandering through a world of shadowy shapes but everything was out of sync, as though she was in a different dimension of time.

"Oh my gosh, look at the time," Judy said. "We've been talking for almost three hours."

Amanda shook her head, feeling a little disoriented. "It doesn't seem like it," she said. "Actually, I've always had a problem with time. Most of the time, I don't believe it exists and the other half of the time, I wish it would disappear." It seemed that someone else had said the words.

"I have to get up early and go to work tomorrow," Judy said, "so I should go home and get some sleep."

"Whether I believe in time or not, I'm still stuck in it and I have to get up early too," Amanda said. "Would you like to meet for dinner before class next week?"

"Yes," Judy answered. "I was just about to ask you the same thing."

Walking to their cars, Amanda said, "I'd like to find out more about my higher self."

"Me too," Judy said. "Let's see what we come up with in our reveries and dreams, and we'll compare notes next week."

"Okay," Amanda replied. "See you then." She had the strangest feeling that a rainbow was smiling at her.

Twenty-Seven

Dream Doorways

Amanda read the paragraph in her dream journal, thinking she'd been half-asleep or dreaming when she'd written the words.

I'm walking through the rain, wondering who I really am, and I'm lost. Everything seems foggy and unreal, as if I'm in a different world. Suddenly the sun comes out from behind a cloud and I see a rainbow that opens up in the sunshine and shows me a path inside its colors. I decide to walk through the rainbow and as I travel through the colors, I come upon a door shrouded in a lavender mist.

Then it seems as if I'm someone else walking through the rain—walking through my dream. I approach the door and stand there for a few minutes, as if I'm unsure about wanting to see what's inside. I try to open it, but it's locked. I sense a strong feeling of fear, but don't know what I'm afraid of.

She shivered. I'm dreaming right now, she whispered. I thought I was awake, reading my journal, but I'm watching myself dream this dream.

Shadowy images of an open-air courtyard with tall columns appeared in her mind. An intense feeling of sadness and despair surrounded her. Closing her eyes, the image went into blackness.

After what seemed like an eternity, she opened her eyes and saw that she was drifting through the universe in a bubble, moving through time and space in her thoughts, but still lost inside the dream. Then she was falling through a rainbow into another world. Not knowing where she was, or even who she was, she knew she had to find her way home.

From somewhere—it seemed far away—she heard the sound of thunder and felt gentle raindrops on her face. As she began to awaken, she saw a pre-dawn mist weave through the colors of a sunrise, reflecting a rainbow that encircled the earth and the universe.

"Follow your dream," the rainbow said, sparkling through the early-morning sunny mist.

Twenty-Eight

The Key to Knowledge

The restaurant was crowded, but Judy saw Amanda as she walked through the door. She waved to her.

"I'm sorry I'm late," Amanda said, sitting down. "I'm almost always late for everything."

"It's okay," Judy replied, smiling. "I had a feeling you'd be late, so I got a table rather than wait for you in the lobby. How'd you do with your dreams and finding your higher self?"

Amanda relaxed into the chair, slipping her moccasins off under the table. "I dreamed about rainbows every night. Just before I went to sleep, I pictured a rainbow and held that image in my mind. All my dreams were misty, but I remembered one clearly. I was walking through the rain and a rainbow invited me inside its colors. When I went through the rainbow, I saw a door into a lavender sphere of light. I felt that I was on the verge of discovering something really important, but the door was locked and I didn't have the key. There was something else about the dream; it seemed as if I was someone else, but I was afraid to see what was inside the door." She shivered.

"I read a few books on spirituality and one said that if you want to become aware of your higher self, all you need to do is to go within the quietness of your mind. Flow with your feelings, be in harmony with yourself and allow yourself to just *be*, then your higher self will appear to you. Another book said that if you want to get in touch with your higher self, listen to your thoughts and feelings and look inside your dreams. Your higher self will begin to talk to you in whispers and dream images. What'd you find out?"

"I talked to Patti about her higher self. Remember, I told you she's into metaphysics?"

Amanda nodded.

"She said it's called a higher self because people believe they have to rise above their physicalness to see their spiritual side, but all they really have to do is look within and see themselves clearly. She said that your higher self is your soul; it's not separate from you or above you. Once you become aware of that, you begin to see how your soul's energy vibrations are expressed through all your thoughts, feelings, and experiences. Your higher self knows everything there is to know and will help you understand the true meanings in your experiences and show you how to uncover the mysteries of life.

"I decided to see for myself if that was true. I did a reverie, telling myself that I wanted to meet my higher self. I saw the ray of light again and when I entered the light, it became brighter, almost dazzling. It seemed to surround me and be within me at the same time. I experienced an incredible, beautiful feeling; I felt like I somehow reached inside myself and touched my soul." She took her glasses off and her eyes sparkled, as if she was seeing the light within her mind and reexperiencing the feeling.

Amanda looked into Judy's eyes. "You really are like a ray of sunshine and I can see your higher self shining through you," she said, seeing a special essence reflected in her eyes. She'd seen a similar light in Renee's eyes last week and wondered if a person's eyes were a mirror of their soul.

Judy smiled at Amanda and put her glasses back on.

"It sounds so easy," Amanda said. "Just look within yourself and listen to the whispers of knowledge in your mind and you'll see the truth and know everything."

"It really is that easy," Judy replied. "I think people make it difficult because they don't take the time to look within themselves or to understand themselves on a deeper level."

"Maybe we should ask Renee about it in class tonight and see what she says."

"Umm, Amanda, did you hear what you just said?" Judy asked.

"Yes. No. What'd I say?"

"You said maybe we should ask Renee about it. That sounds as if you're looking for someone else to tell you what they think, rather than looking within yourself to see what you think."

"You're right, Judy," Amanda said. "Thanks for bringing that to my attention. I wasn't listening to myself."

Judy smiled at her. "Then you said you wanted to *see* what she *says*."

Amanda laughed. "Can I see what I'm saying to myself? It looks like I'm trying to learn how to read images drawn from words. But what does that really mean, and what does it have to do with finding my higher self?" A thought sparkled in her mind. "With all the dreams I had about rainbows this past week, if I were a writer, I could probably write a book." The words *Somewhere Over the*

Rainbow appeared in her mind.

She smiled, remembering the magical times when she was a little girl running through the rain searching for rainbows, knowing she could always find one hiding just beyond a cloud. The joy and awe she'd felt whenever she saw a rainbow enveloped her. "I almost didn't go to work that day it was raining. I wanted to go walking in the rain and find a rainbow, but I really went to work instead of following my dream."

Judy looked at Amanda strangely. It hadn't rained all week. "Maybe somewhere in your mind, you did follow your dream," she said.

"Maybe," Amanda replied. She thought about the key she'd seen in her reverie and the door into the lavender color. Something that Gary had said about the color lavender sprang into her thoughts. *She's really the expression of your spiritual side.* The next time I dream about a rainbow, I'll get the key and open the door, she thought to herself. Then I'll see what's inside the color lavender and what my spiritual side has to say.

Twenty-Nine

Whispers Through a Window

Lavender was going around in circles, looking for herself, when she saw Amanda walking through a misty image of a rainbow.

"Follow your dream," Rainbow said.

The words sounded like a whisper of wind, blowing softly through an open window.

*   *   *   *

Amanda saw an image of a butterfly floating through misty clouds in the universe. Watching the butterfly weave a lavender thread of light through the colors of a rainbow, she heard an echo of a voice whisper words in her mind.

Your dream is woven through the fabric of your life;
spun into a tapestry of words that create a masterpiece
of images painted on a portrait of pages in your soul.

Amanda didn't notice the pencil that magically appeared out of nowhere just then and was placed by an open page in her dream journal.

Half-asleep, she looked out the window, trying to understand the images in her dream. Watching the sun come up over the horizon, seeing the sunlight sparkle through the mist above the rainbow and shimmer through the colors, she reached for the golden key inside her dream, knowing somewhere deep within herself that the key would unlock the secret to her soul.

Thirty

Metamorpheus Light Synergy

"Did you open the door into your dream and find your higher self?" Judy asked Amanda over dinner the next week.

"I dreamed I was a butterfly last night. The dream started me thinking about how a caterpillar changes into a butterfly—about how it weaves its chrysalis and what occurs inside as it metamorphoses into another form. Then I remembered when I was a little girl, I tried to change myself into a butterfly but it didn't work, probably because I couldn't get into the right vibration of energy."

She paused for a moment, looking back into her feelings. "I did a reverie today, imagining that I was a caterpillar changing into a butterfly. As I watched myself emerging from my cocoon into the sunlight, I became aware that as the caterpillar begins to understand its inner nature—as it becomes aware, within itself, that it really is a butterfly—it begins to metamorphose into its true form.

"Now I see that wanting to be a butterfly was symbolic of my desire to be true to my inner nature," Amanda explained. "Being both physical and spiritual at the same time, what I really wanted to do was transform my inner knowing into an expression of my spiritual energies."

"I knew you were really a free spirit all the time," Judy said.

Amanda smiled. "My reverie brought up another memory. When I was in high school, I dreamed up a concept called *Metamorpheus Light Synergy* in science class when the teacher was giving a lecture on gravity and relative energy. I felt there had to be more to energy than he was telling us, and the lecture was boring, so I looked out the window and saw a butterfly and that must have inspired my thoughts."

"You were daydreaming in class?" Judy asked. "Just gazing out the window, transported into your own special world?"

"Yes," Amanda replied. "The words flew into my mind, so I played with them to see what they said. *Meta* means transcending—

going above, beyond, or higher. Another meaning is changed in form. *Morpheus* is the Greek god of dreams. *Light*, in its most natural energy form, is sunshine—universal light. *Synergy* means in cooperative action, and is energy in motion. When I put the meanings of the words together to see the whole picture, they showed that the images in your dreams change form as they transcend the dream—as they rise above dreams into the energy of light and interact with a higher vibration of dream images in another dimension."

"Sounds far out to me," Judy said.

"Would you like to hear the ideas inside the concept?" Amanda asked.

"Of course," Judy replied, smiling. "What are friends for?"

Amanda smiled again. "When you dream, your images rise above physical energy into a parallel form of spiritual energy and then reform into your experiences. As you participate in your dream images in two realms of reality—through your thoughts, feelings, and experiences—your dream images interact between and through and with both physical and spiritual forms of energy in a cooperative motion with matter. This is the parallel part of the concept; there's another part in the form of universal energy.

"The higher part was a little unclear but it seems that when you blend the physical and spiritual images together, you rise into the universal energies of light. Then you can see your true nature and the higher aspects of yourself; you can see who you really are."

Noticing the puzzled look on Judy's face, Amanda searched her mind for an analogy. "When you dream, it's like you're weaving a tapestry or painting a picture as you connect your dream images with your conscious thoughts and experiences. What you're interconnecting is levels of awareness with vibrations of energy. At the center of the design or picture, you see that you're paralleling the physical and spiritual parts of yourself, but you know they're really one and the same because the picture becomes superimposed upon itself and you can see the threads of energy that connect your conscious thoughts and experiences with your inner knowledge in your dream images.

"When you become aware of the images and experiences in your dreams, you can see that all the energy vibrations of your thoughts and experiences are merging and cooperating in harmony with one another as you transcend conscious thought boundaries by going within the spiritual awareness of the images in your mind. All the threads of your experiences, thoughts, feelings, and dream images interweave into knowledge as they come together to form an intricate and ever-changing design that shows a complete picture of all the energy vibrations of your soul in its many physical shapes, spiritual expressions, and universal forms.

"This is the theory. When you put it into motion, it becomes another story. Your dream images and experiences flow in and out of your conscious awareness and come to life as they change vibration and form. Your dreams connect the threads of your inner knowledge and all the images and experiences in your dreams weave themselves into expressions of physical energy in your conscious thoughts, feelings, and experiences as your dreams simultaneously open up and emerge into parallel forms of spiritual and universal awareness and experiences.

"Your physical self is a parallel image of your spiritual self, just as day is a parallel image of night. They're not opposites, because they're opposites of exactly the same thing. They're more like mirror images of one another, reflections of energy in the same design revolving around each other as they evolve into universal enlightenment.

"In your life, as you rise above the physical energy of your thoughts and experiences into your dream images, and the inner awareness of your mind, you know that your dreams are real and your conscious thoughts and experiences are really the dream."

Judy smiled. "So conscious thoughts and real life are just a dream we're having?" she asked, taking her glasses off. "In your dreams, your thoughts and experiences are real, and you're more than you think you are when you think you're awake? And when you transform your dream images into your conscious thoughts and your physical experiences, your dreams become real; they become experiences in your life?"

Amanda nodded, noticing how Judy always took her glasses off when she wanted to see things clearly. "It's uncanny the way you understand things so concisely," she said. "Being inside your dreams is like metamorphosing from a caterpillar into a butterfly because you're setting your thoughts free to express their images in your experiences."

"I wonder what people would think about their dreams and how they'd view their experiences if this concept were well-known," Judy said.

"If this concept was discovered and offered to the world by a scientist, maybe everyone would see that their life is really a magical dream that's interwoven within and through their physical experiences. People might begin to open up a wonderful world inside themselves and pay more attention to their dreams and learn more about themselves by looking into the true meanings within their experiences," Amanda said.

"It's a mystical way of looking at life, but since it's dreaming in another dimension, it's probably too far out for a stuffy scientist to imagine." Reflecting on her thoughts for a moment, she continued. "Maybe a metamorphosed version of Newton or Einstein will come along and shine some light on this concept. But he'd probably have a tough time trying to pull scientific and spiritual thought together."

Judy picked up her glasses from the table to put them back on, but held them in mid-air instead. "Maybe scientific and spiritual thought are parallel images of one another and they only appear to be opposites because they aren't yet in harmony with each other," she said.

"Well, if Newton discovered it, he'd leave out the universal part because he believed in earthly forms of energy, like gravity. If Einstein discovered it, he'd say that your dreams are happening in various forms of energy in space and time, and that your experiences are occurring simultaneously in synchronized vibrations of energy, and that the physical, spiritual, and universal expressions of your soul are all relative to your dreams. But he'd probably forget to say that your dreams are really a vibration of universal light energies reflected in your life."

Judy dropped her glasses on the floor.

Amanda smiled. "If this concept was put into practice, everyone would probably go out of their minds. People might feel as if they were going around in circles and they wouldn't know where to begin to look for themselves."

"Maybe they'd see that a circle is really a continuation, and they'd find themselves in the center of their dream images," Judy said, picking her glasses up from the floor and wiping them clean with a napkin before putting them back on.

"I wonder ..." Amanda mused. "If I look at my rainbow dreams from the perspective of Metamorpheus Light Synergy, then maybe I'm the physical expression of a butterfly, the lavender color is the expression of my spiritual nature, and the rainbow is a universal expression of my soul. By seeing that my life is just a dream I'm having, then I'm really a rainbow playing with the images of being a butterfly and a free spirit." She laughed. "I'm only dreaming that I'm Amanda in a physical form of energy; I'm really a figment of Rainbow's imagination."

* * * *

Rainbow and Lavender looked at one another. "You're the one who put that thought in her mind," Rainbow said.

"I think she captured the principle and ideas of the concept very well," Lavender said, "but she misunderstood a few things in the practical application of it."

"If you remember, I asked you to take your time with it to see into the finer vibrations, but you were in such a rush that you didn't listen."

"I wanted to raise her thoughts," Lavender replied, wishing now that she'd taken her time to completely comprehend the concept before jumping into Amanda's mind with it. I know I'm going to be experiencing the repercussions of this, she thought, until Amanda understands the matter with energy and learns how to see all the aspects of her dream images reflected in her experiences. "Why does energy always return to itself in reformed vibrations?"

"Because energy is, was, and always will be, and because that's what life and learning is really all about," Rainbow answered. "Life is energy in motion, and your thoughts and experiences are all relative to one another." She smiled, wondering when Lavender was going to wake up and see through her experiences into Amanda's dream.

Thirty-One

The Reality of Illusion

"Since this is our last class, I'd like to leave you with some things to think about," Renee said. "I mentioned in our first class that you create your experiences from the inside out through your imagination. I'd like to expand on that by talking about the concept that you create your own reality. I want you to look beyond and below the surface of what I'm saying. Watch how the words picture themselves in your mind and see how you feel about the images they inspire.

"Your thoughts and feelings are very powerful, and your imagination is very magical. Your thoughts and feelings create whatever you imagine. As you shape the images of your thoughts and feelings in your mind, your imagination comes to life in the form and expression of your experiences. Before your reality becomes apparent on the outside, you create it on the inside—in your imagination.

"Your thoughts form your experiences inside your mind. Your feelings nourish your thoughts and allow them to grow into your experiences. You focus your thoughts by where you place your attention. The way you see all your thoughts, how you truly feel about them and what you believe about them, shapes the way you experience your reality. When you put your mind pictures into motion, your thoughts manifest into matter in physical time and space. That's how and when you see the energy expressions of your thoughts.

"Creating your reality works with illusion. It seems to be unreal at first, but you don't have to take my word for it. I'll show you how to see this for yourself: Think about an experience that you've had. Remember it, feel it, and see the images of it in your mind. Look at all the thoughts and feelings that preceded your experience and you'll see how they created your experience. Look at the actions you took to bring your experience into being and you'll see how your feelings and beliefs formed the energy expressions of your thoughts as you watch your thoughts come to life.

"What you're seeing is the visible expressions of energy created from your previously invisible thoughts and feelings. After your thoughts and feelings have manifested into matter, you may notice that, sooner or later, your reality changes into another form or goes in a different direction because energy is continuous and never disappears. It only changes form and its manner of expression.

"If you haven't yet seen your thoughts and feelings in a tangible, touchable way, it's because the energies of physical time move slower than the vibrations of thoughts and it can seem that your thoughts have become *no-thing*, but this isn't so. All thoughts come into *be-ing*. As your thoughts begin to manifest into your experiences, you may see that illusion and reality parallel each other at first or you may notice that they become intertwined—sharing the same energy vibrations as they merge together.

"The real illusion is what you see on the outside; your true reality is what you see and feel on the inside—in your heart and mind. Your thoughts and feelings show you the magic power you have within yourself to create any reality you want. The secret of creating and changing your reality is to know that what appears to be, isn't—and what does not appear to be, is."

Judy took her glasses off and asked, "Isn't that reversed? It seems to me that reality is what you see and illusion is what you don't see."

"Only on the surface," Renee said. "Reality changes all the time."

"So do your thoughts and feelings," Judy replied.

"Your thoughts and feelings change your reality, and you see the images of your thoughts in your mind before they're reflected in your experiences."

"So all you have to do is change your thoughts and feelings, and you change your reality?" Judy asked, beginning to smile.

"Yes. That's why reality is so illusionary."

"Then what you thought was the illusion—your imagination—is really the reality because it becomes the reality, right?"

Renee smiled. "Positive mind pictures will do really wonderful things in your life. Put your imagery in motion, set your thoughts and feelings into action, and watch the energy vibrations manifest into your experiences," she said. "Your experiences are your best teacher."

An idea lit up in Amanda's mind. Turning thoughts into tangible things sounded fun and interesting, and she wanted to try it to see what would happen. She looked at Judy and saw that she was thinking the same thing.

Thirty-Two

Somewhere in Space

Lavender ran across the campus, knowing she was late for the Time and Space class, hoping to slip into the room without being noticed. She wondered why Rainbow scheduled the class at a specific time in a particular place when she was so insistent that time and space were simultaneous. In an earlier class, she'd explained that time was a vibration of energy and space was a dimension of motion. When they were synchronized, all of time and space vibrated in harmony.

Lavender thought that both time and space were warped, and the idea of being *somewhere*, instead of being *here now*, scattered her energies and made her feel as if she was here, there, and everywhere all at once. "Sometimes it seems like I'm *nowhere*, just when I thought I knew where I was to begin with," she muttered to herself.

If I completely center my attention into this present time/space and then expand my awareness, she thought, maybe I can get there on time. The only problem with that was she didn't know how to navigate space to transcend time and was a bit hesitant to leap through an unknown dimension of energy.

There's another way around this, she thought to herself. If I project my vibrations forward into the future, I could be there before I arrive, and then I'll be early, but I could also wind up someplace else and by the time I find out where I am, I'll be even later than I am now and I'll still have to rearrange the future to be in the present. She sighed. There was only one other alternative.

If I coordinate my vibrations back into the past to get an earlier start, I could end up becoming involved with other things and then I'll be behind myself. It seemed like quite a dilemma; there was more to time and space than she could handle all at once. Just thinking about it made her mind spin around in circles, and she felt as if she was in three different places at the same time.

Revibrating her thoughts to the present, she decided not to play with time/spaces. There were so many variables that if she wasn't careful, she could get lost in time or stuck somewhere in space in an infinite number of possibilities. I'll just have to make up the missed time, she thought, hoping Rainbow wouldn't remember what she'd said about flunking her if she was late one more time.

"Lavender," a deep voice called. "Wait up. What's your rush?"

Turning around, she saw Luminous. Her heart began to beat a little faster. She'd been in love with him since the beginning of time, whenever that was. It was so long ago, she couldn't remember when she'd first met him; it seemed she'd always known him.

"Hi," Lavender said breathlessly. "I'm late for the Time and Space class, and my only prayer of passing is to get there on time."

Luminous synchronized his steps with hers. "Want to go to a movie at the drive-in tonight?" he asked. "It's a silent movie called **Thoughts are Tangible Things** and I've heard some good vibes about it." He smiled at her.

"Yes, I'd like to. The movie sounds enlightening," she replied, wondering if Rainbow had dropped a hint to him that she could use some help transforming energy into matter.

Luminous radiated vibrations of light; he was so happy she'd said yes. "I thought we could get some veggies to eat during the movie. I really like broccoli," he said, "ever since I helped you grow it in your garden when you were a little girl."

Lavender laughed. She was so happy to see him again. It seemed that only yesterday they were climbing trees together and today they were just as much in harmony as if they'd never been apart, even though they'd chosen to evolve separately for awhile. "Actually, I'd prefer popcorn," she said. "It's so ... earthy. And it lends an air of realism to watching a movie."

"Let's compromise. You have popcorn; I'll have broccoli."

Lavender smiled. "You're still into illusion, aren't you?"

"Not really," he replied. "It only looks that way. I'll pick you up at eight o'clock."

"Okay. I'll try to be ready on time this time, even though I don't believe in time," she said, looking at the formidable door to the Time and Space classroom.

"There are just some things in life you have to deal with," he replied, laughing. "See you later." Just as he was about to kiss her, Newton-Einstein opened the door from the inside.

"Hi, Lavender," he said in a booming voice that reverberated throughout the room. "I see you're late again."

"Oh, hi Newt. I see you finally managed to synchronize your space," Lavender said politely. "Are you off to earth now for another incarnation?"

"Yeah. The final exam," he replied.

"I wish you well this time," she said, watching as he tripped over his clock and crash landed in slow motion on earth. It was quite alarming to see such an advanced soul trip through time and space, and drop so ungracefully into gravity. As the dust settled, she shouted, "Remember to tell the truth, the whole truth, and nothing but the truth about universal light energy this time. Real people want to know and the super souls are counting on you." As she walked into the classroom and sat down, Rainbow wrote something next to her name in the attendance record.

Thirty-Three

Thoughts Are Tangible Things

"I had a wonderful dream last night," Amanda said to Judy on the phone. "I dreamed I went to a movie called *Thoughts are Tangible Things*. I saw how to flow universal light energy through my thoughts to turn them into real-life experiences. And I also learned that thoughts begin to form in the thin air of ethereal energies."

"Amanda, all your dreams are out of this world," Judy said.

"That's what my mother tells me. Anyway, since it's Saturday and neither one of us has dates, I thought we could go for pizza tonight. I'll tell you about my dream."

"Sounds good to me," Judy said. "See how thoughts turn into real-life experiences just by thinking about them."

Amanda laughed. "In my dream, I had a date with a really super guy. I wish these things would happen on earth, not out of this world. Let's meet over at the shopping mall around four o'clock before we go for pizza. I want to buy a pair of shoes."

"You want to buy a pair of shoes! I'm shocked," Judy said. "I never thought I'd see the day you wore shoes when you didn't have to."

"It's only for appearances. My boss said that if I didn't wear shoes in the office, he'd have to fire me. I told him I was a free spirit and that free spirits don't wear shoes, but he told me to live in the real world. Then I said the firm doesn't pay me enough and I can't afford to buy shoes, so he offered to pay for a new pair instead of giving me a raise."

"But you do wear shoes to work. You just take them off the minute you get there. You've been there for almost three years. Does he really think you'll start wearing shoes if he pays for them?"

"He hopes I will, but I'll probably add them to the collection in my desk drawer."

"Amanda, you really are a free spirit," Judy said. "I've gotta go.

I have an appointment this morning with the optometrist for new glasses."

"Still not seeing things clearly on the outside?" Amanda asked.

"I'll see you at four. And try to be on time."

"Okay, I'll try, but I won't promise. You know how I feel about time."

"Instead of using this money to buy shoes, I'll treat you to pizza," Amanda said, trying to apologize for being late again.

"It's okay, Amanda. Since I know you're always late for everything, I just got here a few minutes ago," Judy said, smiling. "I'm starving. Let's materialize the pizza right here and now out of thin air. Then we can see how tangible thoughts really are."

"Just the thought of pizza makes my mouth water," she said, "but that sounds too unreal. Let's drive over; the pizza will be just as tangible."

"Okay," Judy said agreeably. "But one of these days, I want to create something out of thin air."

After they arrived at the restaurant and ordered their pizza, Amanda said, "I've given your thin-air thought some serious contemplation while we were driving over here."

"I wondered why you were so quiet. What'd you come up with?"

The waitress appeared just then and placed their pizza on the table. "It's hot, ladies, so be careful. Anything else I can get you?"

"No thanks, we're fine," Judy replied.

"Enjoy your meal," the waitress said.

"Pizza, pizza, I want my pizza," Amanda said.

"That's what you came up with?" Judy asked. "You sound as if you haven't had pizza for the last three centuries. I thought you were going to share an amazing revelation with me about creating something out of thin air."

"I do have a thought for you to think about. What would you really like to do with your life?" Amanda asked, biting into her pizza. "Mmm, this is really good pizza," she said. Much better than baby food, she thought to herself.

"You could create a new career out of thin air beginning with only a thought." She looked at Judy. "Unless you want to stay at your job."

"Actually, I've been thinking about quitting," Judy replied.

"If you could do anything with your life—anything at all—what would you do?"

"I've thought about this for awhile," Judy said. "I'd like to live in Africa. I'm not sure why or what I want to do there. I just have a strong feeling that my future will unfold in Africa."

Amanda almost dropped her pizza. "Judy!" she exclaimed in astonishment. "I want to go to Africa too, and I don't really know why either."

"You're joking," Judy said, not sure whether to believe her or not.

"I'm serious," Amanda replied. "When I was a little girl, I dreamed that I lived in Africa and ever since then, I knew it was something I had to do. In my dream, I was in the jungle and I got very sick. My father was there and he showed me a map to find a treasure. Then I was floating on a cloud of light and I saw pyramids and a row of sphinxes by a temple in Egypt."

She looked puzzled for a moment. "I think the Egypt part happened before the Africa part. It was a really weird dream."

* * * *

Lavender looked into Amanda's dream images as she walked into the Temple of Ra. She watched her enter the innermost part of the sanctuary, where only priests who were studying mystical knowledge were allowed. The images began to change in slow motion as shadows wove through the dream and she saw an open-air, circular courtyard surrounded by evenly-spaced columns.

In the center of the courtyard was a large, round, flat-topped stone inscribed with symbols around the outside. Beyond the courtyard were steps leading down to a lake. The scene stood still and silent, a shadowy reminder of her lifetime in Egypt.

Lavender shivered deep inside her soul, feeling an overwhelming sense of fear. She knew she'd seen and experienced something terrible there, but couldn't remember what it was. Her throat began to hurt.

* * * *

Amanda pushed the images out of her mind, somehow knowing she'd see them again. Africa seemed to blend into Egypt and she didn't know how or why. She shivered, feeling a tremor of fear. "I must have spaced out for a moment. I was watching some shadowy images from that dream," she said, coughing to clear her throat. "Doesn't it seem like an incredible coincidence that we both want to go to Africa and neither one of us knows why?"

"I don't believe in coincidence. There must be a reason or a higher purpose for it," Judy said. "I think we're destined to do this together. I just feel it. Let's go," she said impulsively.

"Okay," Amanda agreed. "Maybe the reason is so I won't have

to wear shoes anymore. I'll just wander around the jungle barefooted."

"Do you really want to go?" Judy asked, not quite believing that Amanda was serious.

"Yes, I really want to go and I'm serious, Judy. It's so awesome that we both want to go to Africa, even though we're not sure why we want to go there. It's a little scary for me, but I'd like to find out what it's all about."

"Umm, Amanda, let's be realistic," Judy said, with a sinking feeling. "How are we going to get there? It would probably take a long time to save enough money." She sighed with disappointment. For a few minutes she'd imagined that going to Africa was something that could really happen and had felt joy in her thought. "There's not much of a possibility that we'll ever get there," she added wistfully.

Amanda smiled. "Let's think positive. If we look into illusion instead of what only appears to be reality, I'm sure we'll think of something. After all, thoughts are tangible things."

Judy laughed. "I know how we could get to Africa," she said. "We could create the way there out of thin air."

"That's a really great idea," Amanda replied enthusiastically. "Thoughts float around in thin air. Before they become tangible, they're sparkles of universal light drifting through ethereal energies in time and space until you see a thought and accept it. Once you accept a thought, you can shape it—through your feelings and beliefs about it—to fit your energy vibrations by forming the thought into exactly what you want.

"That's where imagery comes into the picture. Thoughts immediately inspire images, feelings, and ideas. When you focus your awareness into the feelings and images inside your thought, you open up ideas and begin to create the circumstances that reflect your thoughts," Amanda said, all in one breath. "I learned that from the movie last night."

"Do you mean that your thoughts aren't really yours?" Judy asked. "They just somehow appear magically somewhere in the universe and you reach into time and space and grab the first thought you see floating around in thin air and decide to explore it?"

"Your thoughts belong to you because you choose them and you can do anything you want with them once you accept them," Amanda replied. "All your thoughts radiate energy and you tune into your thoughts very carefully and precisely. It occurs instantaneously in harmony with your energy vibrations."

Sounds like an invisible Think Tank drifting through outer

space, emanating rays of energy toward earth and zapping unsuspecting people with illusionary thought/images, Judy thought to herself, trying not to laugh. Some of Amanda's dreams were just too far out of this world to be believable.

"I can see that you don't believe me; it's written all over your face. And you don't need to put your hand over your mouth to cover your smile."

Judy burst out laughing. "I'm sorry, Amanda. I don't want to hurt your feelings, but sometimes I can't tell if you're joking or serious. You have a very unique way of looking at things and I enjoy listening to your dreams, even though I think some of them are strange."

Amanda smiled. "You didn't hurt my feelings. I like that you think whatever you want and that you see my dreams in the way that's right for you. I enjoy looking into my thoughts and ideas, and exploring my dreams. It's like looking through an open window into my mind. It's fun and it always proves to be very interesting."

She looked directly into Judy's eyes. "Thoughts are vibrations of energy and are so light-transparent that you can see right through them. The Think Tank isn't located in outer space and it doesn't zap unsuspecting earth people with illusionary thought/images. It's in inner space and is more like an intangible idea center floating through a clear, blue sky, where you can creatively choose exactly what you want."

Judy smiled, not the least bit embarrassed that Amanda had seen her thought. "You didn't tell me you were secretly developing your psychic abilities," she said.

"I've been meditating every day to open up my inner awareness," Amanda replied. "It just sort of happened over the last few months since we finished the Imagination class. I feel as if I'm more aware and open to the energy around me and within me, and I sense the vibrations of energy. In a way, it's like reading a book between the lines; you only have to look through the words to see what the images are saying."

Judy munched thoughtfully on her pizza. "Maybe your dreams are your way of exploring and unearthing the mysteries of the universe. Tell me more about tangible thoughts."

Amanda smiled, delighted to share her dream. "Thinking is a flowing process in harmony with energy. When you first think of something, the thought is composed of universal light energy. If you accept the thought, it moves into the ethereal energy of thin air. As you continue to think the thought, it gathers both universal and earthly energy. As you put your feelings into the thought, the vibrations of the thought begin to form images inside your mind.

"When you tune into a thought and individualize it in your imagination, by your beliefs and feelings about it, related thought/images and ideas in the same vibratory range of energy become accessible to you. This opens up a world of possible expressions for your thought. As you become aware of the energy vibrations connected with your thought, in the form of images, ideas, and feelings, and you begin to act on them, the expression of your thought becomes more substantial."

"I'm beginning to get the picture," Judy said. "Tangible things originate from universal energy that becomes shaped and molded into matter by your thoughts. As your thought flows through the vibrations of your images and feelings, your thought becomes tangible and your imagery becomes visible, right?"

"You must have seen this movie before," Amanda said, "because you just described how to transform energy into matter."

"What happens if you change your mind or decide you don't like your thought?" Judy asked.

"If you change your mind, the thought revibrates into a different focus of awareness and opens up avenues of energy in the direction of your changed thought. If you don't like your thought, or don't do anything with it, the thought disappears into another dimension of energy."

She paused for a moment, listening to words that appeared in her mind. "Your thought doesn't really disappear; it begins to vibrate in other realms of reality and manifests in proportion to the original power you've given it."

"Do you mean that everything you think will actually happen somewhere, sometime?" Judy asked. Sounds serious, she thought to herself.

Amanda nodded. "Every thought becomes real."

"I wonder what happens to the unseen energies of your thoughts," Judy said. "They'd probably appear in your life when your vibrations are most in tune with them and say surprise; you created me and now here I am," she said, answering her own question.

An image of pages and paragraphs flying through the universe ran through Amanda's mind. "I imagine that your thoughts would probably scatter and separate into image pieces that drift through time and space in different dimensions, and their expressions would roam through other realities. You'd have to find all the pieces of your thoughts and images, and put them together if you wanted to see all their energy expressions.

"The interesting part would be that all the pieces were doing their own thing and going in their own direction, so by the time you found all the pieces of your thoughts, images, and feelings, they would have had experiences of their own."

She smiled. "It would be like playing a game called *This is Your Life: Understanding the Illusions of Your Reality*. There are lots of twists and turns in the form of fate and different paths to follow, but the purpose of the game is to discover what's real and to find out what life is truly all about. In the course of the game, you gather all the energy expressions of your thoughts by picking up the pieces of your experiences and putting them into their proper perspectives.

"There are different levels of skill and lots of choices. You earn credits or debits, depending on how you play the game. To move forward, you have to completely immerse yourself in your feelings and learn from all your experiences. You're not supposed to cheat, but you can if you want to. If you cheat, or if you refuse to learn, you have to go back and do it over again.

"You're allowed to use hindsight, insight, and foresight to help you only if you believe what you see in those images. You choose how to play the game by creating any reality you want, but you do have to follow a few rules.

"First, you choose all your experiences and your responses to them. There are no accidents. You do everything on purpose.

"Second, all your thoughts and feelings manifest into expressions of energy in one reality or another, whether you're aware of them or not.

"Third, time doesn't exist in linear spaces of past, present, and future. Everything occurs simultaneously.

"Fourth, all your thoughts, images, feelings, and experiences are connected through vibrations of energy. Each and every one of them influences all your other thoughts, images, feelings, and experiences, either directly or indirectly. If you change anything in your life, then everything even remotely related to or associated with that particular thing changes proportionately—even things that have already happened."

* * * *

Lavender watched her energies flutter and fragment in a sudden spiral of wind that blew out of nowhere. "Sometimes Amanda is just too free-spirited," she mumbled. "What's the matter with her mind, thinking that life is a game and scattering pieces of her thoughts all over the universe? She knows better than to fool around with energy."

"Lavender, can you see that Amanda's thoughts are mirroring

your thoughts, and that your perceptions of her thoughts are influencing both her perceptions and your experiences?" Rainbow asked.

"The way Amanda sees the thoughts I share with her make me feel as if I'm being pulled in too many different directions all at once and I'm flying here, there, and everywhere through the universe trying to collect the scattered pieces of my experiences." Lavender sighed, knowing that the vibrations of Amanda's thoughts could become very confusing if she decided to roam through realities that she didn't yet understand.

"I haven't been this dizzy since my cloudy mind cold when I felt like I was coming apart at the seams. How on earth am I going to pull myself together and connect my thought/images with all their expressions? And where am I going to put the energy vibrations of the experiences that she's creating with the thoughts she's playing with?"

Rainbow smiled, taking a brighter view of Lavender's thoughts. Putting them into her own perceptions, she said, "Studying spirituality requires a dedicated search for knowledge, but I do wish you'd lighten up and see the fun side of life once in awhile. You're beginning to take your assignment of helping Amanda rediscover her true spiritual nature much too seriously."

* * * *

Amanda laughed, thinking it was fun to play with her imagination. "Seeing the illusions of your reality is one thing; watching them appear in your life is something else. It's a matter of putting your thoughts and their images into motion so you can see how energy really works as it manifests into your experiences. That's what makes the game fun and interesting.

"To win the game and put all the pieces together, you have to know what's real and you have to completely understand all your experiences in every vibration of awareness and on every level of reality, both seen and unseen. Then you've mastered all forms of energy because you've learned how to be in harmony with universal light energy and you've unified all your experiences by synchronizing the energy vibrations of your thoughts, feelings, and actions with the vibrations of your soul. After you've put all the energy expressions of your experiences into their proper perspectives of time, space, matter, and motion, you know who you really are and what life is all about. You have a complete picture of yourself."

* * * *

"Lavender, are you watching Amanda's words?" Rainbow asked, wondering if she knew that Amanda had just unearthed a universal understanding by playing with her thoughts. But Lavender didn't seem to be listening; she was running around the earth and the universe simultaneously trying to catch the pages and paragraphs in her manuscript and Rainbow's insight was apparently lost as an unexpected gust of wind blew her question away.

* * * *

"I didn't mean to go off on a tangent like that," Amanda said, "but I wanted to see how to play the game. The thoughts popped into my mind, so I explored them. I like the ideas about knowing what's real and mastering energy. I think life is meant to be taken seriously and while you can have fun with your experiences, energy isn't anything to fool around with."

Judy looked at her and rolled her eyes toward the ceiling. "Amanda, sometimes I think you get lost in space, then you always come back down to earth. But now you have me wondering. What if the game of life is real? If every thought manifests in some level of reality whether you're aware of it or not, then what did you just create by playing with those thoughts?"

A picture of all her thoughts going in a million different directions all at once as their images simultaneously roamed through both the earth and the universe interacting with their energy expressions ran through her mind. She watched herself chasing after her thought/images as they tried to fly somewhere over a rainbow. It was like trying to catch free-spirited butterflies on a windy day.

The scene was so funny that she began to laugh. This could be a lot of fun if I look at it the right way, she thought. It could be very interesting and ultimately, very enlightening. But then again, it could become very confusing.

"It looks like I created lots of multi-dimensional thought vibrations and scattered the pieces all over the universe," Amanda replied. "Now their images and expressions are probably playing hide 'n seek and I'll have to find them somewhere in my experiences and talk them into being serious before they get into trouble."

"Maybe the images and expressions of your thoughts will come back to you and ask your advice on how to play the game," Judy said. "I've heard that whatever you think and do returns to you in one form or another."

"I've heard that too," Amanda replied. "It seems to me that life is like a circle that returns to itself in ever-evolving levels of awareness. Can you imagine how infinite all those levels must be?" She opened her eyes wide, as if she was seeing a picture so vast that the energy of the images overflowed the frame.

Judy took her glasses off. "I never realized that thoughts could have so many possible energy expressions," she said. "There's more to thoughts and creating your own reality than meets the eye."

Amanda nodded in agreement. "The movie summed up how thoughts turn into tangible things by showing a larger-than-life thought on the screen."

As the images of your thoughts vibrate into the energy expressions of your experiences, Your Thoughts Become Tangible Things.

Thirty-Four

A World of Words

Amanda was absorbed in thought for a moment, watching an image slip softly into her awareness. "The movie showed magical thoughts that hang around forever in your mind, traveling through time and suspended in space, just waiting for you to recognize them and do something about them," she said. "Magical thoughts are like a mystical mindscape of images that weave in and through your dreams and flow into your feelings."

Judy smiled, seeing an image of sunlight shining on a path. "I know I have the power to make my thin-air thought about Africa come true. Show me, step-by-step, how a magical thought manifests into a physical experience."

Amanda smiled, feeling that both she and Judy were about to unravel the illusion of reality. "You have to follow the thread of your thought from origin to outcome. Thinking a thought occurs so fast it's done in the blink of an eye. Manifesting a thought into a tangible thing occurs over a period of time because physical energy vibrates slower than universal energy."

A rainbow appeared in her mind and she saw herself walking barefoot in the rain through a dream as pages and paragraphs began to form into an image of a book. "Suppose you want to write a book," Amanda said. "That's the sparkle of universal energy and is like a light bulb turning on in your mind."

* * * *

Lavender looked at Rainbow and smiled. "Did you hear that?" she asked, shimmering into vibrations of energy that reflected universal light in the form of rainbows. "Amanda is starting to pay attention to her dreams." She beamed brighter and brighter, feeling in tune with the essence of her soul. "I'll share my pencil with her," she said. "We can write the book together when she wakes up from her dream."

* * * *

"If you accept that thought, you'd begin to absorb the energy of it in your mind by putting your feelings into your thought. This amplifies and flows universal and ethereal energies into earthly energy as it flows around and through the thought that's in the process of forming. As you look into the energies of your thought, it begins to show itself in ideas and images.

"In your mind's eye, you might see a picture of an open book or your images might show you the cover of your book, or you may feel the intangible essence of your book begin to flow through your awareness," Amanda explained. Just then she felt a tingle of energy in her right hand, like the form of a pencil. She looked quickly but saw nothing in her hand.

"If you're thinking about creating an experience, like going to Africa," she said, "your images might show highlights of your experience as it forms itself in your mind in the shapes of how you perceive it happening."

"As we create the way to Africa, we'll see images of the experience in our mind before it actually occurs in our life as it gathers energy in the process of manifesting, right?"

Amanda nodded. "And we'll also become aware of ideas and insights that will help us open up those particular vibrations of energy."

"This is so exciting," Judy said. "It's like watching the previews of a coming attraction for a mind movie you really want to see and experience."

Amanda softly rubbed the first two fingers of her right hand with her thumb. They felt warm and the tingle of energy was still there. She smiled at Judy's enthusiasm about Africa. "You're really getting into the spirit of things, aren't you?" she asked.

"Yes, I am. I can see it all now, even though I'm not sure what I'm looking at." An image of a tropical garden in a rain forest appeared in her mind. She could almost smell the flowers and feel the moisture in the air.

"I just saw an image of a very peaceful garden," she said. She closed her eyes, seeing it clearly. "It looks like a garden of harmony, where nature is perfectly in tune with itself." She breathed in the essence of the garden, exploring its energy. "I can hear the sound of a small waterfall that's in the center of some rocks beside lush, flowering bushes. The clouds float through a deep blue sky and shimmer in the sunlight as they reflect rainbows."

The garden she's seeing in her mind is a place I've been to in one of my dreams about Africa, Amanda thought to herself.

Judy smiled, delighting in her imagery. "It's so beautiful," she said, opening her eyes. "I feel as if I'm inside my image, as if I'm in a place that really exists. I know it's a sacred place because I can feel a special kind of energy flowing through every part of the garden."

It was only a dream, Amanda thought. But Judy wouldn't know about the sacred magic unless she'd been there and actually experienced it. She decided not to say anything, even though it was uncanny that Judy had described the garden so accurately. Then she remembered that the movie had said that time and space are simultaneous—that you can experience the past and the future in the present by synchronizing your awareness into certain thoughts, dreams, or experiences.

"What's the next step to turning thoughts into tangible things?" Judy asked.

"Depending on what you want to write about and how you decide to develop and form your thought, you'd choose and open up related thought/images that correspond with the subject of your book."

"Or your experience," Judy said.

"Right," Amanda replied. "That's how your thoughts gain depth and dimension in space and how your images begin to vibrate in tune with your energies." She felt the illusionary form of a pencil in her hand again, but knew it wasn't really there. "Words are the energy expressions of a book and their images shape themselves according to what you want your book to say. As you open up and explore your thought, you begin to shape and sculpt your ideas and images into a tangible expression of energy.

"Putting your thought into motion is accomplished by picking up a pencil and writing the first word," she said, seeing a picture of words in her mind that paralleled into a portrait of pages. "You develop your images by generally grouping your ideas and insights together. This creates the format and structure for the chapters in your book and builds the foundation for the physical expression of your thought.

"The next few steps are very closely connected," Amanda said. "The experiences are so intertwined with each other and the interweaving thread of energy is so subtle that it's difficult to tell where the energy of one experience leaves off and the other begins.

"As you continue to write your book, you begin to fine-tune your images by putting your words into the picture of your book and seeing the energy of the words in action as you flow your idea/images through a moving mindscape. It's like you're putting yourself into the picture by seeing and feeling your words in motion.

"As you give the thought your full attention and center your awareness into clarifying and revising your words, you focus your energies into the same vibratory rate as the theme and tone you've chosen for your book. Then specific idea/images that are directly related to the subject and expression of your book begin to flow into your mind."

Amanda felt a surge of energy gently surround her and flow through her. It felt like sparkles of light were dancing in her mind. "It seems as if your book somehow magically comes to life as energy begins to gather in a definite frame of thought and starts to vibrate into your experiences."

* * * *

Lavender saw Amanda being drawn into a dream image of a rainbow. It seemed as though she'd entered a world created with words—a mystical mindscape of pages and paragraphs, where her dream became real.

* * * *

Amanda smiled. "You're in your own magical world and it's very real. You experience yourself writing your book in a dimension of *being-ness*. It's a truly enchanting place, where time and space don't matter—where only the world that the words create, exists."

As Judy listened to Amanda's words, she felt as if she was in the center of a sunrise, somewhere in Africa. "What happens next?"

"As this magical world of images and experiences open up within the energy vibrations of the words, you travel inside your mind to a place where the words and images are interchangeable. At first you feel as if you're in two separate worlds at the same time, but then the worlds begin to blend into one another as your words merge into images. I'm not sure exactly how it happens—whether you blend your energies into your words and the images they inspire, or whether your book forms its essence around you—but you can really feel the vibration and expression of your book as it shapes itself into your experience of writing it."

Amanda saw several images inside her mind and felt as if she was in three different places at the same time, experiencing three separate realities simultaneously. Part of her awareness was with Judy, centered into their discussion of magical thoughts. Another part of her awareness was in a misty image of a universal classroom, where she was sneezing at dusty words and refusing to trade in her pencil for a cosmic computer.

And in a third part of her awareness, she was holding what looked like a pointed brush made from a hollow plant stem that she used to draw pictures of words in a book she was writing. It wasn't really a book; it was more like a very long piece of paper that she rolled as she wrote on it. Somehow she knew that it contained secrets of knowledge.

Suddenly her throat began to hurt. She thought it was because she was talking so much and was afraid she was going to lose her voice. She took a drink of water, but her throat still hurt. She sensed that she'd so completely immersed herself in her inner world that she was physically experiencing the images in her mind; they seemed to be just as real as the discussion she was having with Judy. "I feel as if I'm dreaming while I'm awake," she said.

Judy smiled. "I feel as if I'm mind-tripping into my thoughts and images, opening up levels of awareness within myself. It feels like I'm in a higher realm of energy, as if I'm traveling on a ray of light. It's like a journey into the center of myself." Looking at Amanda thoughtfully, she said, "Sometimes I wonder if you're really an ancient philosopher who is now hiding in the disguise of a mere mortal."

* * * *

Lavender felt a whisper of wind echo deep inside her soul. A shadowy image of the philosopher writing pictures of words on papyrus paper floated through her mind as she watched her pencil transform itself into a frayed reed-pen that he held in his hand. Her throat began to hurt and she felt afraid.

* * * *

"What makes you say that?" Amanda asked, feeling an odd tremor of energy go through her body, coupled with a foreboding sense of fear.

"It's just a feeling I have about you," Judy replied. "Some of the ideas and theories you come up with seem very philosophical and in a way, remind me of discussions we've had before because I somehow recognize what you're saying. Must be déjà vu or something."

"We may have traveled this way before," Amanda said. "During the intermission, there was a preview for another movie about past lives and probable futures, and there was an entire segment on parallel lives that I missed because I went to the refreshment stand for popcorn and my date got broccoli."

"Amanda, what if your dream occurred in a parallel dimension of reality, and you're remembering what you've experienced in another level of your awareness?"

Amanda shrugged her shoulders. "It could be true," she said. She looked at her hand. "A few minutes ago I could have sworn I was holding a pencil in my hand, but I'm not." Maybe I am dreaming, she thought to herself.

"What if you were a writer in a past life, and you're just now synchronizing your awareness and energy vibrations into that experience?"

"It's a possibility," Amanda replied. "But since we're talking about how to create a book out of light energy and thin air, it could be a subconscious reaction to our discussion." Somehow that didn't feel quite right. "Maybe I really am a reincarnated writer," she said slowly. A voice inside her mind whispered, "The pencil is real."

Drifting into her thoughts, she saw fragmented images of a map appear in her mind. She wondered if the map her father had shown her in a dream about Africa was the same map she was seeing in her thoughts right now. The dream had happened so long ago it seemed like another lifetime. Searching her memory, she tried to remember what he'd said about the map. Something about a dig site in Egypt and looking for a hidden treasure. He seemed to know exactly where they'd find it; he'd mentioned a temple by name.

Just as she was about to put some of the sketchy pieces of her dream images together, Judy said, "With the example of writing a book to show me how thoughts become real, I think you really are a writer."

Judy's voice seemed to come from far away. With an effort, Amanda redirected her attention from the map images into their discussion. *"From the pictures in your mind come words,"* she replied. She had a feeling she'd read those words somewhere before and tried to remember where she'd seen them. They sounded philosophical—like words in an ancient text.

A shadowy image of an old, bearded man appeared in Amanda's mind and she felt an indefinable echo of fear. Looking into his eyes, she saw a sadness that permeated her soul. He tried to speak, but there was no sound.

"Amanda, are you all right?" Judy asked. "You look frightened, as if you've just seen a ghost."

"I saw an image of someone who was trying to tell me something. I think it was something I didn't understand before, and it's important that I know what it is now, but he couldn't talk." Tears welled up in her eyes.

"Maybe you saw the spiritual essence of a past self."

"Maybe," Amanda replied. "But the image is gone now."

"Back to your book," Judy prompted.

"Where was I?"

"You were telling me how your book begins to come to life as your thought begins to become tangible," Judy replied.

Picking up right where she'd left off, Amanda said, "As you become in tune with levels of energy that reach beyond the realm of your conscious thoughts, you open up a universal source of awareness and you're able to understand that awareness within yourself because you're synchronizing your energy vibrations with the vibrations of universal light energy. When you're in tune with those higher levels, it seems that your book takes on a life of its own and begins to write itself."

She felt as if she was reading the words from an imaginary book in her mind. Her thoughts and images were becoming more real every moment and she couldn't seem to separate her dream images from her thought/images. It seemed that there was a thread of energy continuously flowing through the tapestry of her thoughts and dreams as it simultaneously wove the images together.

"That sounds as if you're aware of the thoughts and images of your higher self," Judy said. "It's as if you're completely connected with everything you know on a spiritual and a universal level. Does the book come to life and begin to write itself because you're so in tune with a universal source of energy or does your higher self write the book?"

Amanda saw an image of a rainbow reflected in her mind. "Your higher self is the connecting thread of energy that flows universal energy, in the form of images, ideas, insights, and inspiration into your awareness," she said. "In a way, you become your higher self as you merge into the energy vibrations of universal awareness—as you blend yourself into levels of energy that vibrate in tune with expressing the essence of your book.

"When your thought reaches this point, sooner or later, it manifests into reality in the form of a book that you can now hold in your hands and read. You have a tangible energy expression of a magical thought that you created out of universal light energy and thin air."

She felt as if she was somewhere inside a dream, walking barefoot through the rain looking for answers to what life is all about and who she really was. The words *Somewhere Over the Rainbow* flowed into her mind. I wonder if my life is a book I'm in the process of writing? She smiled to herself; it was a special smile she understood somewhere in a magical place inside her soul. What if I've already written the book and now I'm in the process of reading it? I wonder if I have the power to paint pictures with words—to rearrange the pages and change the chapters into rainbow colors of knowledge that show vibrations of universal light? It might be fun to explore that idea, she thought, seeing an image of herself writing pages of pictures. I could create a world with words—a mystical mindscape of images. "Maybe I'll write a book about my rainbow dreams," she said.

Judy smiled. "You've had the thought before," she said. "It would be a truly magical book," she added. "Now that I see how to make my thin-air thought come true, I know we'll get to Africa somehow, but what are we going to do when we're there?"

Amanda shrugged her shoulders. "I haven't got the foggiest idea. Let's just go with the flow and see what happens. Our discussion about thought energies has been absolutely awesome and my brain is beginning to get boggled." She started laughing.

"We're really creating our trip to Africa; we're making it happen out of thin air, right here, right now, right in front of our eyes," Judy said, laughing. "It seems so unreal. Why are we laughing about it?"

"Probably because it's either the right thing to do or we're both out of our minds," Amanda replied. A feeling of fear loomed in her mind, casting a shadow into her thoughts. She shivered instinctively, without knowing why. She decided to look her fear right in the eye; she wanted to see through the shadowy images and knew that Africa was an important step on her journey to remember who she was. She wiggled her toes, practically feeling the jungle under her bare feet.

"I feel so peaceful about this," Judy said. An aura of light seemed to emanate all around her like a bright ray of sunshine. "The path that I've been seeing in my reveries is the path that leads to Africa," she said.

Thirty-Five

Possibilities and Probabilities

"Why does Amanda want to go to Africa? I don't want to go," Lavender said to Rainbow. "Can she go without me? I think I'm going to be sick."

"What are you afraid of?" Rainbow asked, seeming to disappear into a shadow as a cloud misted through the universe. "Do you want to fail her now or do you want to help her find the way to Africa?"

Lavender heard Rainbow's thought that she'd failed once before, even though Rainbow didn't say it. That's why she'd died from malaria and had chosen to experience Africa again.

I didn't fail; I just changed my mind and decided to leave, Lavender thought silently to herself. Shadowy images of her experiences in Egypt misted in and out of her awareness. Her throat began to hurt and she felt an overwhelming sense of fear.

It seemed that Rainbow was having difficulty talking and Lavender could see that she was afraid of something too.

"I know I died before I accomplished what I set out to do, but why does Amanda need to go to Africa to continue my previous purpose?" She hoped Rainbow wouldn't answer the question.

"It's much more involved than that," Rainbow said. "She wants to accomplish more than a previous purpose. She's honoring a past-life promise with Judy and she's also deciding whether to open up the space for her soul mate to reappear, as well as exploring myriad other opportunities in the process of remembering who she really is and discovering what life is all about." She paused for a moment. "And most importantly, both Amanda and her father are trying to help you open up and remember your spiritual knowledge."

"How can Amanda help me?" Lavender asked. "I'm supposed to help her. And what does her father have to do with Africa? He's just a reincarnated archeologist who wants to look for hidden treasure in Egypt."

Rainbow smiled. "Amanda is beginning to change what you

think is the future to reshape the past. All those theories and principles you thought I left out in my lecture on reality creation have now turned into what you're both experiencing. It's all just theory until you apply the principles by putting the possibilities and probabilities into practice."

Rainbow's vibrations shimmered in the sunlight. "It looks as if you're side-stepping the truth and not seeing the direction of your destiny. Every time you change your thought perspectives or misunderstand the images and energy vibrations of your experiences in Africa and Egypt, Amanda responds by changing her perceptions of your thought/images. That's why her dream doorway is revolving in circles instead of evolving into enlightenment."

"But Amanda rearranges energy every time she changes her thoughts or shifts her focus of awareness, and I feel like a butterfly being tossed about in the wind." Deadly fear was setting in and she didn't know how to stop it.

"Sometimes she feels exactly the same way, but doesn't really know why yet," Rainbow said.

Lavender felt as though she was losing control; the energy of her fear overpowered her and clouded her ability to think clearly. She looked at Rainbow and started to hiccup.

"You're both influencing each other's thoughts by pulling in opposite directions and this causes disharmony between your vibrations. When you feel out of tune with yourself, this affects Amanda's perspectives, which in turn affects your perceptions. If you'd look at the polarities of the situation you're sharing, you might see that you're both revolving around the same circle," Rainbow said breezily.

Lavender knew her energies were unsynchronized, but couldn't seem to pull herself together and get her bearings. She thought Rainbow was being rather airy about the whole situation.

"Lavender, sometimes I think you enjoy living in what you think is two dimensions at once but I wish you'd see that they're both one and the same, not separate," Rainbow said. "Then you'd see that your almost-earthly errors and experiences are really steps toward the truth about your spiritual nature." She smiled again, but Lavender couldn't see her through the misty clouds that were blocking her view.

"But I am living in two dimensions at once," she insisted. "And they really are separate because they're parallel worlds of one another." Circular images spiraled around her thoughts as they wove through her energy vibrations. Trying to straighten out her thoughts, she remembered that Rainbow had told her time and time again that the earth and the universe were mirror images—duplicate dimensions of one another. And she also remembered one time when Rainbow said that time is simultaneous and all experiences are synchronous.

"Lavender, have you started working on your master's thesis yet?" Rainbow's voice interrupted her thoughts.

"No, I haven't starting writing it yet," Lavender replied. It's too infinite and the topic is too massive, she thought irritably. She didn't know when she'd find the time to begin it, much less complete it, even though she couldn't graduate her soul until she'd written her thesis on ***Time and the Two Separate Worlds are Really the Same.*** Rainbow had suggested the topic when it appeared that she was having trouble in the Time and Space class.

Lavender sighed. "I have too many things to do all at once," she said. Time was running out and she knew it. Tuning into Amanda's vibrations, she thought to herself, I don't have to deal with Africa yet, and I won't have to deal with it at all if she changes her mind or can't find the way there. Then she won't open up the images of Egypt.

"But you know she will," Rainbow said, reading her thoughts. "She's already seen the map in her dream images."

Lavender remembered the map from her lifetime in Africa and knew that a treasure was hidden near a temple in Egypt. She tried to turn off the shadowy images that loomed silently in her mind.

"You're seeing the shadow side again," Rainbow said. "The bright side includes Egypt and Amanda plans to find the truth. She's exercising her free will to remember her spiritual knowledge. You're the one who is experiencing fear. She's exploring that fear by looking into her thought/images and turning Africa into an adventure of awareness—a journey within herself to remember who she really is and who she was before. And that's a big part of what life is all about."

"Yeah, but she doesn't know what I know," Lavender said, feeling powerless as she watched her thoughts scatter into duplicate dimensions simultaneously, each image vibrating to a separate level of energy and awareness.

"Maybe she knows more than you think she does," Rainbow replied.

Lavender couldn't come up with anything to say to that. It was probably true, at least for now, and she couldn't think of any more excuses or arguments. She sensed the energy moving in Amanda's thoughts and knew she could rearrange her own images in any form she chose, but there were so many pieces of the picture floating around that she didn't know where to start or how to put them all together.

"Your thoughts aren't as far apart as you think they are," Rainbow said, smiling at her.

Shaping her thoughts into a semblance of togetherness, Lavender saw that she really was in control of her destiny, even though it didn't look like it because she didn't want to accept responsibility for her reality. She knew that Rainbow was going to show her a few more insights and she didn't want to hear them.

"Amanda is having difficulty opening up the future because you're reluctant to see the past," Rainbow said. Her voice seemed to reverberate into echoes of energy. "That's why it looks like she's stuck in the present and can't find the way to Africa, because you can't make up your mind."

"I'm more than reluctant; I'm terrified," Lavender said, seeing the shadowy images of her past-life pictures begin to take shape and form in Amanda's mind as they spilled over into her experiences. She knew that Amanda was going to Africa, with or without her cooperation, where she'd begin to recognize her soul and be able to read the map that would lead her to Egypt, where her future would unfold into understanding and open up into knowledge when she was able to clearly see her past.

Lavender closed her eyes and hesitantly stepped into Amanda's images, knowing she was opening the past she'd locked inside her.

Rainbow hugged Lavender. "I know how scared you are, but seeing the truth will set you free. And Lavender, I've always known that you're a brave soul. You agreed to face this when you chose to reincarnate as Amanda."

Lavender knew that Africa was really going to happen in Amanda's life and knew, with every part of her soul, that she would be there.

Thirty-Six

The Mundane and the Magical

The intercom beeped on Amanda's desk as soon as she arrived at work. "Will you come in here please, Amanda?" Mr. Parker asked.

She kicked off her shoes and walked into his office. "I know I'm late, but my clock stopped last night when the electricity went out because of the thunderstorm." She smiled. "Maybe the lab guys could develop a time-awareness clock that runs on universal energy so that lightning would zap people out of bed when it's time to get up and go to work," she suggested.

Mr. Parker smiled, then sighed. "I'm very sorry to have to say this, Amanda, but my supervisor insists that I fire you because you're continually late and you refuse to wear shoes in the office, even after you've been given repeated warnings."

"Thank you, sir," Amanda said, shaking his hand. "The best things always seem to happen to me on rainy days. I was even born on a rainy day. I remember looking through a window and seeing a rainbow." She smiled again.

Mr. Parker laughed. "This isn't the reaction I expected. Most people respond with negative feelings when they get fired."

"I have so many better things to do with my life than to be unhappy," Amanda said. "This opens up a world of possibilities that I might not have had the courage to explore if you hadn't fired me."

"Now that you're really a free spirit," he said, smiling, "what sort of possibilities are you going to explore?"

Amanda laughed. "I'm probably going to Africa. That seems to be my next step to wherever my life is going to lead me."

"Gary, what are you doing home from school this early?" Amanda asked. "And why are you wearing your Indian clothes?"

"Our assignment in Creative Arts class was to create something natural and aesthetically pleasing, and to explain why we chose our project, so I planted a few trees in the center of the campus and gave a consciousness-raising class to help people become more aware of the earth's natural ecology. I offered the teacher a new way of thinking and the students a new way of learning by showing them how to understand and tune into the rhythms and balances of nature," he said, smiling. "The teacher gave me an 'A' for my art project. She said the trees were beautiful and looked completely natural planted in the ground. Then she sent me to the principal's office for digging up the campus without permission.

"The principal didn't know what to do with me, so he sent me home for not following the dress code. He said the trees could stay, but the school system isn't ready for this form of environmental education and that I have to learn how to live within traditional limits. He said being different was dangerous to other people's opinion of me, and that it was no use trying to change old ways of thinking. I told him I couldn't change anyone's thoughts; they have to do that for themselves. I just wanted to offer them a natural way to look at life." He smiled again.

Amanda laughed and hugged her little brother. "I love your individuality and your peaceful nature, but isn't fourteen a bit young to be pursuing your life's purpose?"

"I'm only fourteen on the outside," he said. "Anyone can discover their destiny at any time just by looking inside their thoughts and following their feelings."

Amanda sifted his words through her mind. What do I really want to do with my life? she asked herself. If I tune into my spiritual nature, I'll know what my real purpose is, she answered herself. "I wonder what Africa has to do with the shadowy images I see in my thoughts."

"Why don't you take a closer look and see?" Gary suggested as the phone rang.

"Hi, Judy," Amanda said.

"How'd you know it was me?"

"Just a feeling."

"I have some wonderful news to tell you," Judy said. "I quit my job this morning. I'm ready to go to Africa."

"So am I," Amanda replied, knowing it was really true. "I got fired this morning. How's that for coincidence?"

Judy laughed. "Somehow it seems like fate, but you must have planned it on purpose. All we have to do now is find the way to Africa."

Amanda looked out the window. A flash of lightning lit up the sky and illuminated a dream image of a rainbow inside her mind. I'm ready to follow my dream, she thought. "Let's go for a walk in the rain to get our thoughts clear on finding the way to Africa and knowing what we want to do when we're there," she said.

"Sounds super," Judy replied. "I'll meet you at the park in ten minutes."

"I'll be early this time," Amanda promised. "I have my shoes off and I'm ready to go."

* * * *

"I suppose you're going to blame me that Amanda got fired from her job today."

"You're certainly being negative about her experience, Lavender," Rainbow said. "And no one is blaming you for anything. You're feeling that way because you choose to feel that way. If you look at what really occurred, you'll see that you're helping Amanda discover her destiny because it's your destiny too, and she chose to be fired so she could free herself to go to Africa."

Lavender was mystified for a moment, then she began to see what was really happening. It took every ounce of courage she had not to turn around and run away.

"Of course there were several other possibilities Amanda could have chosen but since you're still a bit reluctant to find your way to Africa, she gave some of her power away by allowing other people to apparently make a decision she'd already made but was hesitant to put into motion. If you'd been more willing to open up and explore your experiences in Egypt, she would have quit her job instead of being fired," Rainbow said.

"If Amanda goes to Africa and then to Egypt, she's going to get hurt and so am I," Lavender said, feeling shaky by the turn of events.

"You're seeing shadows, instead of looking into the light," Rainbow replied. "Amanda's future experiences in Africa and Egypt hold just as much potential for healing as they do for hurting. Your last lifetime offered the same possibilities," she added. "You're just getting in your own way and tripping through your thought perspectives."

"I know I'm off-balance," Lavender said. "I feel as if I'm stuck in the middle between the past and the future, lost in a shadow somewhere between the earth and the universe. It's a hell of a predicament to be in." She felt like crying, but knew she had to raise her spiritual energies and clear her mind if she was ever going to find her way out of the shadows that surrounded her soul.

"You created all of this," Rainbow replied. "And you're

responsible for everything in your reality, including the way you feel about Amanda's experiences."

"I know I create my own reality," Lavender said. "I just don't want to be responsible for the negative situations and for the things that go wrong."

"But you are responsible for everything you experience," Rainbow said. "That's how you gain control of your power—by acknowledging and accepting responsibility for your actions and the situations you create. When seemingly negative things happen, it's either because things are out of balance and need to be corrected or because you're going against the natural rhythm and flow of your spiritual choices. Either way, it creates a feeling of separateness and disharmony within yourself which is mirrored and expressed in your experiences.

"A soul always strives for balance and harmony. It's inherent within their nature. You can regain your power by looking into your experiences and seeing the reasons why they're happening to you. Being inside your experiences and completely immersing yourself in your feelings gets you into the flow of your free will, where you understand your choices and you know why you created your experiences.

"As you accept and understand current circumstances, and honor your previous choices and creations, you begin to apply your power by allowing your feelings and experiences to become positive learning experiences that help you understand your soul. You must feel peaceful within yourself and at ease with your experiences before you can empower yourself to create new or better circumstances, or to change previously-existing situations. Otherwise, all you do is repeat versions of the same experience and revolve around in unchanged circles instead of evolving into universal awareness and enlightenment."

A thought lit up in Lavender's mind and the image reflected a parallel light shrouded in shadows. "The philosopher I saw while I was searching to know what's real—the one who offered me the scroll when I opened the door into knowledge—lives in a parallel life in Egypt, doesn't he?"

Rainbow nodded.

"I met myself face to face, didn't I? And my past experiences in Africa, when I decided not to see through the shadowy images of Egypt, have caused and created this repeat cycle in Africa, right? And Amanda's future experiences will parallel my past experiences to create an expanded experience of two separate lifetimes in Africa that will blend into one another, right?" Lavender asked, seeing it clearly in her mind.

Rainbow nodded again. "It's interesting that all your answers are inside your questions."

I'll probably continue to parallel myself until I learn how to merge my energies and my awareness into all my experiences, Lavender thought to herself.

Rainbow looked directly into her eyes. "I'll share a very special secret with you, Lavender. As you allow yourself to be in harmony with yourself, you tune into your true spiritual nature."

"If I look through the shadows, I'll know the truth about the philosopher and I'll be able to remember my spiritual knowledge," she whispered.

Light filtered softly through her shadowy images of Egypt as she began to reawaken the awareness of her experiences as a high priest turned philosopher. She knew she'd turned off the light, creating the shadows that surrounded her soul, but couldn't remember why. An almost-overwhelming feeling of fear spun through her as the images began to show themselves. They were like a horrible nightmare.

She closed her eyes, choosing not to see those experiences right now. But she'd seen the light of her soul begin to emerge and watched as the light grew brighter, illuminating the way that would lead Amanda into finding the truth.

Music flowed into her mind. Maybe I died and went to heaven, she thought to herself.

Somewhere, over the rainbow, clouds are clear.
There's a place that I dreamed of, once in a time now here.

Someday I'll wish upon my star and wake up
with a rainbow all around me.

Where light is bright and truth is clear,
that's where I'll find me.

Why is Amanda singing that song again? she wondered. Listening to the words and melody of the music vibrate into her thoughts, she sensed a magical feeling of harmony inside her soul. "It's time for me to expand my horizons and explore all the energies of my experiences," she said to herself. A thought that she was ready to find peace within herself flowed gently into her mind and she knew that the beginning of her journey was only a few steps away.

* * * *

"I see why you love walking in the rain," Judy said. "It's so peaceful."

Amanda smiled, feeling the wet softness of the ground beneath her feet as she squished the mud between her toes. She turned her face up to the sky and breathed in the freshness and pure energy of the air, loving the feel of the gentle raindrops on her face. It was something she'd done as a child to feel connected with the energies of the earth and the universe.

"What's that song you're singing?" Judy asked. "The melody sounds familiar; I know I've heard it before."

"*Over the Rainbow*," Amanda replied. "I sing the song to myself when I want to center my energies and get my thoughts clear. I change the words to fit my feelings. It helps me be in tune with myself."

As if the universe was in harmony with Amanda, the sun came out and the clouds began to clear. Looking up at the sky, she saw a beautiful rainbow. "It's so magical," she breathed in awe, watching the sun's rays shimmer into prisms of color. She felt as if she was being drawn inside the rainbow, flowing through the colors as she floated into the lavender light at the top of the rainbow. It was like being inside a dream.

"It seems that the rainbow came out just for you," Judy said.

Amanda smiled, feeling a wonderful sense of inner peace and harmony—a feeling of being in tune with the essence of her soul.

Taking her glasses off, Judy looked up at the sun, directly into the light. "I was just thinking that if we look at finding the way to Africa from a higher point of view, and we flow universal energy through our thoughts, we'll be able to see the way to Africa."

"When you said you wanted to make your thin-air thought about Africa come true, do you remember your imagery and how you felt?"

"I saw the sun shining on a path and I felt very peaceful inside."

Amanda smiled again. "We've said several times today how peaceful we feel inside," she said. "If we follow our feelings, and take that inner peace a few steps further, we can expand our horizons at the same time."

Judy returned her smile. "Are you thinking what I'm thinking?"

"Yes," Amanda replied. "I know how we're going to get to Africa and what we're going to do while we're there."

"We'll join the Peace Corps," they said in unison, laughing and hugging one another with joy.

Judy looked up at the sun again. "We reached into the universe to find the way to Africa and it was within us all the time, just waiting to be recognized."

Amanda smiled at the rainbow in the sky. "I feel so free, like a child who's been granted a wonderful wish," she said. It's like watching a dream come true, she thought, knowing that she was taking the beginning steps on a magical, mystical exploration into enlightenment, and that she was ready to follow her dream—ready to journey somewhere over the rainbow to find her soul.

Thirty-Seven

A Mystical Mindscape

Amanda picked up a pencil, wondering what to write. Images of words appeared in her mind and she knew she'd read them somewhere before. A waterfall of words cascaded around her, creating rainbows everywhere and she literally couldn't find a place to print them, so she drew pictures of the words and put them in pages of an open book and waited to see what would happen, even though everything seemed to be happening all at once.

Lavender opened a window in the Time and Space classroom and the sudden gust of wind scattered the images all over the place. She sighed, seeing the pages and perspectives in her book rearrange themselves again. Life is just too changeable, she thought to herself.

"Lavender, you're the one who wants the eraser on your pencil so you can revise your thoughts and reshape your experiences if you decide to change your mind," Rainbow said.

Lavender's thoughts turned like pages in a manuscript that was in the process of being rewritten. She watched the next chapter and the one next to the duplicate one preceding the parallel one curve into time tangents and saw that a chapter written in a past life was blank, even though she knew the words were there because she'd seen the writing before. Then she noticed that the chapter before the chapter before this one metamorphosed more than several chapters later into more than several chapters and two separate worlds simultaneously more than once.

And previous pages a few chapters ago began to look like pictures of sketchy shapes as they formed the foundation for her thought/images that later turned into experiences. Then she noticed that another chapter written in magical words was beginning to blend into the present chapter because she could see the images were all filled with shimmering sparkles of universal light energy vibrating together and becoming superimposed upon one another, inspired by a stream of subconsciousness that flowed through her mind.

And the end of this chapter could be the beginning of this

chapter if Amanda would make up her mind once and for all whether to read or write her book, and the chapter following the next chapter looked like an open book that was so real you could see the words magically come to life all by themselves. And the entire book, from cover to cover, was centered on the chapter in the middle, which was really the first chapter and the final word, but it kept going around in circles like a revolving door that went both ways somewhere inside the rainbow, except Lavender refused to wake up from her dream and Amanda thought she was still sleeping.

Once upon a time, when she could almost see her nearly-remembered knowledge through cloudy images, she saw that Rainbow was pretending to be herself in a parallel perception of herself in a vibration of universal awareness. But in the here and now, she couldn't tell who was who because she thought she'd been writing the preceding paragraph but when she read it later, she discovered that it was partly about her and it was beginning to dawn on her that she and Amanda were really one soul, sharing a journey home and everything was all the same difference anyway.

Or maybe the mistake had slipped by her awareness because there were so many pieces of paper in the picture and you couldn't be perfect all the time. If you were, you wouldn't have to reincarnate to correct your mistakes but that was only half of it, and if she wasn't writing this book, then who was putting the words on paper and playing with the images in her mind? And she knew, at least she thought she did, that she was a free spirit, Amanda was a butterfly, and Rainbow was ... Well, Rainbow was a rainbow. That was obvious. But then again, appearances could be deceiving and you always had to find the truth for yourself and maybe you were really more than you thought you were to begin with.

When it looked like the focus of the book was going to drift into Amanda's imagination, everything began to fall into parallel places after she found the light library and started researching one of her past lives when she thought she'd lived in Egypt before she dreamed about following a rainbow. It was a mundane thought that opened into a magical world of words and showed her a few more insights into imagination than she'd seen before. Meanwhile, during all the writing and scrolling of paper and papyrus, she and Judy were waiting for a letter so they could go to Africa.

In her free time, Amanda planted a broccoli garden in her back yard and tried to be as real as her imaginary friend by changing into a butterfly in the breeze. And before she got too old or too serious to play anymore, she ran through rainbows and climbed trees with a shaman before she realized that life was just a game of Illusion.

Then she began painting a portrait of pages with a pencil that didn't really exist yet.

Lavender wasn't sure if she was exploring the mystical images of words or if she was experiencing the mystique of writing, but she was almost sure that she was lost in time, stuck somewhere in the pages of a picture that flowed over her frame of awareness and she'd misplaced her pencil and the eraser had completely vanished into thin air. Her Alpha/Omega computer didn't work anymore because she'd crashed out a microchip from the universal source of power by breaking a cosmic commandment. And then there was the time she stretched the truth too far into another dimension when she tried to follow her future and shine a light on some shadowy spaces and the reverberating repercussions from the echoes of energy still hurt.

Just as Amanda was about to sneeze at a few dusty words that were floating around in her mind, Lavender began to sniffle, wishing upon a star that she could remember her spiritual knowledge. Although she was feeling better now than before, she wondered if she could reuse her cloudy mind cold as an excuse not to read an ancient scroll in her misty memory, but knew Rainbow would remind her that she'd woven the energy vibrations of her thought/images into her experiences and tied the threads together with seams of illusion and that she was responsible for all her creations. But she had a terrible feeling of fear that a spiritual shadow was looming up in front of her.

Hoping the clouds would begin clearing before she started repeating herself again or rearranging her energies into another form, she began to daydream in class about metamorpheus light synergy but the scientific view was too earth-bound and limiting, and she preferred a lighter, more spiritual approach. Besides that, she wanted to expand her horizons and find a golden key to knowledge in the center of the sunrise.

All day and night, during the span of today, tomorrow, and yesterday, she'd been searching for herself, looking here, there, and everywhere—even somewhere over the rainbow. Between traveling through past-life pages and tripping through paragraphs and looking in the real world and learning the secrets of nature and exploring the mystery of magic, there was the real possibility that none of this was happening—that it was all probably a dream. It was a little confusing and time was running together, both before it occurred and after it happened while it was in the process of going around in circles and spiraling into past, present, and future spaces as it scattered in all directions into every vibration of energy at once.

And she knew something was the matter with energy and was feeling spaced out because there was trouble with time, but the reality of illusion had her running around in circles and parallel perceptions. She would have liked to stop for a minute and catch her breath—she was so dizzy—but Amanda was spinning down to earth and wanted to practice the freedom of flight and read the *Scroll of Knowledge* before she became hopelessly lost in earth energies and fell into her tangible thoughts or got stuck somewhere in space and ended up somewhere in nowhere. And the sentences were so long.

As if all of this and most of that wasn't enough, it was raining and she couldn't clearly see the rainbow hiding behind a cloud even though she knew it was there and she heard a whisper through a window but the door was locked. She wished that either the sun would come out of its shadow or that she could have a vacation in a lavender sphere of light, or at least learn how to rise above herself to see a real rainbow, or take a journey into awareness to discover the direction of her destiny or find a garden of harmony to relax in for a few lifetimes. It was just too much to handle all at once in the first place. And in the second place, all she wanted to do now was apply a few principles of peace in her life. But before she did that, she was hungry and had a taste for pizza.

"If only Amanda would talk to me," Lavender said to herself. There's so much I could tell her if she would just wake up and see the light within herself. She's wandering through duplicate dimensions and dream doorways, in and out of a mystical mindscape of images in search of her soul. I know there's a spiritual side to all of this. Maybe I'll go to school in the universe and study spirituality instead of playing with images of illusion to find out who I really am and who I was before, she thought silently to herself. The energies of earth were circling around her, and they were either revolving into raindrops or evolving into the edge of enlightenment.

Rainbow wove into her misty thoughts and through her shadowy images, carrying a lavender thread of light and spinning ever-changing pictures of a masterpiece, singing a song. Lavender couldn't recognize all the words, but the melody was familiar.

"Lavender, in your spiritual search for knowledge, the truth is something you've always known, even though you haven't always been able to see it." Rainbow smiled brilliantly. "If you want to unearth the mysteries of the universe and graduate your soul, then I suggest you master energy in all of its multi-dimensional forms and vibrations by completely opening up and understanding your spiritual knowledge while Amanda learns how to apply that knowledge in all of her earth experiences." With those words, she disappeared into a cloud with a silver lining, vibrating to a higher level of awareness.

Rainbow is playing mind games with me by radiating thought/images from a realm of reality that only appears to be just beyond my reach, Lavender thought to herself. It seems to me that she's exploring the energies of words and expects me to read their images and recognize their true meanings for myself. I wonder if she's a writer.

Thirty-Eight

The Trouble With Time

Lavender couldn't seem to get herself in motion this morning. She'd overslept, watching Amanda dream about a library with books that came to life when they were opened, and now she was late for the Time and Space class again. She gathered her energies around her and rushed across the campus. Walking into the room, she noticed that all the other students were on time and wondered if she was the only one who had a problem with time.

Rainbow breezed into the room and began her lecture. She seemed a little out of breath, as if she'd been running. "One expression of energy on earth has been labeled *time* and placed within limited applications of its many multi-dimensional forms and vibrations. The proper term for time is energy, and like energy—time is, was, and always will be. But at the same time," she said, "time does not exist. Time is an illusion of energy, but this doesn't change the reality of it for a soul who believes in time."

Why did time ever have to be invented? Lavender wondered. The only place that time really mattered was on earth, and then it was only important because most people still believed that time existed. I'll bet time was created as a bad practical joke by someone with a scientific sense of humor, she thought, wondering if Newton-Einstein had anything to do with it.

"To see through the illusion," Rainbow continued, "let's look at a few ways that time is viewed on earth. Some reincarnated souls see time in a clock/calendar vibration in order to provide a structure for their experiences. Other souls comprehend the concept that time is both non-existent and simultaneous, but have placed a paradox on that perception and haven't allowed their awareness to grow into a universal understanding. And too many souls seem to be stuck or lost in a linear concept of time," she added.

"To understand time as it relates to space in an earthly vibration of motion, envision time as a spiral coiled within the space of a circle. Viewed in this way, you see that as time vibrates, it ripples and repeats itself in related spaces. Circles and spirals both have a flowing rhythm of motion, but a spiral is like a circular parallel of itself with individual and synchronous characteristics and qualities. A spiral, set free, can move in many directions. It has the ability to transcend space, whereas a circle has no place to go but around itself over and over again, always revolving and returning to the same space.

She smiled. "Going in circles will make you dizzy. Traveling through a spiral will take you in the direction you decide to go—forward or backward, higher or lower, or side-to-side—depending on your manipulation of space and the way you maneuver through the motions of matter."

Lavender noticed that her perceptions of time were beginning to wobble, and watched her perspectives slide in and out of her thoughts while they slipped through spirals of space. I wonder if time is warped around the edges? she thought.

"Because time is composed of energy, as are all things, its motion is directed by thought. Your perspectives and perceptions will influence the way time appears to you. If you believe in past, present, and future, then time will show itself in that illusion though you'll often see divergences to your beliefs. This occurs because your perceptions can limit your view of the real properties and qualities of time.

"The true nature of time is a flowing rhythm of motion, showing itself in synchronicity with the matter of your experiences. Everything in the earth and the universe happens simultaneously in vibratory rates and forms of energy. If you try to capture or change the expression of time to fit your frame of thought and your focus of awareness, it doesn't change the real nature of time; it only changes the way you experience time.

"The same is true for parallel selves." Rainbow looked at Lavender, wondering if she was paying attention. "I know that some of you feel it's easier to keep track of them if you place them in a limited, linear framework or if you view them separately from yourself and see them as existing in a duplicate dimension of energy. Then you think you always know where they are, and what they're doing, but you do tend to lose them from time to time."

I wonder why that happens, Lavender thought. I've only lost Amanda a few times, and that's because she's got a mind of her own and decided to go in another direction—something that parallels are never supposed to do. Maybe she disappears into another realm of matter once in awhile, or travels in a different vibration of time where I can't see her because I'm looking in the wrong space.

"When you recognize that time is simultaneous, and you

synchronize space with matter and motion, you'll always be able to find your parallel self," Rainbow said, wondering why no one in class had synopsed her lecture into the one word that would explain everything clearly. She wanted to say that the word was harmony, but knew her students had to become aware of the word for themselves before it would mean anything. She moved to the open window into the energy of the sun, radiating rays of light into prisms of color as she continued her lecture.

"What I said is only partially true. A parallel self remains parallel until you recognize that they're synchronous with you, just as space looks like a parallel circle placed within itself in the form of a spiral until you see its synchronous and simultaneous nature. When you see the reality of your parallel self, you'll see the truth about your spiritual nature at the same time. Until then, you'll see your parallel self in what appears to be a mirror reflection, and your thoughts and experiences will be seen superimposed on duplicate images in parallel places."

Lavender couldn't seem to get her thoughts straight and felt as if she was losing her perceptions of matter and motion. She noticed that her thoughts were falling out of their perspectives into simultaneous spaces, and that time was slipping away from her as it stretched out of sequence. Beginning to feel dizzy, she wondered if she was stuck in a circle of time or a spiral of space, or if Amanda was stuck in a parallel perception of matter and motion. "I'm having a little trouble with this," she said.

Rainbow laughed. "I'm not surprised. Look at your thoughts and their perspectives. Your time/spaces are a little warped around the edges, and your perceptions of your parallel self are still in the dark ages," she said. "You're trying to separate and straighten space and motion while you put time and matter into sequence. You could turn time, space, matter, and motion into a cosmic catastrophe if you're not careful." She smiled. "You might even throw the whole rhythm of your universe out of sync."

Rainbow wondered if Lavender was ready to see the truth about herself. "You've been viewing Amanda as your parallel self and I've gone along with your perception because it's what you choose to believe. If I told you that you were really living on earth instead of in the universe, you'd probably tell me that I'm dreaming and refuse to accept it. That's why it appears that Amanda is experiencing earth energies, instead of you. But now I feel that you're advanced enough in your studies to see Amanda as who she really is, and to see yourself as who you really are. And Amanda has already said she wants to understand her true spiritual nature."

Lavender looked at Rainbow, wondering how she knew about those thoughts that surfaced from time to time. Every once in awhile, she did wonder if she was Amanda, and was becoming increasingly curious about who Rainbow really was. She pushed the thoughts aside. "Amanda is my parallel self," she insisted. "She's the one who is stuck in a physical body, not me. I'm a free spirit."

Rainbow shimmered in the sunlight. "I'd like you to experience the energies of matter in motion to help you understand the synchronous and simultaneous nature of time in relation to the directions, dimensions, and destinies that you chose to explore in parallel spaces in a circular vibration of time," she said. "Your homework assignment is to write a research report on a past life that both you and Amanda feel requires a universal understanding and an earthly balancing."

"When is this research paper due?" Lavender asked, not realizing that her question showed she was stuck in a linear continuum of time. She wondered why Rainbow was smiling.

"You can turn it in whenever you decide to experience it," Rainbow answered. "This report will show you some of the reasons you chose to reincarnate—to place part of your energy essence on earth. To complete the assignment, you'll have to synchronize your awareness with Amanda's awareness. You might even learn how to harmonize all the energy vibrations of your soul," she said, vibrating rainbow colors all around her.

Lavender knew that now was the time to remember Egypt because Amanda had dreamed about a library last night when she thought she was sleeping. The book she'd started to read had shown her images of a life in Egypt, and now she was wondering about reincarnation and had decided to begin her research today. She had a feeling she'd been a philosopher; that feeling had begun when she'd seen an image of an old, bearded man who offered her a scroll.

Lavender remembered when the philosopher had offered her the scroll and she'd refused it. But Amanda had accepted it and wanted to read it to see what it said, but the hieroglyphics remained a mystery. Lavender knew the scroll contained secrets of spiritual knowledge and she was curious about it too; she couldn't remember a word of it.

She decided to stop by the Light Library after class to open the book to the chapters on Egypt, even though she was still reluctant to see or read anything about her life as a philosopher. But Amanda was looking forward to learning more about her life in Egypt and Lavender had already agreed to overcome her fear and help her find the truth.

Thirty-Nine

Library of Light

Amanda was walking around what appeared to be a college campus when she saw a spiral stairway composed of rays of sunshine shimmering into the universe. Placing her foot on the bottom step, she felt a gentle wave of energy flow through her. Traveling up the stairs, a vibration of energy softly radiated upward from her feet, sending sparkles of light through her entire body. She began to feel as if she was floating a few inches above the steps, gliding through emanations of energy, weightless and free, flowing into higher realms of light.

At the top of the stairs she saw a brilliant light that illuminated the entrance to a library that was created entirely with the vibrant energy of the light itself. Rays of universal light emanated everywhere through the open windows. Vibrations of light formed the floors and the walls. Beams of sparkling energy supported the arched ceiling; in the center was a domed skylight.

A magical aura surrounded the library; ethereal energies of pure awareness softly reverberated through the vast array of books. A hushed stillness echoed within the library even as it shimmered with energy, with the knowledge contained in the books that filled the shelves and lined the walls. She listened quietly. The books talked in whispers of wisdom and murmurs of mystical knowledge.

The rows of books appeared to be endless, as if they went on forever. Walking through the aisles and the alcoves, she saw that there were books on every subject imaginable. It seemed that the library contained all the knowledge that had ever been spoken, written, or recorded, in all the world and the entire universe since the beginning of time, since the beginning of thought.

Running her fingers over the titles of the books, she found that she could read them within her mind. The books were written in a universal language that she understood easily, just by touching the books or looking at the pictures on the covers. The words and their images danced into her mind, creating a symphony of sound vibrations, and within the music and the melody, she understood the knowledge inside each book.

Continuing to walk through the library, exploring the energies of knowledge, she noticed another stairway with seven steps that vibrated with a light that shimmered and sparkled with energy, as if it were alive. There was a sacred feeling about this light; it seemed to contain an essence within itself. The vibrations emanating from the light were filled with images of color that had shape and substance. It looked like a beautiful blur of rainbow colors forming into prisms of light.

Looking into the light, she experienced an emotion that went beyond words and thoughts. More than anything else, she wanted to be part of that light. She wanted to rush into the light, to become the essence of the light, yet felt that she might disturb it if she rushed, so she waited, respectfully and reverently. The light opened up and invited her in. Stepping into the light, she was filled with a feeling of awe and wonderment and pure joy.

Each step of the stairway vibrated in harmony with the colors of a rainbow. Walking slowly up the stairs, she paused on every step—feeling the energy, hearing the unique vibration, the tone and experience of each color. Ascending the stairs and absorbing the colors within her body and her mind, she felt her awareness expanding and knew that she was traveling a stairway that led her into the true essence of herself.

Reaching the top of the stairs, she saw that the higher echelon of the library was a loft containing the written records of every soul's existence and she knew, with a magical sense of inner knowing, that these books vibrated with an energy that was unique to every soul and could only be opened and read by that particular soul.

In the center of the loft was a table with an open book and a lamp that glowed with a lavender light. Next to the table was a comfortable chair. She walked over to the table and looked at the book. It was dusty, as if it hadn't been opened for a long time and the knowledge within had been still and silent. It seemed that the library had been waiting for her to discover it, and the open book was waiting to be read.

Knowing that the book was about her soul, she looked at the chapter title. *Experiences in Egypt.* As she read the words, they began to vibrate on the page, then to radiate with a soft glow of light, emanating into rays of energy that formed images that swirled into thoughts and sparkled into a special kind of knowing within her mind. Touching the words, her hand began vibrating with energy.

Picking up the book, she relaxed in the chair. Holding the open book close to her heart for a moment, her body began to vibrate with a radiant energy. She felt as if she was being drawn inside the pages as the words vibrated and resonated in her mind, moving in rhythm and harmony with the flow of spiritual and universal energy. It felt as if a gentle current of energy was flowing through her, releasing a higher power within. She heard a soft humming sound inside her mind, and as the energy continued to flow through her, she knew her awareness was completely opening up inside of her, beginning to surge and soar through every part of her body, mind, and soul.

As she read the chapter title again, the words formed an image of a pyramid. She touched the pyramid, feeling the texture of the stone. It was solid. The pyramid was real; it wasn't an image that disappeared into shadow when she blinked her eyes. *The words formed real pictures.* It was like magic. When she read the words, they formed pictures that came to life—three-dimensional images that vibrated from the pages into her experience—resonating with an energy that was inspired by the words inside the pages.

The book was energy in motion, and the words had magically transported her into Egypt. Looking at the clear, sun-drenched sky above her, she felt the warmth of the sun on her face. Breathing in the warm, dry air, she smelled the scent of lilies intertwined with roses. She heard the sound of water softly lapping on a shore and knew there was a lake nearby.

Looking around her, she saw a row of sphinxes leading up to the entrance of a temple and she knew, without going inside, that there was an open-air, circular courtyard in the center. A feeling of fear began to surround her slowly, imperceptibly at first, but then it grew stronger, almost overwhelming. The sand was hot beneath her bare feet, yet she was hesitant to move.

She'd seen this picture before. She'd dreamed the shadowy image several times, but this time it was more than a dream image or a misty memory. It was real. She knew she'd been here before and at the same time, she was here now, experiencing it all over again as if it were happening for the first time.

Suddenly the scene went into darkness and the book closed, as if someone had slammed it shut and turned off the light, and she was in the local library, curled up in a chair. She took a deep breath. The experience had seemed so real.

Forty

Principles of Peace

Amanda was at the library most of the morning doing research on Egypt—looking through pages that pictured pyramids and temples—when she had a feeling that the letter from the Peace Corps would arrive today. She rushed over to Judy's house.

Judy was sitting on the lawn holding the envelope addressed to both of them. She waved it at Amanda as she pulled up the driveway. "The mailman delivered it thirty seconds ago. Your sense of time is improving," she said, smiling. She opened the letter and they read it together.

Dear Ms. Invue and Ms. Millenum:

You are both invited to join the Peace Corps in Africa for a two-year term to work side-by-side with the people to cultivate their crops.

"We're going to Africa," Judy shouted, jumping up with joy. "We're really going!"

Amanda laughed. "This is so perfect. I get to help grow a huge vegetable garden," she said, experiencing a feeling that she hadn't felt since she was a child. She thought of her imaginary friend and smiled, wondering if he'd somehow magically appear in one of the leaves.

The letter explained the specific peace project they'd be assigned to and stated that their training would occur on-site in Africa under the guidance of Philip and Sara Bridges, experienced Peace Corps volunteers who'd served there for a year. The remainder of the letter provided information on required immunizations, a list of suggested items to take with them, local customs and lifestyle, and their travel arrangements.

The sun sparkled through the clear, blue sky, splashing rays of light on the wings of the airplane. Judy looked out the window, watching Africa appear before her eyes. I'm really in Africa. It's more than an image in my mind; it's *real*, she thought, still a bit awed by the power that had changed a thin-air thought into a tangible experience.

As the plane circled the airport, Amanda looked out the window, trying to see everything at once. On its landing approach, the plane flew through a misty cloud, then through a beautiful, double rainbow. Stepping off the plane, she experienced a strong feeling of déjà vu. I've been here before, she thought, but nothing looks familiar; it just *feels* familiar.

The Bridges were waiting for them at the airport. "You must be Judy and Amanda. We recognized you from your happy smiles. All Peace Corps volunteers seem to have friendly faces. I'm Philip and this is my wife, Sara," he said, smiling and shaking both their hands at once.

"Welcome to Africa," Sara said, giving them both a big hug. "How was your flight?"

"It was incredible, especially when I saw Africa," Judy replied.

"The landing was super," Amanda said. "The plane flew through a double rainbow; it was like being born all over again." That seemed like a strange thing to say, she thought to herself, wondering why she'd said it.

Sara smiled. "Our village is only a few miles from the rain forest. If you don't mind the mosquitoes, the forest and flowers are beautiful and you can always see a rainbow there."

Amanda shivered suddenly, although it was quite warm. "Is that the only place you can find a rainbow?" she asked.

"It sounds like a wonderful place," Judy said.

"When we get to the village, we'll help you get settled in," Philip said. "Tomorrow is the big day for planting. You can unpack and rest for awhile if you'd like, or you can go for a walk through the village. Everyone is looking forward to meeting you."

"You'll be sharing a lovely bamboo house with a thatched roof," Sara said. "It's very comfortable and has all the conveniences of home: Hand-woven rugs for a floor, two fold-up chairs and a shipping crate for a table, cots to sleep on, an oil lamp, and window curtains made from leaves."

"It sounds charming," Amanda said. "It's a good thing I left all my shoes at home, but I guess we shouldn't have brought make-up and nail polish, and we probably won't need our hairdryers, will we?"

Sara laughed. "We tend to be very natural here," she said.

Piling into the jeep, along with their suitcases and supplies for the village, Judy felt completely at home. The road toward the village was the same path she'd seen so many times in her imagery.

Amanda looked over at Judy and squeezed her hand, knowing how much being in Africa meant to her. Suddenly she remembered Morpy, the caterpillar she'd found when she was a child, and sensed that Africa was a step on her path that would lead her into finding her ultimate destiny.

When they arrived at the village, children crowded around the jeep, waiting for the candy that Philip pulled from his pocket. Shyly smiling at Amanda and Judy, they ran to hide behind their parents. The village leader came forward to greet them. Offering his hand, he helped them step down from the jeep. Smiling warmly at Amanda, he said, "You know the spirits of seeds. Please, you will help us plant the first seeds?"

"Yes. I'd be very happy to help," she said, returning his smile.

The next day, at the first light of dawn, the elders placed a circle of stones around a sacred area that represented their land. A small child brought Amanda a handful of seeds which had been blessed by their shaman. Kneeling, she placed the seeds tenderly into the earth, then gently covered them. The village leader raised his arms and face to the sky, as if in prayer. As he lowered his arms, he reached his hands into a bowl filled with rain water and sprinkled the ground inside the circle just as the sun came up over the horizon. The villagers began to dance and sing, chanting for the union of the nature spirits with the sun god and the rain goddess.

After the ceremony, Philip said, "No outsider has ever been included in their planting ritual before. The chieftain must have sensed a special, inner quality about you, and known that you would understand and respect their beliefs about the powers of the earth and the universe."

Amanda smiled. "I feel very honored that I was allowed to help. I grew a vegetable garden when I was a little girl and my mother thought it was magical because it grew so fast. Maybe that's why he asked me."

Sara smiled. "It's part of their belief that as you give to the earth, the universe gives to you. Before the first seed sprouts, everyone who helps with the planting will receive a spiritual gift that symbolizes the harmony of the earth with the universe. The gift, whatever it may be, is in tune with a desire in your heart and brings joy to your soul," she said.

"Phil and I helped plant the crops last year, then we went to the rain forest. We found a beautiful place where we experienced a feeling of inner peace. That was our gift. It helped us become aware of what's really important in life. We're going there again today after all the seeds have been sown. Would you both like to come with us?"

"I'd love to go and see the rain forest," Judy said.

"How about you, Amanda?" Sara asked. "I can almost guarantee you'll see a rainbow there."

"I'm deathly afraid of mosquitoes," Amanda replied. She looked over at the trees that bordered the village and smiled. "I'll climb a tree later today. I used to do that when I was a little girl and I felt that it somehow connected me with both the earth and the universe."

Judy was surprised at Amanda's response. It was so unlike her to refuse the chance of seeing a rainbow.

"Ladies, we can't stand around talking all day. We've got work to do. Who wants to learn how to drive a tractor?" Philip asked.

"I do," Judy replied.

"Me too," Amanda said. The tractor and other farm equipment looked so out of place here that she laughed.

Forty-One

Realms of Reality

Amanda watched the sun sparkling through the leaves of a tree. Rays of light danced with the soft breeze to form ever-changing patterns on the leaves. One moment the design showed ripples and waves of sunlight, the next moment it looked like a person was sitting the tree.

It's just an illusion, she thought, watching the sunlight and shadow interplay on the leaves. Suddenly she realized that there really was a person in the tree. "Hi, up there," she said, waving. "Who are you?"

"I'm a shaman," the person in the tree replied.

"Are you real?" she asked. "There for a moment, I thought you were an illusion."

"I'm real," he replied.

Catching a better glimpse of him, noticing his blond hair and the blue jean cut-offs he was wearing with a purple jersey that had *Deva—33* printed on it in large, white letters, she said, "You don't look like a real shaman. You look like a star athlete."

"I played football in high school, but I imagine that the school I went to was quite different from the ones most people attend," he said, beginning to climb down from the tree. "What does a real shaman look like?" he asked.

Amanda shrugged her shoulders. "I don't know; I've never seen one before," she said, smiling.

"Are you sure you've never seen a real shaman?" he asked.

Amanda laughed. "I'm positive. I've never seen a shaman, but there's something about you that seems familiar. I feel as if I've seen you somewhere before."

She thought for a moment, searching the images in her mind. "You remind me of the imaginary friend I had when I was younger." Her words surprised her. She'd never told anyone, except her mother, about her friend. "I first saw him as a light in my broccoli garden and he seemed very real to me." She smiled again, feeling completely comfortable with him. "What is a shaman and what do they do?" she asked.

"A shaman is someone who understands the energy of nature, and they work in harmony with nature to do magical things," he said. "But the things they do aren't really magical; they're perfectly natural once you understand and apply the power of energy."

"I used to be able to do magical things when I was a little girl. I even named my dog Magic, so I'd always remember how real magic is. By the way, my name is Amanda. Do you have a name or should I just call you shaman?"

He jumped down from the tree and tenderly held her hand in both of his. "My name is Adam."

Amanda looked into his eyes and recognized him immediately, knowing, incredibly, that somehow this shaman was her imaginary friend. She struggled with believing and not believing, wondering if her birthday wish about wanting her friend to be real had come true after all this time. Somewhere inside her soul, she knew it was him and that he'd always been real. Her heart began to soar with joy and she threw her arms around him and hugged him.

"You'd love the rain forest, Amanda," Judy said. "We found a very beautiful garden there and the sunlight reflected a really awesome rainbow. It's the same garden I saw in my mind the first night we talked about Africa."

She smiled and her eyes sparkled. "It's like a sacred sanctuary where you can get in touch with the true nature of the earth, and you can feel the essence of your soul. I experienced a tremendous feeling of harmony there today. It was so wonderfully magnificent that words can't truly describe it."

"You look like an ethereal spirit of light," Amanda said, smiling at her. "You've found your soul; I can see it in your eyes, but it's more than that. There's something different about you." She looked at Judy closely, then laughed. The difference was so obvious she was surprised that she'd missed it. "You're not wearing your glasses. Did you lose them?"

Judy smiled again. "No, I'm seeing things more clearly now," she replied. "What did you do today?"

"I found a new friend. I was climbing trees with a real-life shaman and remembering how to see through the appearances of illusions. The truth is, I found my old friend, not a new one. He only appears to be new, and I didn't really find him; he was never lost." Amanda smiled, glowing with happiness and joy.

"My friend, Adam, reappeared in the leaves of a tree today, the same way he disappeared when I was a little girl, except he didn't really disappear. I just couldn't see him for awhile because I forgot the secrets of universal light," she explained. "I've invited him to dinner tonight. I'll introduce you to him then."

Forty-Two

The Butterfly in the Breeze

"I brought you a present," Adam said, handing Amanda a leaf. She turned it over gently, noticing the chrysalis underneath that was just beginning to open. Together they watched the butterfly emerge.

"She's beautiful," Amanda said. The butterfly perched precariously on her finger, its wings drying in the air. "Look at her coloring; she has an iridescent hue of lavender woven all through her. I'll name her Lavender but I don't want to keep her prisoner; I want to set her free." She smiled. "She's like Morpy. She's just like me, somewhere inside her soul."

A soft breeze circled around her. "Fly, free spirit, on the wind. Find a magical rainbow and follow your dream," she whispered. Sunlight shimmered on the butterfly's wings as she opened them and began to fly, floating on a gentle current of air, then soaring into the sky, disappearing into the universe through a misty cloud.

"Thank you, Adam. This is one of the most special gifts anyone has ever given me," Amanda said.

Adam smiled. "I wanted to give you something you'd treasure, like a rainbow."

Amanda looked at him thoughtfully. "What have you been up to, all this time since I've seen you last?"

"All this time?" he repeated. "I thought you'd know everything there is to know about time by now."

Amanda laughed. "I'm not sure how time really works, but I do have a theory running around in my head."

"Tell me about it," he said, sitting down comfortably on the ground.

Amanda sat down next to him. "I used to think that time marched forward, but now I'm beginning to think that it goes around in circles. As you go into your future, maybe you're really entering your past and you can get lost in time or stuck somewhere in space if you're not exactly centered in the present."

"What makes you think that?"

"Some of my earlier experiences look like they're repeating

themselves—happening all over again—but they change expression and feeling as they reappear in the form of my present experiences," Amanda replied. "It's as if the past energies of time and matter are somehow changed or rearranged in the present because my memories seem to be a lot more than just memories."

She smiled. "I have a feeling that I could probably reshape my future experiences now—if I have a mind to—even though it looks as if they haven't happened yet." She paused for a moment, then said, "But maybe they have. Maybe I'm just not aware of them."

"I'm beginning to think that your theory is more than a theory," Adam said.

"It's a possibility," she replied, considering the thought. "Maybe the vibrations of time are all really the same; they're synchronous and simultaneous, all at once." A diagram of circles and spirals drawn on a chalkboard appeared in her mind. The design of the drawing began to fluctuate, as if it was flowing with energy, rearranging itself into ever-changing patterns and pictures of motion and expression.

"If a thought, or a feeling or an experience, is similar to or reminiscent of another experience, then time and space could become synchronized with matter at a revolving point of energy when you focus your awareness into that experience," she mused. "If that were true, then all your experiences would become timeless because they would exist simultaneously in related vibrational spaces of past and future energies that are interwoven and in tune with your present awareness."

Now I see what the diagram shows, she thought to herself. The circles travel through time and the spirals move through space, like ripples of energy touching and connecting feelings. Suddenly new images—light sparkles and parallel lines—appeared in the diagram as if someone was in the process of drawing them. Looking at the images, trying to see how they fit into the whole picture, she felt a powerful sense of inner knowing open up inside of her.

The sparkles of light are thoughts coming together, and the parallel lines are levels of awareness merging with experiences. She smiled, seeing how it all worked so perfectly in harmony. "When you center your attention into the *here and now* of whatever you're thinking, feeling, or experiencing at any given moment, then the energies of time, space, matter, and motion blend together to become a fluid dimension of energy that flows in, around, and through your experiences, bringing the past, present, and future together."

* * * *

So that's how time and space are simultaneous, and how matter and motion become synchronous, Lavender thought in amazement, wondering how Amanda had unraveled and understood the doodles in the drawing before she did. She smiled, impressed with her awareness. I'll put her perceptions in the thesis for my master's degree, she thought to herself, realizing that Amanda had also discovered how spiritual energy blends into both universal and earthly energy.

* * * *

"Where'd you come up with that theory?" Adam asked.

Amanda shrugged. "I probably dreamed it at some point in time. Or maybe I took a Time and Space class in the universe. But I haven't had time to test the theory yet—to apply it here on earth. So for now, I prefer to see time in a straight sequence. It makes life much easier to handle." She smiled. "Bring me up to date on everything you've been doing since I was a little girl and don't leave anything out."

"To make a long story short, I've been living in the illusions that I created to experience life on earth," he said.

"You're really going to make me see through our time apart all by myself, aren't you?" Amanda asked, laughing. She turned toward him. "Let me look deep into your eyes so I can see your soul." She cradled his face in her hands. "We were always together—in our feelings and thoughts of one another—even when it looked as though we were apart."

He put his arms around her and kissed her. "I love you, Amanda. I always have and I always will."

Forty-Three

Today, Tomorrow, and Yesterday

"Amanda's in love," Lavender said dreamily. "But who is the shaman that just appeared out of *nowhere*? He wasn't even in Africa the last time I looked."

Rainbow smiled. *"No-where* is really *now-here*, and people tend to mispronounce it all the time. You remember Adam, Amanda's broccoli buddy, and how could you forget who he is when he was ..."

"I know who Adam is, but who is the shaman?" Lavender interrupted. "I searched everywhere in Africa, but he wasn't anywhere to be found."

"Synchronize the vibrations of space with the matter of your experiences as you flow your thoughts and feelings through the motions of time," Rainbow said.

"I'm trying to see everything at once, and be everywhere at the same time, but the past and the future are blurring into the present."

"You're trying to be *somewhere*, instead of being *nowhere*," Rainbow said. "Center your attention into your experiences and clearly focus your awareness in the present. Look inside your feelings in the here and now."

Lavender opened up her thought/images and feelings, then smiled. "I could swear on the face of reality, absolutely, without a doubt in my mind, that only yesterday—or maybe it was the day before—Adam was sitting next to me at the tangible movie, holding my hand and buying me popcorn during the intermission," she said. "But I still want to know who the shaman is."

"He's Adam. And how could you ever, even for a moment in time, forget who Luminous is?" Rainbow asked, surprised at Lavender's lapse of mind. "Even if he does seem to disappear into an ever-evolving higher vibration of light once in awhile, and you think you can't get there from here, how could you really forget what he looks like?"

"He changed his appearance into a new form," Lavender replied. "He looks the same as Adam now, but it's been such a long time since I've seen him that I didn't recognize him right away." She smiled. "Does that mean I'm in love too, or am I just dreaming?"

"Maybe you need to work on your memory," Rainbow suggested. "The thesis for your master's degree on *Time and the Two Separate Worlds are Really the Same* is due the day before tomorrow."

"Thanks for reminding me, but I thought it was due the day after yesterday," Lavender said, looking for an excuse to turn it in late. "I didn't realize you wanted it right here and now. You know I don't like to be rushed or put into a time frame, and I don't know when I'll be able to find the time today to write it."

"You seem to be a little unaware today and your attention seems to be wandering," Rainbow said. "Are you suffering from PMS again?"

"No, I'm not suffering from Probable Mental Slowdown," Lavender replied irritably. "It's just that I thought I was in love for a few minutes and it was a nice illusion. And then you brought reality into the picture." Maybe I can turn back the hands of time and reexperience it again when Rainbow isn't looking, she thought to herself. All I have to do is go inside the energy of the memory and then I'm there. The thought gave her an idea but before she had time to say it, Rainbow was talking.

"If you'd take the time to write your thesis from the thought/images in your mind, you might see that it's already in the process of writing itself," Rainbow said.

Lavender wondered why Rainbow thought that her thesis was in the process of writing itself. Didn't she know that if she saw that the words were already written, it would be completed? All she had to do was read her thought/images, not write them again. Maybe she's stuck somewhere in the present, she thought to herself, and she can't see how magical the words really are, and how they come to life when you read them and look between the lines. But she does seem to know more than I do—that's why she's my teacher—so maybe I should go along with her perceptions.

She took a deep breath, trying to work it up into a full-blown sneeze, but then realized that there weren't any more dusty words; they were all alive with energy. "I know I have to complete my thesis right now, and I really do want to get my master's degree and graduate my soul," she said, "but I'm still in the middle of the research paper on my past life in Egypt."

Following her feelings into that memory and losing track of

where she was, she went flying off on a tangent. "NOW I know who the shaman is!" she exclaimed. "He was in Africa before and I didn't recognize him then because I never saw him the first time. By the time he appeared, it was too late and I was unconscious."

"Then how do you know who he is now?" Rainbow asked.

"Because the future is reflecting the past," Lavender replied.

"Huh? Run that by me again, will you?"

"It's all happening now," Lavender explained. "But things have changed."

"Huh?" Rainbow repeated. "Then who is the shaman?" she asked. "I thought he was Adam."

"But that's the whole point, don't you see? He is Adam," Lavender said. "When Amanda turned off her inner knowing when she was a child, he seemed to disappear into the light of the universe. After his brief reappearance as a throat specialist, he went to Africa for the second time. With his present background as a shaman, he decided to return again to reexperience being a natural healer—to acquire even more knowledge through practical experience and to teach spiritual aspects of healing with universal light energies in a physical environment—and to renew his relationship with Amanda and share her destiny if she decides to pursue her spiritual purpose in this life.

"But Amanda couldn't see him way back when, because she'd gone somewhere else for awhile. I think she was out of her mind, even though she heard him talking to her, telling her about the magic inside her soul."

Lavender smiled to herself. "I knew who he was all the time. He wasn't Adam yet, because he was a shaman then." But he's a shaman now too, she thought, watching the images revolve in spiral circles, rippling through her thoughts, like sparkles of energy. The chalkboard in the Time and Space class appeared in her mind and she saw that the parallel lines she'd drawn were beginning to merge.

Lavender shimmered into the sunlight and smiled at Rainbow. "Are you who I think you are, or are you someone else?" she asked. Watching her thoughts superimpose themselves on the images of her pages, she saw that her manuscript, together with the book that Amanda was writing about her dreams, was rearranging itself again and knew that she was getting ahead of herself for the second time since yesterday. There's always tomorrow, she thought hopefully, simultaneously thinking that everything was all too much to handle today.

"Lavender, where are you now?" Rainbow asked. "You seem to be lost somewhere in the present."

"I know I'm repeating myself, but I also know that sooner or later I'll find myself again," Lavender replied. Picking up her pencil, she tried to erase half the past/present/future words on the piece of paper, but the eraser wasn't working. That wasn't surprising. The eraser hadn't worked for a long time, ever since she became aware that she was painting a picture of her soul with her pencil and writing the images of her spiritual knowledge with words.

"Lavender, are you painting parallel pictures as you write your words again?" Rainbow asked.

"Maybe that's what happens when you rewrite the beginning at the end, or when you write the end before you begin, or when you write the same thing twice, repeatedly, rephrasing the middle over and over again, or when you write three things all at once," Lavender answered, watching the words dance on the page as they formed magical images in her mind, simultaneously exploring a mystical path that the words created.

If all my experiences are timeless and I'm *now-here*, then I'm on a journey home—following my dream and watching the words lead me into a magical world somewhere inside my soul—going into the past, present, and future simultaneously, and seeing my energies synchronize themselves here, there, and everywhere at the same time, she thought to herself as she smiled at Rainbow. "See ya at the rainbow's end," she said.

Forty-Four

The Spiritual Side

One minute Lavender was writing her past-life research report; the next minute she was lost somewhere in a shadow in Egypt, searching for the missing pieces of her memories. She felt the wind echo through her soul as it began to revolve into a whirlwind of motion and matter, spinning into a powerful vortex of energy. Then she was falling, spiraling through a surrealistic time/space that seemed to be filled with fear and spiritual pain as her experiences in Egypt surrounded her. She struggled with the shadowy images, trying to speak, but there was no sound.

Knowing she was caught up in the middle of her past-life memory, frightened almost out of her mind and desperately looking for a way out of the soul trauma she'd chosen to reexperience to gain understanding and evolve her soul, Lavender centered her awareness into Rainbow's vibrations in the revolving spiral of energy that seemed to echo everywhere at once. It was silent and still in the center of the vortex and she felt as if she was suspended motionless somewhere between the past and the present, not sure of which direction to choose.

Lavender sensed Amanda shaking with fear. She seemed to be caught up in a powerful vortex that had spun her into a surrealistic time/space and she, too, was motionless, apparently lost, looking for a doorway.

"It took great courage to share your knowledge in Egypt," Rainbow whispered to Lavender. "Find that same courage again and overcome your fear, so Amanda can remember the knowledge that's locked inside your soul."

"Why does Amanda have to remember and reexperience the events in Egypt?" Lavender asked. "Can't she—I—we—" The energy was beginning to circle around her again and she felt overwhelmed by her fear. "Can't she change her mind?"

"Yes and no," Rainbow replied. "She's seen part of the memory and created the opportunity to open up and explore that particular experience—to change her past misunderstanding into present awareness and future enlightenment. But with her free will, she can choose to close the door into knowing and turn off the experience."

Just like I chose not to remember it when I lived in Africa before, Lavender thought silently to herself.

"If she decides not to experience the past now, it may become a future possibility instead of a probable reality in her present life. She can open up and explore the memory only when she's tuned into a particular vibration of spiritual energy. It may be an opportunity that comes only once in this lifetime, and she must have the courage to face it by opening up her awareness and expanding her vibrations to encompass the experience."

Clouds gathered, obscuring the light from the sun and shrouding Rainbow's words into nightmarish shapes and shadowy images. It looked as if a powerful storm was in the process of forming. Thunder rumbled through the clouds as lightning flashed across the universe, illuminating an insight in Lavender's soul.

As the energy reverberated into echoes, Lavender said, "I'm the one who has to reexperience the events in Egypt—to understand my feelings and balance those energies—because I chose to be Amanda in her—I mean my—present incarnation. I've been seeing her as my parallel self when she's really the physical energy expression of my soul. She's not separate from me; we're one and the same, aren't we?"

"Yes," Rainbow replied.

Lavender watched the clouds move across the universe and cover the earth. She heard the ripping sound of thunder; it sounded like the clouds were being torn apart. Then there was stillness, nothingness. Waiting for the cleansing rain to begin, she heard only silence; a cold, deadly silence that shadowed the darkness and echoed through her soul. She was more frightened than she'd ever been before.

"It's your fear showing itself to you," Rainbow said. "It appears to be menacing and overwhelming because you're feeding it your energy; you're giving it the power to exist. You've turned off the light of your awareness and now you're struggling with yourself to see through the shadows you've created that surround your soul.

"You've come full circle, Lavender, and experienced both sides of silence. It's time to step up your spiritual awareness into a vibration of evolvement and enlightenment. It's time to see what really happened in Egypt, and to understand why it happened. You need to heal your spiritual hurt and harmonize the energies of your soul. Then you'll be free to share your knowledge again," Rainbow said. "It's time for you to face your fear—to see through the shadows.

"Amanda's desire to remember her spiritual knowledge and to find the missing pieces of her soul have guided her into the shadows. You opened the vibrations in Africa before, wanting to reexperience the memory, but then you allowed your fear to overpower you and hold you back. You changed your mind and chose to carry your Egypt experiences into this lifetime. To evolve your soul, you *must* allow yourself to clearly see through the shadows into the complete awareness of those experiences because they have not yet been understood and healed."

Lavender looked at Rainbow with anguish and terror in her eyes, knowing that Amanda was exercising her spiritual birthright to know the truth about her experiences in Egypt **now**.

"She won't be able to see the truth about the philosopher unless you're able to see it too," Rainbow said.

Lavender shivered deep in her soul, trying to release her fear as she opened up her awareness and watched Amanda walk through the open door in her dream. A glowing light, like the flicker of a candle flame, began to illuminate the shadowy images of Egypt and Lavender saw the essence of her soul reflected in Amanda's eyes.

As Amanda crossed the threshold into the shadows, she seemed to take on the image of the philosopher. Lavender blinked her eyes rapidly; her vision was blurring through the tears in her eyes. Feeling a deep sense of sadness and despair, she knew she was feeling Amanda's emotions, yet she felt so peculiar, as if she was someone else and was experiencing her soul in another vibration of energy, in a parallel place and time. The philosopher was speaking to her, but she couldn't hear him above the echo of wind that blew through her soul.

Forty-Five

Duplicate Dimensions

Amanda and Judy wrapped themselves in blankets, listening to the heavy downpour of rain pummel the thatched roof and splash in the mud puddles outside. The wind seemed to echo everywhere at once. Flashes of lightning lit up the universe as the sound of thunder rolled in the clouds. The light from the oil lamp cast a warm glow through their bamboo house, creating a cozy atmosphere. It was a perfect night to share inner thoughts and reflections.

"Every once in awhile, I feel that I've somehow stepped back in time," Amanda said. "Sometimes I feel as if I'm living in a parallel place."

"Is it our surroundings and the way of life here?" Judy asked. "This village probably hasn't changed very much in the past few centuries."

"That might be what triggered my feelings to begin with because the environment is similar to the place that I feel I lived before, but it wasn't in this village."

"Reincarnation?" Judy asked.

"I'm beginning to believe that reincarnation may be a reality. The day we arrived, I had a strong feeling of déjà vu and lately my feelings of having been here before are becoming stronger. I keep seeing images of another place and time in Africa; I'm not sure where, though."

"Maybe you're experiencing déjà vu because we envisioned Africa so many times in our mind," Judy said.

"That's not it, exactly," Amanda replied. "I've had dreams about living in Africa before, but the images were fragmented and sketchy. I told you about one of my dreams when we first talked about coming to Africa, remember?"

Judy nodded.

"I had that dream again last night," Amanda said. "This time, most of the pieces came together and the images were clear. I dreamed that my father was an archeologist in Africa and I was in charge of the workers on his crew. He showed me a map to find a hidden treasure and said that our next dig site was near the Luxor Temple in Egypt. A short time after that, I became very sick. He was taking care of me, placing a cool cloth on my forehead and telling me to get better." She shivered, suddenly seeing a shadowy image loom in her mind.

"Even though it was only a dream, it seems curious that he'd mention a temple by name unless he was somehow connected with me in a past life in Egypt. What's interesting about this is that ever since I was a little girl, he's wanted to go to Egypt on an archeological expedition to look for hidden treasure. He almost quit his job one time to do that, but my mom talked him out of it." She smiled. "I remember it because I thought he was ready to be real."

She was quiet for a few minutes, looking through the dream images and memories in her mind. "I think I lived in Egypt before I lived in Africa, and my dream is showing me a path that leads from my past life in Africa into my past life in Egypt, except I didn't go to Egypt because I died." She shivered again.

"How did you die?" Judy asked.

"I'm not sure," Amanda replied. "That part of my dream wasn't clear, but it seemed more as if I changed my mind and decided to leave that life." She hugged her knees to her chest. "I feel I'm repeating something; it's as if time and space are flowing together, and I'm somehow transcending time and traveling through a duplicate dimension. I think I was innately guided to return to Africa so I could go to Egypt because I didn't go there before."

A sudden gust of wind blew the door open and Amanda felt an echo of fear blow through her soul. She got up and closed the door, making sure the latch was securely in place.

"That was spooky with the door opening like that," Judy said. "Maybe it's symbolic. Maybe a door just opened into your past life—into a duplicate dimension." She smiled at Amanda, noticing that she looked frightened. "So your past is the future that you're going to explore in your present, right?"

"Maybe time doesn't move in a straight line," Amanda said. "Maybe it moves in circles—returns to the same spaces." She pulled her blanket closer, trying to ward off the feeling of fear that began to surround her. "I'm searching for myself," she said, "so I can know more about who I am, and find out who I was before."

"Are you really going to Egypt, or are you going to travel there in your dreams?"

Amanda shrugged. "It seems to me that they're both the same." She took a deep breath, as if she was summoning all her courage. "I've had a few dreams about a philosopher who lived in Egypt. In one dream, he gave me a scroll of something he'd written." Tears filled her eyes as she remembered the emotions of sadness and despair she'd felt when she'd seen him. She began to cough, suddenly finding it difficult to speak. "I think I was that philosopher and that I misunderstood my experiences there. I got a feeling from him that there are some events I need to remember so I can change them somehow, but I don't know what they are."

Judy handed her a tissue and listened quietly, sensing that Amanda was beginning to open her memories and that she needed to bring her past-life feelings up to the surface so she could see inside her soul.

"Every time I see an image of Egypt, it's shrouded in a shadow and I can't see it clearly. I feel afraid, as if something terrible happened but I want to know what it is." She coughed again. "Whenever I become aware of an experience that's connected with the philosopher, my throat begins to hurt—just like now. Then it seems as if someone turns off the light and I can't see or remember anything else."

"I think you're getting close to seeing what you experienced there," Judy said softly. "I think I was there too; I have a feeling that I knew you when you were that philosopher."

Amanda looked into Judy's eyes, seeing a far-away image mirrored in her own mind. "I remember you," she said slowly. "We spent a lot of time together, talking about and exploring the power of spiritual knowledge, and then you were—they—" Her eyes grew large, filled with the horror of what she was seeing in her mind. She drew in a ragged breath. "Oh Judy, I'm so very, very sorry," she said, sobbing. "They tortured you and then they stabbed you, over and over again. There was blood everywhere. I saw them kill you and I couldn't stop them."

The wind blew the door open again and Amanda felt as if she was falling into shadowy spaces and dark dimensions that seemed to hold only spiritual pain as the past-life experience opened up into her awareness. An unearthly terror wrapped itself around her.

Judy saw the terror in Amanda's eyes and tried to move toward her, but an invisible force held her back. It seemed that Amanda was in the center of a swirling vortex of wind that spun around her while it also held her suspended motionless. It was as if an energy vibration of time was occurring simultaneously in the past and the present, and the past was somehow interacting with the present. A pinpoint of light began to flicker and emanate from Amanda's eyes and Judy sensed that she was somewhere deep inside her soul.

Amanda's voice was an anguished whisper. "They killed you

because I shared my knowledge with you," she said. Her body began to shake; it seemed that the swirling vibration of energy was flowing through her as she saw and felt her experiences. "They killed all my friends and my followers—they forced me to watch—told me it was ..." she was shaking violently now, "... all my fault."

Amanda's words and emotions opened up Judy's full memory of the event that Amanda was reexperiencing. She felt calm and detached as she watched herself die, seeing her spiritual essence rise above her body. It was like watching a movie replaying scenes in her mind, except she was completely aware of everything that was occurring and knew what everyone in the picture was thinking and feeling.

"Amanda, it wasn't your fault," she said soothingly. "I remember it now. The courtyard. The priests. They wanted to keep the knowledge secret, to enslave people to their will by taking their power away. You shared the knowledge, wanting everyone to have the right to search for their inner truth and to find their own spiritual power. They killed me; not because of you, but because of me. I refused to be silent about the knowledge I'd learned.

"You were a high priest in the Temple of Ra. You broke your vow of secrecy and left the temple because you believed that knowledge must be shared. The priests tormented you with the murders to keep you silent—to keep you from teaching the secrets of knowledge that would set people free to find the truth within themselves. They told the crowds that only priests were allowed to use the knowledge and that if anyone else dared try, it would mean certain death."

Judy sensed that Amanda was going deeper into the memory and tried to focus her attention into the present. "Look at me, Amanda, and listen to what I'm saying," she said. Amanda's eyes were like dark, liquid pools of fear and pain, reflecting the anguish and horror she was experiencing. "You're here now. I'm here too. We're friends again, learning together and finding spiritual knowledge. You're remembering a past-life experience."

As Judy watched helplessly, Amanda struggled against an invisible bond that held her prisoner in her memory—struggling to free herself from the mental anguish and spiritual pain that held her soul locked in the throes of fear. She placed her hands across her mouth in a protective gesture, then suddenly she screamed; it was a scream of agony that reverberated through the village and ripped through her soul. She began to gag, coughing up blood as she fell limply to the floor.

Philip and Sara came running into their house through the open door, looking startled and disheveled, abruptly awakened from sleep by Amanda's scream. "What's wrong?" they both asked at once.

The fear and horror Judy had seen in Amanda's eyes terrified her more than anything else. "We have to help her," she cried hysterically, afraid that Amanda was dead.

Sara was already kneeling by Amanda, gently turning her head to the side and wiping the blood from her mouth. Philip put his hands on Judy's shoulders, trying to calm her. "Judy, tell me what happened," he said quietly.

"I don't know what happened," Judy said, crying. "We were talking about something horrible she remembered from a long time ago and I think she somehow went inside the memory, went completely into the past and reexperienced it." Her voice was shaking. "Is she all right?"

"She appears to be in shock, but I'm sure she'll be all right. She probably hurt her throat or bit her tongue when she screamed; that's why she's bleeding," Sara said, covering Amanda with the blanket to keep her warm. "If she doesn't regain consciousness in a few minutes, we'll take her to the hospital in town."

Judy sat down next to Amanda on the ground and reached for her hands, holding them gently in hers. She immediately felt a vibration of energy flow between them and sensed that she was connected with Amanda on a spiritual level, though she could no longer see into the memory and didn't know what was occurring with her.

Sara put her arm around Judy to comfort her. "I studied psychology in college and from what you've said, it sounds as though Amanda became traumatized by the events in the memory and lost consciousness due to her fear. Your subconscious mind has a built-in safety valve that protects you from reexperiencing any extreme physical, mental, or emotional pain of a memory. Her mind probably turned off the memory and closed down her awareness of it as a protective measure," she explained. Judy didn't seem convinced.

"Amanda will be just fine," she said reassuringly. "It's almost impossible to supersede that filtering mechanism. Memories can seem very real, especially when you become emotionally involved with them, and they can sometimes cause temporary physical responses. But it's only a memory."

It's much more than a memory, Judy thought to herself, knowing that Amanda's soul had somehow traveled through time and space, and entered a duplicate dimension where her past-life experience was happening all over again in the present.

Adam appeared in the doorway, then went over and sat by Judy. "Amanda chose to reexperience this," he said quietly, "so she could see through her experiences in Egypt and remember the truth about her soul." He smiled at Judy, then looked at Sara. "She'll come around by herself. Her voice was hurt, but will heal itself naturally. Just let her be," he said, standing up and leaving as suddenly as he had appeared.

Sara smiled. "He has the most amazing habit of just appearing out of nowhere. The villagers say he was a shaman a hundred years ago and that he returned in a new form, but he's really the same one as before."

"It's probably true," Philip said, fingering the latch on the door. "Judy, did you open the door after Amanda screamed?"

Judy shook her head no. "The wind blew it open twice. The first time Amanda closed it and the second time, it stayed open."

"That's odd," Philip said, trying to move the spring lever. "The latch is stuck in the closed position and the door should have been jammed shut." He went outside to check the handle on the door. Stepping back in, he said, "It stopped raining and the sun is coming up. You girls must have been talking all night."

Judy wondered what happened with time and where it had gone. It was early evening when she and Amanda had started talking about déjà vu and dreams, and it seemed that only a few minutes could have passed, yet more than nine hours were missing.

"I really love sunrises," he said. "When I was little, I'd get up early every morning just so I could watch the sun come up over the horizon. It looked like a regal god with mystical powers that spreads universal light all over the earth." He smiled. "It seemed to me that the first rays of light were like little sun spirits that danced at dawn, welcoming in the new day. I even thought that there was a magical place inside the center of the sun and if you could travel a sun ray to get there, you'd find something wonderful," he said. "It's funny, the things you believe when you're a kid."

Judy smiled at him, surprised that he felt the same way she did about sunrises.

He went outside again and looked up at the sky. "Oh, wow! This is incredibly beautiful. Come and look at this," he said, holding out his hand. "This has to be the most unusual rainbow I've ever seen. It's *shimmering* through the mist in the sky and radiating sparkles of light everywhere. It looks like the sun is raining a rainbow; that's the only way I can describe it."

Sara got up and walked outside with him. Judy stayed next to Amanda, afraid that if she let go of her hands, she'd lose the energy connection with her. Knowing how special rainbows were to her, she said softly, "Amanda, I wish you could see the rainbow."

Amanda's eyes began to move rapidly behind closed lids and Judy wondered if she was really looking at the rainbow, somewhere inside herself. A few minutes later, her eyelids began to flutter and when she opened them, Judy could still see the pain and fear in her eyes. Amanda squeezed her hands tightly. She tried to talk, but there was no sound. She took several deep, shuddering breaths, trying to release the anguish that surrounded her soul.

"After they tortured and killed my friends and followers, they cut out my tongue and banished me, saying my punishment was to live in silence with the blood of my followers on my hands," she said in a whisper. "But that didn't stop me from communicating. I wrote all my knowledge in a scroll, but then they discovered it and killed me. And then they must have destroyed the scroll." She sighed with absolute despair. "They took away my friends and my writings—everything I'd treasured—and I promised myself I'd never share my knowledge again."

Her eyes filled with tears of sadness, but there was a recognition in them. "Because of those experiences, and because of that promise, I turned off my spiritual knowledge and left part of my soul there. That's what the philosopher wanted me to know." She smiled through her tears. "That's why I'm here now—to remember my knowledge and find my soul—so I can share my knowledge again." Suddenly anger and helplessness flashed in her eyes. "I hate those priests," she said vehemently. "I hate them for what they did."

"Amanda, don't let it hurt you any more," Judy said softly. "You've traveled through some very painful past-life experiences, but now you're ready to understand the philosopher you were." She smiled. "He can help you remember your knowledge and find your soul in your rainbow dreams."

Forty-Six

Past-Life Pages

Lavender looked at Rainbow in horror. "They killed so many people, then they cut out my tongue and exiled me," she whispered.

Rainbow nodded. "Then you wrote the *Scroll of Knowledge*."

"But they destroyed it. My words were lost," Lavender sobbed in despair. "Writing the scroll was the only solace I had because I felt the knowledge would be preserved for other seekers of truth. But when they killed me, all my knowledge was lost—gone into nothingness, like dust." She shuddered and closed her eyes, as if the picture in her mind hurt too much for her to look at.

"The spiritual pain you're feeling, both then and now, is one of the reasons it's been so difficult for you to read your past-life pages and to open the images of Egypt, but you know inside your soul how valuable the knowledge is and you care deeply about sharing it. That's why you wrote the scroll, and why you're writing your book, so you can remember your words." Rainbow smiled at her through the tears in her eyes.

"Your words didn't vanish into dust; they're inside your soul. Look within yourself; you'll see that you're already rewriting the scroll in a new form. You're sharing the knowledge with Amanda, so that she, in turn, can apply it in her life and share it with others. As she lives the knowledge in all her thoughts, feelings, and experiences, she'll be able to clearly see her soul and to understand her true spiritual nature. She'll be free to open up and pursue the path that will lead her into her destiny—to speak and share the secrets of knowledge. She wants to be a teacher of truth, just like the philosopher."

Forty-Seven

Journey Into Awareness

Amanda saw a butterfly caught in a swirling vortex of wind. She ran toward it to free it but the butterfly disappeared, shimmering into sparkles of light before it vanished and she wasn't sure if she'd seen it at all. Lately she'd been seeing things that weren't really there, and it seemed that someone else's nightmares were merging into her dreams.

Ever since she'd entered that shadowy space—that strange dimension of time that reverberated with echoes of energy—where she'd seen and felt her experiences as a philosopher, she felt out of sync with herself and now she couldn't seem to differentiate between illusion and reality, or between the past and the present. All her experiences and memories seemed to blend together into the misty images of her dreams, and she felt as if part of her awareness was stuck somewhere between her dream images and her everyday experiences. They both appeared to be the same and she began to think that she was living in two separate worlds simultaneously.

Whenever she spoke, it was in soft whispers. She seemed afraid to talk, as if she'd reveal secrets that were better left unsaid. She spent most of her spare time alone, seeking solitude to explore her thoughts and feelings, and to write her experiences in her book. She noticed something unusual about her pencil. It never needed sharpening; the point never wore down the way a real pencil would and the eraser didn't work, even though it was new.

Every morning when she woke up, she found words interspersed with symbols that looked like hieroglyphics in her dream journal—words and symbols that she didn't remember writing. When she looked at the symbols and read the words, they drew pictures in her mind, leading her into a world of images that wove threads of mystical experiences through her thoughts.

Sometimes she felt as if she was traveling through the universe, knowing everything there was to know and yet she felt she knew nothing when she returned because she couldn't describe her feelings or translate her experiences into words that accurately reflected what she'd discovered. When she tried to put her experiences into words, the images became misty pictures that either completely dissipated or formed a mosaic maze of scattered pieces in her mind.

She told Adam what she'd been experiencing, hoping he'd be able to help her understand it, but he only seemed to make matters worse. "Your misty images and nightmares shadow the truth you're afraid to see, and your laryngitis hides the knowledge you're afraid to speak. You're playing a game with illusion, Amanda. You're really going deeply within yourself and metamorphosing your awareness; you're becoming real and being true to your nature. You used to play with illusion when you were a little girl," he said, smiling. "Do you remember how the game goes?"

Amanda nodded. "It's a very intricate and interwoven game of energy that patterns and weaves the tapestry of your thoughts and feelings into the expressions of all your experiences." There was more to it than that, though. There was a parallel part that she hadn't completely understood because she thought it was a dream. It hadn't seemed real at the time, but it appeared that you could see a mirror reflection of yourself by looking into the images of your soul in vibrations of universal light. An image of a butterfly fluttered into her thoughts.

"It's like being a butterfly and setting your spirit free." She sighed, remembering when she'd tried to transform herself into a butterfly so she'd be free to express her true spiritual nature. It hadn't worked. Half-formed images and nearly-remembered mystical knowledge of the sun god, Ra, flashed through her mind.

"It's a silly, pretend game about the appearances of reality and I don't want to play. I just can't believe I'm a butterfly in real life," she said, turning off her past-life experiences and inner knowing. The images of the philosopher became a dark blur in her mind, along with the surrealistic time/space that was filled with shadows and haunting memories.

* * * *

Lavender seemed to return from her travels in Egypt, but Rainbow could see that part of her was still missing, drifting through the misty images and shadowy shapes in Amanda's mind.

"Why is Amanda having nightmares about her experiences in Egypt?" Lavender asked. "I keep trying to show her secret symbols of knowledge in her dreams, but she's not sure if they're real or if they're figments of her imagination and fragments of thoughts and feelings from all the memories floating through her mind."

"Amanda isn't accepting her experiences in Egypt on a spiritual level of awareness. She's reliving the events in nightmare form to help her overcome her fear. She wants to see the whole picture, but changes her mind every time the memory gets real," Rainbow said, smiling at Lavender's attempts to be helpful. "She's not ready to empower herself with her full spiritual knowledge or to recognize all the energies of her soul."

"I think she's suffering the after-effects of the shock of seeing the memory, but she feels reluctant to talk about her past-life experiences," Lavender replied, not realizing that she still felt reluctant to voice her fear or to clearly see through the shadows she'd surrounded her soul with. "Intellectually, she accepts the experiences but she needs to integrate her acceptance on all levels of her awareness and transform her spiritual pain into understanding, so she can change the energy vibrations of the events. When she does that, they'll turn around into a beautiful healing experience that will allow her to clearly see into her soul and open up her spiritual knowledge. Then she'll be able to see her true nature and find out who she really is—I mean who I really am."

* * * *

It was the same nightmare, happening all over again. Shadows were reaching for her, looming out of the darkness, begging for light. Amanda woke up screaming in silence; there was no sound. She got up and looked through the window. A full moon lit the sky and a mist was moving slowly through the pre-dawn hours, gently enshrouding the earth. Shivering, she dressed in blue jeans and an oversized sweatshirt, then opened the door to go for a walk through the mist.

Just before dawn, Philip saw her sitting beneath a tree. He'd been getting up early every morning to watch the sunrise. Walking over to her, he said, "It sure is foggy this morning; it makes everything seem unreal. When I first saw you out here, I thought you were a ghost." He smiled.

"Sometimes I really feel that way—as if I'm a ghost walking through a foggy mist in a dream," Amanda whispered.

"How's your laryngitis today?" he asked. "Any better?"

She shook her head no. "I guess I don't have much to say lately."

"Sara and I are becoming quite concerned about this," he said. "It's persisted for several weeks. We'd like to take you to the hospital and have the doctor look at your throat. Maybe you hurt your vocal chords when you screamed that night."

Amanda put her hands protectively over her mouth. "I know you want to help me, but I won't allow anyone to put anything in my mouth to look at my throat," she said in a raspy voice. Dropping her hands into her lap, she smiled at Philip, feeling silly for acting like a little girl and covering her mouth. "I had laryngitis when I was younger and it somehow got better all by itself, and I know it will now."

An image of a beautiful garden, encircled with a rainbow appeared in her mind and she felt as if she was flowing through the energy vibrations of the rainbow. Sunlight shimmered brilliantly through the colors and she felt a special magic and harmony flow through her soul. "I'll find my voice somewhere inside a rainbow," she said to Philip.

He looked at her, thinking that her answer was strange, then smiled. "Whatever you think is best," he said. "Sara and I would like to help in any way we can, though."

Judy walked over to them, stretching her arms toward the sun and looking upward into the sky.

Just then the sun began to come over the horizon, splashing rays of light everywhere, radiating vibrant hues of gold and orange into the universe and reflecting pearl-like tones of peach and mauve on the bottom of the clouds. They were quiet for a few moments, enjoying the sunrise.

Judy smiled, breathing in the light from the sun. As she lowered her arms in a circular motion, an aura of light seemed to vibrate around her. "Have you found your way into the center of the sunrise yet?" she asked Philip.

"No," he answered, "but someday I really will learn how to travel a sun ray to get there."

"Just breathe in the energy of the sun and *be* the light," Judy said. "Then you'll see that the center of the sunrise is within the center of yourself."

Amanda smiled at both of them, remembering a pre-birth promise she'd made to herself. From a foggy, misty, almost-forgotten memory, Rainbow's words whispered in her mind. "Follow your dream," she said.

Forty-Eight

Parallel Places

Walking barefoot through the rain, Amanda heard the words and the melody of her favorite song weave softly through her thoughts.

Somewhere, over the rainbow, clouds are clear.
There's a place that I dreamed of, once in a time now here.

Someday I'll wish upon my star and
wake up with a rainbow all around me.

Where light is bright and truth is clear,
that's where I'll find me.

Fragments of images fluttered through her mind as the rain turned to mist. Wanting to see the truth about her soul, she tried to put all the pieces of her experiences and feelings and thoughts and dreams and memories into their proper places, hoping to achieve a clear, complete picture.

Images of a dream flowed into her mind. She was walking through the rain, traveling inside the colors of a rainbow, searching to find herself, to know who she is and what life is really all about. Inside the color lavender, she saw a mirror image of herself reflected in a sphere of light and remembered when the color had taken her on a tour of the universe.

"Hi, Lavender," she said. The sphere shimmered, radiating sparkles of light that gently vibrated through her soul.

Amanda thought she heard someone calling her, but the voice was an echo calling to Lavender, whispering through the winds of time as she listened to the sound of raindrops tapping softly on a window. *This dream is real,* she thought to herself. Suddenly the dream burst into rays of light, like a magical sunrise in her mind.

An image of Lavender taking her to see a sunrise came clearly into focus and Amanda saw that there was more to that dream than she'd seen before. Lavender had gone into the center of the sunrise and returned with a golden key. She gave her the key, saying, "This is your key to spiritual knowledge that you placed inside a rainbow right after you were born."

Amanda felt the warmth of the key in her hand and knew that the key opened a mystical door somewhere inside her soul that unlocked her inner knowing and showed her the way into her true spiritual nature. Watching the sunshine sparkle through the early-morning misty clouds, reflecting a rainbow, a magical insight began to dawn within her. She began to see the light within herself and at the same time, began to see Lavender in the same light. *Now I know who I really am. I'm Lavender.*

She felt as if she'd just awakened from a long sleep, but knew she was waking up to her spiritual self and that she'd found a magical piece of the picture—a piece that fit perfectly into a masterpiece. She smiled, watching memories and dream images of Lavender float into her mind. It was like reading an open book that showed a picture of her soul, painted and penciled with words that were woven into and through the tapestry of her life, with threads of energy connecting all her thoughts, feelings, and experiences together.

Lavender shows me my spiritual side in my feelings, and I see all her experiences in my thoughts and dreams, Amanda realized, recognizing how often her dreams had paralleled her thoughts and experiences in one form or another. She's been writing the words and symbols in my dream journal; she's been showing me the secrets of my soul. It's her shadowy images of Egypt that I see and feel in my nightmares.

Just then a cloud covered the sun and obscured the light. A shadowy image of the philosopher slowly began to shape itself and walk through the mist. Amanda knew she was looking through Lavender's eyes and seeing her images, but wasn't sure if she was dreaming or if she was awake.

Lavender appeared to be lost, searching for herself in a world that seemed to be unreal. The shadow followed her wherever she went, haunting her awareness.

"The truth is hidden in the shadows," Amanda said, but her voice was silent.

Lavender was running from the shadowy shape, trying to find a place to hide, but there was nowhere to go. Fear loomed through her thoughts as she turned to face the shadow. As the shadow began to encircle her, she took a U-turn outside of herself and ran into a door, but it was locked.

"I want to know what's real; I want to understand my true spiritual nature." Lavender's words echoed in Amanda's mind. She offered Lavender her key and watched her open the door. Just inside was the philosopher, standing in a shadow. He began talking to her, explaining why the experiences in Egypt had happened, but Lavender wasn't listening. Amanda heard him clearly, though.

"In a lifetime prior to Egypt, you refused to share spiritual knowledge and used the power only for yourself," he said. "Then, when you were me, you openly shared your spiritual knowledge by showing people how to find their own power—to see and know the truth within themselves—and you balanced that karma. You've paid the price for silence with silence. You didn't see this before because you didn't want to see the hurt you mistakenly thought you caused others, and you haven't allowed your feelings to speak—to say what hurts you in both those lifetimes. You've learned your lesson and now you're suffering needlessly because of your fear."

There were tears in his eyes as he continued to speak. "You turned off the light of your spiritual awareness when you chose never to share your knowledge again because of your experiences in Egypt. See through the shadows into the light, Lavender. Face your fear and the spiritual pain that you've kept locked up inside you. Accept your feelings and understand them. Forgive the hate you feel toward those who helped you learn the lesson you chose to learn, and heal your feelings that caused you to fear sharing your knowledge again. Change that choice you made."

He smiled sadly at Lavender, knowing that she wasn't listening and that his words were apparently lost. An image of a butterfly caught in a swirling vortex of wind flashed into Amanda's mind. "Set yourself free and evolve into enlightenment." He reached toward Lavender, offering her the scroll. She refused it and the philosopher turned to her. It seemed that he could no longer speak.

Amanda had seen this image before, but hadn't been aware of all the pieces in the picture. He offered her the scroll and she watched herself walk through the open doorway in Lavender's dream and accept it.

As she crossed the threshold and walked through the shadows, she entered a world filled with knowledge and light. Holding the scroll close to her heart, she knew she'd seen the truth about her soul and found her spiritual knowledge. Knowing that she held a wonderful treasure in her hands, she opened the scroll to see what it said, but couldn't decipher the words. She knew she had to find a way into and through Lavender's fear.

"I'm going to help Lavender face her fear," Amanda said to the philosopher she once was. Her voice was almost clear—only a trace of the laryngitis remained—and her throat didn't hurt anymore. It must be the magic somewhere inside the rainbow, she thought. But she knew that her voice wasn't really all better yet; the harmony of the melody was missing and the vibrations were out of tune.

She turned to Lavender and took her hand, trying to guide her through the shadows into the light, saying, "I want to read the scroll and remember our spiritual knowledge. I'm going to help you accept your—I mean my—our experiences in Egypt. Your fear is holding you prisoner in your memory. It's time to heal what hurts. It's time to wake up and set your spirit free."

Lavender looked at her with fear in her eyes.

"Lavender, what are you so afraid of?" Amanda asked gently. "Tell me what hurts so I can help you heal it."

Lavender shook her head no, covering her mouth with her hands.

"You have to let go of the pain inside your past-life experiences and face your fear," Amanda said. "You're getting hung up on misunderstanding your memory. If you're going to act childish about this, then I'll just have to take matters into my own hands."

An ethereal mist slowly began to circle around Lavender. She looked like the foggy ghost in her own dream. Amanda shivered deep inside her soul. The wind echoed everywhere at once, sending sparkles of lavender light shimmering in the misty air and spinning through her. She felt dizzy and disoriented.

"A mosquito bit me," she said, slapping her right arm. She looked at the bump forming on her arm and gasped. Her skin was the color of dark copper. She looked around her. She was in a jungle, helping to excavate an ancient ruin.

"Many mosquitoes here," the worker next to her said in a foreign language that she understood.

* * * *

It appears that she's changed her mind about seeing through the shadows and remembering her knowledge, Rainbow thought silently to herself. "Lavender, follow your dream," she said softly as she curled up into a sphere of light. The words echoed in Amanda's soul, whispering through the winds of time.

* * * *

Amanda woke up in a cold sweat. She couldn't clearly remember her dream, but an image of a mosquito kept buzzing around in her mind. Suddenly she saw the philosopher, shrouded in a shadow and felt a fear deep within her. She shivered, knowing she had to go to Egypt.

Judy sat up, not knowing what had awakened her. Rain was tapping on the window leaves of the bamboo house. She looked over at Amanda; she was curled up, hugging her knees to her chest.

Lighting the oil lamp, Judy said softly, "Tell me about your dream."

"I had a nightmare again." Amanda shivered. "A mosquito bit me and then my rainbow disappeared into a lavender sphere of light," she said. She felt an echo of fear go through her and had an uncanny feeling that a ghost had just walked through her soul. A flicker of light began to emanate from her eyes as she looked at Judy. "I want to find my rainbow," she said.

"After the sun comes up today, I'll take you to the garden in the rain forest," Judy said. "You'll find your rainbow there." She sensed that there was something different about Amanda and looked at her closely. It seemed as if she was looking through someone else's eyes—not hers. "Are you cold?" she asked. "You keep shivering."

"I feel icky," Amanda replied. "I've only been sick once in my life. I had a cold when I was a little girl, but this time I feel much worse. My head is hot and I'm dizzy. Judy, I'm really scared; I don't know what's happening to me and I don't feel like myself anymore."

Forty-Nine

Misty Memories

From half a world away, in the middle of the night, in the middle of a dream, Jim reached for the phone. "Mr. Millenum, your daughter has malaria. She was admitted to the hospital an hour ago," a doctor's voice said. "It appears to be serious. She has a high fever and is drifting in and out of consciousness."

"I'll be on the next plane," Jim said, seeing an image of himself placing a cool cloth on Amanda's forehead.

"Who was on the phone?" Beth asked, pulling the blanket over her head when Jim turned on the light.

"Amanda is very sick and I'm going to Africa," he said, slowly hanging up the phone. "She has malaria."

Beth sat up so fast that she nearly fell out of bed. "I'm coming with you," she said, starting to cry.

Jim put his arms around her. "Beth, honey, I know you want to, but you can't," he said gently. "You don't have a passport and you haven't had the required shots. I have. The business trip I took to Brazil last month," he reminded her. "Will you call the airline for me while I pack?"

A few minutes later, Gary knocked on their bedroom door. "I heard the phone ring. What's wrong with Amanda?" he asked.

"Come in, Gary. She has malaria, and your father is going to Africa," Beth answered in a trembling voice.

"She'll be all right," Gary said to both of them. "I just feel it. She never did like mosquitoes. I'm surprised she let one bite her."

"When the phone rang, I was dreaming that Amanda was someone else and that she had malaria," Jim said. "It seems so strange." Somehow I knew, he thought to himself, wondering how.

"There's a plane leaving in two hours," Beth said. "Can you be ready by then?"

Jim nodded. "I'm ready now," he replied. I just hope I'm not too late this time, he thought to himself. Please, Amanda, don't die, he prayed silently, hoping somehow that she could hear him.

"Wake up, sir. We're about to land."

Jim opened his eyes and looked at the flight attendant, feeling disoriented, not knowing where he was for a moment. Then he remembered. "I must have been dreaming," he said, still half-asleep.

"You were mumbling about excavating some ancient ruins in Africa, then you started talking about sphinxes and secret hiding places in Egypt. Are you an archeologist?" she asked.

"No," he answered. "I'm a lawyer, but I was dreaming that I was an archeologist, looking for a long-lost treasure." An image of showing Amanda a map to a temple flashed through his mind.

She smiled. "Please raise your seat to the upright position and fasten your seat belt."

He wondered how Amanda was doing. During a stopover in Paris to change planes, he'd called Beth and her condition was the same. He'd been in the air for the last nine hours and had no idea how she was now. I'll find out soon enough, he thought. Trying to put the worry out of his mind, he thought about his dream and the images he'd seen in his dream the night before.

Then he remembered the dreams he'd had when Amanda was a child. It seemed that the dreams were connected, but his memories of them were fragmented and misty. Somehow he'd known her when he was the archeologist he'd just dreamed about being.

There was something else about the dreams—something about Egypt and a bloody knife. He remembered when Amanda had a cold that developed into laryngitis and a throat infection. The doctor had talked about a possible tonsillectomy. She'd been so frightened, refusing to open her mouth so he could examine her throat, whispering through clenched teeth that all her friends would be dead and she wouldn't be able to talk anymore.

Suddenly he saw Amanda's face superimposed on the face of an old, bearded man who was talking about spiritual knowledge and power. And then ... he couldn't remember any more. There was just the image of a bloody knife and a terrible feeling inside him, as if he'd seen something horrible.

The dreams hadn't made sense then, but now they were beginning to show a picture of a past life together. I must be out of my mind with worry, he thought, shaking his head. Now I'm starting to imagine that Amanda and I lived before in Africa and Egypt. The thought returned him to the dream he'd had last night.

He looked out the window at the misty clouds, absorbed in his thoughts. What if reincarnation really happens, he wondered. Then my dreams and feelings would make sense. And if souls did return to earth to finish something they'd begun earlier or to correct something they'd left hanging in the balance, as the theory went, then maybe that's why Amanda came to Africa—to explore something she'd left unfinished—and why I've wanted to go on an archeological expedition to Egypt ever since she was a little girl. But how do all the pieces fit together, and how do I fit into the picture now? Before he could come up with any answers, the plane had landed.

"Mr. Millenum, I'm Adam Deva, a friend of Amanda's," Adam said, extending his hand. "She's in a coma now and the doctor isn't giving a prognosis, except to wait and see. They've done everything they can; now it's up to her. She has a strong will though, and I believe she'll be just fine. I'll take you to see her right away."

"Thank you," Jim said, shaking his hand, wondering how Adam had picked him out in the crowd of passengers, and how he'd known that he'd be on this plane. He must have talked to Beth, he thought to himself.

Walking through the airport terminal, he felt as if he was inside a dream and that the dream was happening again but this time it was different; some of the images were changed. He looked at Adam. "Have I met you somewhere before?" he asked. "You look familiar."

Adam smiled. "I was a throat specialist for a short time about twenty years ago before I left the States and came to Africa."

Jim nodded. Amanda's sore throat. The coincidence was uncanny. "That's probably where I met you. Small world, isn't it? Strange that you were there then, and you're here now. Are you with the Peace Corps?"

"No," Adam replied. "I came to Africa so I could lead a more natural way of life."

Taking a closer look at Adam, Jim said, "I don't want to offend you, but you look as though you just graduated from college. Life in Africa must agree with you."

"It does. And no offense taken. A lot of people have told me that I don't look like who I appear to be."

"I can't shake the feeling that I've seen you somewhere else too." He smiled at the image that appeared in his mind. "I know this sounds crazy, but I had a dream that Amanda and I lived in Africa before in a past life, and that she had malaria. I took her to a shaman, hoping for a magical cure. You remind me of that shaman."

"I'm a shaman now," Adam said. "And you remind me of an archeologist I knew a long time ago."

Jim was astonished but kept his composure, trying to sort through his thoughts and feelings. What Adam had said was a confirmation of his dream. Maybe it's more than a dream, he thought to himself.

"The jeep is parked right over there," Adam said, pointing across the street. "We can put your suitcase in the back. It's only a twenty-minute drive to the hospital from here."

An undercurrent of dread swept through Jim. "Adam, could these dreams and past-life memories be real? Could the experiences have really happened? It seems so incredible to me."

"If you'll keep an open mind and be willing to explore your feelings about your dreams and memories, you can find out for yourself," Adam said. "Let your thoughts be free from any preconceived beliefs for awhile and see what you come up with."

"Considering everything I've become aware of in the last two days," Jim said, "I think I'm open to anything that could provide some clues or answers to the jumble of thoughts running through my mind. I don't know much about reincarnation or how it works, but I've read about past-life ties and karmic connections. Amanda collected a lot of books on the subject before she left for Africa and I read a few of them. I've felt a special bond with her ever since she was born, but I never considered the possibility that we could have had a past life together until now."

"Why don't you start with your dreams about living in Africa before," Adam suggested. "What do you remember?"

Gathering the information from his dreams, he said, "You tried to help Amanda—she was a man; the foreman of my crew—become well by telling her about the magic within herself. Something about her natural ability to heal her body, mind, and spirit. But she died. Do you know why?"

"It's my feeling that her soul was too sick to care. The malaria, both then and now, covers her fear of remembering and completely accepting all of her experiences in Egypt. True healing comes from within, on a spiritual level, healing the cause for a real cure. Because her spirit was so disheartened about what happened, she couldn't face and overcome her fear then, so she chose to leave that life."

How does he know about Egypt? Jim wondered. I haven't mentioned that part of my dream to him. Maybe Amanda said something, he thought to himself. If she remembers the same things I remember, there must be more to the dreams, and to the events that are happening now, than just a very strange series of coincidences.

"It isn't really the malaria that was and is making her sick. It's her fear of seeing those experiences within herself and speaking her true feelings—saying what hurts, voicing her fear and pain. Being in a coma, she can go deeply within her soul to become completely aware of her experiences and her reaction to them, and to decide what she's going to do about them now. She's repeating her earlier experience in Africa to try to accomplish what she wasn't able to do before because of her fear."

"So fear is the real cause of Amanda's malaria?" Jim asked.

"Fear is a powerful emotion, but it can be used as a catalyst for change. When people don't face their fear directly, they create illusions to indirectly experience and express their fear," Adam replied. "Amanda is looking through lifetimes of illusion to see what she's truly afraid of. Only by accepting her fear and understanding it, and changing the way it manifests, can she become completely well."

Jim was quiet for a few minutes, mulling over what Adam had said. "Then the malaria provides a way for her to see inside her soul this time, but last time it was a way out. So she reincarnated and returned to Africa to face her fear of what happened to her in Egypt?"

"Based on everything she's told me, it seems to be one of the reasons," Adam replied. "Why do you think you were with her in Africa before and why do you feel you're connected again in this life?"

"I'm not sure what my part in this is, except it's somehow tied up in what happened to her in Egypt. When Amanda was a little girl, I think she remembered some of her experiences there. She was trying to face her fear, even then. And I had a feeling that I had to help her in some way." A sense of despair came over him. "I don't know what happened to her there, but I have this terrible feeling inside me," he said.

"Try to go inside that feeling," Adam said. "It will help you open up your memories. The events you saw and experienced will come back to you and you'll know how to help her. Listen to what your feelings tell you; let them form into pictures in your mind."

A look of horror crossed Jim's face. "They cut out her tongue." That's why I kept seeing the image of a bloody knife, and why I was so upset about her possible tonsillectomy, he thought to himself. "I was there in Egypt. I saw it happen," he said, becoming very agitated.

"What else do you remember?"

"Sphinxes. Secret hiding places," he said, watching images appear in his mind. "The map I showed Amanda in Africa; I knew where we could find a treasure. I drew that map from a memory of when I was an architect in Egypt." He took a deep breath. "I had dreams about digging for hidden treasure in Egypt when Amanda was younger," he said. "I thought the dreams were inspired by something I'd seen on TV, and that my desire to go to Egypt was due to a sense of adventure because I was fed up with my job."

Jim was quiet, looking into his thoughts. "I'm beginning to understand the dreams and my feelings. It's all coming back to me," he said. "She was a high priest, but called herself a philosopher. She spoke of truth and light, saying that knowledge was the way to freedom, that knowledge lights the way on your path—on your journey home to your true spiritual nature. She said you could know the truth within yourself and find your own way; you could empower yourself with your own remembered knowledge. She encouraged people to look for the truth within themselves, to see the real meaning of their life inside their thoughts and experiences.

"But the knowledge she shared was secret and the priests wanted to keep her silent. They ..." He covered his eyes with his hands, as if he was trying to blot out what he was seeing. Slowly, he continued. "They killed everyone who refused to renounce what they'd learned. I watched them do it. I escaped death because I denied what I knew inside me to be true.

"She tried to explain why she'd broken her vow of secrecy, why she'd shared the knowledge. The priests refused to listen and said her punishment was to live silently in exile with the blood of her followers on her hands, that it was her fault they were dead. That's when they cut out her tongue.

"About a year later, when I was working on the entrance to the Luxor Temple, I saw a few priests bring her into the open-air, circular courtyard. I came up the back steps by the lake and hid behind one of the columns and watched. She held a scroll in her hands, close to her heart, and they took it from her. Then they stabbed her. Just before she died, they threw the scroll on top of her body, saying they'd burn the knowledge with her. I knew how much the knowledge meant to her, and to me, so I took the scroll after they left and hid it inside one of the columns that were being built near a row of sphinxes by the front of the temple."

"That's something Amanda doesn't know. She thought the scroll was destroyed and that the knowledge was gone forever. And that thought has caused her a great deal of spiritual pain. She dedicated her whole life in Egypt to learning and sharing mystical knowledge. And now, in this life, she's trying to remember that knowledge. She wants to share it again, so that people will be free to know their true spiritual nature."

"But somewhere inside of her, wouldn't she somehow know

that the scroll wasn't destroyed?"

"Not necessarily. If she closed down her soul awareness, then the events that happened after her death in Egypt would be a blank for her. The hospital is on the next block. I'll drop you off at the door, then park the jeep and come in. Amanda is on the third floor, in the intensive care unit."

"Thanks," Jim said. "For everything."

"Hi Judy," Jim said, walking into the room. "It's nice to see you again."

"Mr. Millenum, I'm so glad you're here," Judy said, getting up from the chair beside Amanda's bed. "I talked to your wife about two hours ago. She wants you to call her after you've seen Amanda and talked to the doctor. I'll leave you alone with her now, and I'll let the doctor know that you're here."

Jim looked at Amanda laying on the bed, her face deathly pale on the pillow. He leaned over and kissed her forehead, then sat down beside the bed and held her hand. Tears filled his eyes. "Amanda, please don't die this time," he whispered. "I know you can hear me, that your soul is listening. I was with you in Egypt. I saved the scroll you wrote and hid it inside a column in front of the Luxor Temple.

"Remember the map I showed you when we lived in Africa before? I couldn't remember what the treasure was then; I just knew it was something valuable. Please care enough to get well. We can go to Egypt and I'll show you where your scroll is. Please return to life so you can share your knowledge again. Find the magic somewhere inside your soul."

The doctor walked into the room, followed by Judy and Adam. "Mr. Millenum," he said, "I'm Dr. Hasam. Amanda's condition is quite serious. Her heart stopped once but we were able to revive her."

"She's had malaria before," Jim said, overcome with emotion.

"She had malaria before?" the doctor repeated, startled. "Her blood tests didn't show any antibodies. When? How long ago?"

"In a past life," Jim answered.

"A past life? Oh, you mean when she was younger," the doctor said. "I can contact the physician who took care of her and get the medical records, find out what treatment was pursued and the drugs that were administered. That might be very helpful to us now. What hospital was she in?"

"She wasn't in a hospital. She was in a garden," Adam replied.

The doctor looked at Adam. "This is no time for games," he said.

"He's not playing a game," Jim replied.

"Mr. Millenum," Judy said, "before we brought Amanda to the hospital, she said she wanted to find her rainbow and I told her I'd take her to a garden in the rain forest here. When she was drifting in and out of consciousness, she was talking to someone she called Lavender about a garden and a magical rainbow, urging her to wake up and face her fear, then she asked Adam and me to take her to the garden again. She said hospitals were for sick people who wanted to be sick and that she wanted to be well.

"I've been to this garden; there's a very special magic there. I think the rainbow is part of her soul and if she could connect with the rainbow in the garden, maybe she could heal herself." There were tears in her eyes as she continued. "And if she does choose to die, I think she'd rather be in a garden, close to nature in the warmth of the sun. Please, will you let us take her there?"

"Yes," he said, remembering that her voice had returned in a garden when she had laryngitis as a child, and that she'd said she'd gotten better because she believed in rainbows. Maybe the rainbow is the magic within herself, he thought.

The doctor shook his head no. "I strongly advise you against taking her out of the hospital. I know you're feeling very emotional right now," he said gently, "but Amanda's life is hanging by a thread and the only chance she has to survive is right here."

"I'm taking her to the garden," Jim said. "I know she has a better chance there."

Fifty

Choices and Changes

"I'm just sick about this," Lavender said. "How could Amanda let this happen again?"

"You created it," Rainbow replied. "Remember when you weren't looking forward to Amanda coming to Africa because you knew she'd remember Egypt? You knew at the same time that Africa held just as much potential for healing as it did for hurting. You chose to explore the hurting; Amanda chose to explore the healing. Because of those seemingly opposite choices, you're unsynchronized and out of harmony with yourself. Blend your spiritual and physical energies; get yourself together here. Now is not the time to fall apart."

"How can I take responsibility for all of this and pull myself together at the same time when it's obvious that I'm sick?" Lavender asked. "You can see that I have malaria."

"I don't believe that," Rainbow said. "It's only an illusion. You think you're sick and that's the thought you're expressing now."

"I'm not really sick? It just looks that way?" Lavender asked. I sure feel sick, she thought.

"Lavender, get real. You're playing a game with illusion, but the game is deadly serious. As a matter of fact, it can kill you. I wish you felt better."

"Me too. Being sick is no fun. But how can I make myself well?"

"Face your fear and see what you're truly afraid of. Fear is only a vibration of energy and that energy exists in any form you create for it to exist in. Amanda is trying to turn the fear around to see what it really shows. She wants to change the energy of your fear by rearranging the way it expresses itself. You could help her by meeting her halfway."

"I'll think about it," Lavender whispered, watching her thoughts and images waver between Amanda and herself.

"Every thought and feeling, and every action and reaction, that you and she have affects this energy. All vibrations of energy exist here and now—in the present—even when they seem to be happening in the past or the future. Your thoughts, feelings and choices are what really matters. The repercussions and echoes of energy affect and alter what appears to be past experiences and future realities in present choices. Once a choice has been made, all the energies related to that choice revibrate and change accordingly. This is how the past can be changed—by rearranging the energies of thoughts and feelings—by changing thought perspectives and image perceptions. Then the vibrations of energy and the expressions of experiences change to reflect current choices."

I knew she was going to give me a lecture, Lavender thought to herself.

"But you already know about the energies of choices and changes, and how they take shape and show themselves," Rainbow said. "You clarified it for me when we were talking about nowhere."

"Speaking of nowhere ... Oooh. I feel so sick. I just want to curl up into a lavender-colored sphere of light and rest in peace for an eternity. On second thought, maybe not that long, just a couple thousand years or so until I feel better. I'm so dizzy, Rainbow."

"You're dizzy because you're going around in circles, repeating yourself."

"I'm not the only one," Lavender replied. "I saw you curl up into a lavender sphere of light when Amanda chose to get bitten by a mosquito. That's what gave me the idea in the first place."

"I've made a few mistakes every now and then," Rainbow said. "And I've misunderstood some of my experiences. And I'll admit that some of my perceptions have been a bit off center and out of sync from time to time. I'm not perfect yet. Sometimes I don't see the whole picture clearly. I was looking at a past-life piece before and it seemed that you'd changed your mind about seeing through the shadows and remembering your spiritual knowledge, but then Amanda told me to wake up."

"But Amanda is dying now, and part of me is dying too."

"Lavender, listen to me. Part of you isn't dying. The part of you that is changing its form is the physical energy expression of yourself that you created to give your soul the opportunity to live in the light instead of dwelling in darkness. You can still choose to see through the shadows that you've surrounded your soul with."

"But everything is getting darker and I can't see anything. What's happening to me, Rainbow? I'm so frightened. I really feel like I'm dying."

"You're allowing your fear to overpower you," Rainbow said. "Face your fear. It's the only way to live. Change that choice you made in Egypt when you turned off the light of your soul and closed down your spiritual awareness. Choose to speak and share your knowledge again. It's why you decided to be Amanda this time. Let your desire for truth and knowledge be stronger than your fear. It's only the darkness that is death. This is the turning point—your last chance in this lifetime. Choose now. See the light within your soul and come into the light."

Thunder rumbled across the sky as clouds covered the universe. The wind echoed everywhere at once, reverberating through her soul. Lavender was shaking deep inside herself as the darkness began to swallow her up. "Amanda, help me," she cried. "I'm scared to death."

There was a bright flash of lightning as Amanda reached for her. "Lavender, I'm just as scared as you are but we can do this together. Tell me why you're afraid and let me help you. If we can face our fear and heal the hurt we feel, I know we'll be able to see the light inside our soul and remember our spiritual knowledge."

Rain began to fall as the thunderstorm let loose with all the power of the universe. "Amanda, you're fading in and out of the picture. I can't see you clearly. There are too many clouds and the images are wavering."

"You're losing physical energy, Lavender," Rainbow said, "but you still have time to renew yourself. Voice your fear."

Lavender knew that Amanda was trying, with all her heart, to see the truth within herself that she'd kept hidden in shadows for such a long time. "I'm afraid people will be persecuted for their beliefs. But I'm more afraid that if knowledge is kept secret, people won't be free to find their own truth and to see what's truly inside them," she whispered from the depths of her soul.

"That's the spiritual pain that hurts so much, Lavender. The priests wanted to keep you silent—to keep the knowledge from being shared. Let go of that pain. It's only a shadow; it isn't real. It's time to heal the hurt—to make it all better. It's time to let the light reflect the true image of your soul."

Lavender wavered between shadow and sunlight, trying to make up her mind.

"I'm afraid too," Amanda said. "I'm afraid that the spiritual knowledge you and I care so much about and want to share again will be lost to silence. Please wake up and see the light."

Lavender heard the sound of raindrops tapping softly on a window. Opening the window, she noticed that the rain had turned to a gentle mist and it was nearly time for the sunrise. "But what if people won't listen, or will refuse to see the light within themselves?

Then the knowledge is truly lost."

Amanda smiled at Lavender. "That's your true fear—not listening to yourself and not seeing your own light—not knowing the truth within yourself. It's time to change that fear, to choose to save our knowledge and share it again. That's what our dream is all about."

Lavender heard a voice echo deep within her soul and turned around to see the philosopher. "Having and applying spiritual knowledge is freeing and empowering," he said, standing in the sunshine. "Step out of the shadows into the sunlight and set your spirit free."

As Lavender stepped into the sunshine, the light became brighter, sparkling through the early-morning misty clouds, reflecting a rainbow.

"Walk through the rainbow with me, Lavender," Amanda said. "There's a beautiful, magical garden that I want to share with you."

Fifty-One

Garden of Harmony

The garden sparkled with a vibrant warmth and energy that Jim felt immediately as he carried Amanda into the garden and laid her gently on the soft, green grass. Sitting beside her, he looked up at the sky and saw a rainbow shimmering in the sunlight as a few puffy, white clouds floated leisurely through the azure blue sky. The sound of a waterfall nearby was soothing and relaxing. He smiled at Judy. "I can feel the magic here," he said. "It's so peaceful and beautiful; it's a wonderful place to be."

"The two things that Amanda loves most are gardens and rainbows," Adam said.

"I remember the garden she grew when she was a little girl," Jim said. "She insisted on growing broccoli in the back yard, saying that the earth wanted to grow food next to the flowers, and that the food would be happy because the flowers would be happy too." He smiled again. "She also said she had a friend who lived there, but my wife and I never saw him." Glancing up at the rainbow, he said, "She used to tell us that she was a rainbow in real life and that she could fly through the colors." Suddenly he put his hands over his face and began to cry.

Judy sat down next to him, putting her arm comfortingly through his. "Amanda is here now, in this beautiful garden with her rainbow. Somehow I know that the magic will heal her."

* * * *

"Amanda, I remember this garden," Lavender said.

"You were here before, the last time you lived in Africa," Amanda replied. "I remember seeing this garden in your dream. But you weren't listening to yourself then, and you refused to face your fear."

Lavender looked around the garden. "Everything is so vibrant and healthy, and in harmony with the natural essence of itself." She smiled. "Is that why you brought me here?"

Amanda nodded. "It's time to heal all the hurt and pain we feel inside our soul. It's time for us to come together—to be in tune with the essence of who we really are."

"I used to think you were my parallel self," Lavender said. "I saw you as separate from me, but now I see that we're one and the same."

"Do you ever wonder who Rainbow really is?" Amanda asked.

"I have a feeling she's more than who she appears to be. She's more than my teacher and your higher self, but I haven't found the time to explore that feeling yet," Lavender replied.

"I have the same feeling," Amanda said, smiling. "Maybe tomorrow, we can look into it to see who she really is. But now I want to heal myself on both a physical and a spiritual level. To do that, I need your help."

"All we have to do is change our feelings," Lavender said. "The malaria is only an illusion that I created to mask my fear of seeing my experiences in Egypt on a spiritual level of awareness because of the pain I felt inside my soul. But now I see the truth in the matter so while you're healing yourself, I'll make my voice better."

"Wait a minute, Lavender," Amanda said. "We have to do both things together at the same time."

"You're right," Lavender said in agreement. "It's amazing how quickly you can slip back into old ways of thinking without seeing what you're doing. We need to change our thought perspectives, and the way we see things, so we can see them are they really are. We're physical and spiritual at the same time. We need to look at the whole picture, not separate parts of it."

* * * *

Wanting to get a clear view of everything, Lavender looked up at Rainbow. Looking back at Amanda, she saw that the garden appeared to be different and felt as if she and Amanda were worlds apart when they'd been connected only a second before. "Why isn't Amanda seeing the garden in the same way I see it?" she asked.

"She's experiencing the garden in its physical form while you're seeing the garden from a spiritual level," Rainbow replied.

But how can I be spiritually separate from myself? Lavender wondered. Maybe it's just a slip of mind, a parallel perception, she thought, trying to understand why the same thing appeared to be different at the same time. Looking at Rainbow again, she said, "Amanda and I want to heal ourselves. How can we do that if we're separate? She said we need to get together on this."

"Health is true harmony of body, mind, and spirit in a universal sense. Healing occurs when you tune into yourself and allow your energies to flow naturally, like the rhythms of nature," Rainbow said. "Look at this garden and see how the earth and the universe cooperate in harmony. Bring that awareness inside you; turn on your inner knowing and let it flow within yourself to heal and harmonize all the energies of your body, mind, and spirit. Then you'll be able to heal the past-life hurt and find your voice in the sacred magic of your soul."

* * * *

Feeling out of touch with herself and knowing that Lavender was lost somewhere in her dream, Amanda went inside the color red in the rainbow and began to walk through the vibrations of energy, looking for her soul.

Entering the color orange, she saw the garden she was in now blend into the garden Lavender experienced when she lived in Africa before and knew that the garden was the same, even though it appeared to be separate—a parallel image superimposed upon itself.

The sun shone warmly, vibrating in harmony with the energy of her inner knowing, in tune with the color yellow inside the rainbow. Knowing that she was part of a sunrise, she felt the golden key that she held in her hand begin to vibrate in a magical, mystical flow of energy. A ray of light illuminated a door in Lavender's dream. Opening the door, she watched her walk through the shadows into the sunlight.

Continuing through the rainbow into the color green, she saw the garden inside her feelings and watched it become much more vibrant than before. The garden was pulsing with life and energy, and she felt perfectly in tune with the vibrations inside her heart, in harmony with her true spiritual nature. As the energy flowed into and through her body, she felt the realness of health replacing the illusion of malaria—renewing her body and her mind, refreshing her spirit.

Feeling lighter, she flew into the sky—into the color blue inside the rainbow. Hearing the vibrations of her voice return, she knew that Lavender was listening to herself.

Feeling free, she floated into the color indigo and saw her spiritual knowledge opening up. As all her knowledge flowed into her awareness, she began to read the words that she'd written in the *Scroll of Knowledge*.

Flowing ever so gently into the color violet inside the rainbow, she watched Lavender merge into a synchronous physical/spiritual expression of herself, vibrating in harmony as she flowed into the light of her soul, somewhere over the rainbow.

* * * *

Rainbow smiled at Lavender. "Amanda has allowed the magical energies within her body and her mind to heal herself. Now it's up to you to cure the cause and complete the healing. Change the energies of your experiences in Egypt by embracing and accepting them, then turn them around into a wonderful experience of learning. Go with the flow of your feelings through the rainbow into the light of your soul."

Walking through the color red inside the rainbow, Lavender sensed the spiritual separateness of herself. Feeling lost in a misty image of a physical world looking for herself, she watched Amanda begin to walk through the colors of a rainbow, following her dream.

Entering the color orange, she saw herself experiencing a tropical garden in a rain forest in Africa for what appeared to be the second time. Seeing through the parallel image, she knew that time and space were co-existing simultaneously, and that everything was all here and now.

The color yellow inside the rainbow—inside a sunrise—vibrated with the energy of her inner knowledge. A ray of sunlight illuminated a golden key and she saw Amanda open a door in her dream that led into a realm of enlightenment, into a real world of spiritual knowing. As she walked through the doorway, her experiences in Egypt began to open up in the light of the sun and the shadows that surrounded her soul began to change into misty images.

Inside the color green, inside her heart, she touched her true feelings and saw the real healing begin. Feeling a vibrant energy flow through her as she became perfectly in tune with her spiritual nature, she watched all the illusions and misty images about herself become clear.

The soothing warmth from the yellow rays of sunlight, combined with the vibrant energies of the green garden, emanated from within and radiated through the rainbow, forming a sky-blue color that bathed her throat with vibrations of energy. As the energy flowed in harmony with the vibrations of her voice, she listened to the philosopher speak inside her soul. Completely accepting and understanding all her experiences in Egypt, she began to weep, releasing all the fear and pain she'd held within herself for so long. The tears were purifying and her spirit was renewed and refreshed.

Knowing that she was really free, she floated into the color indigo in the rainbow as all her spiritual knowledge opened up and flowed into her awareness. Turning on the light of her soul, she watched Amanda begin to read the *Scroll of Knowledge*.

Feeling the magic of the words draw her into the color violet inside the rainbow, she saw Amanda in her lavender sphere of light, vibrating in harmony with herself. Together they flowed into the universal light of her soul.

* * * *

"I just had the most wonderful dream about a rainbow," Lavender began as Amanda said, "I just watched a rainbow dream become real."

"We've come together inside the rainbow," Lavender said, jumping up and down with joy. "Amanda, now we can be who we really are."

Rainbow smiled, shimmering in the sunlight above the garden.

Fifty-Two

Better Now Than Before

Amanda opened her eyes. "There's a rainbow all around me," she said in a soft, dreamy voice. She looked at her father. "I heard you talking to me; I heard every word you said. When you told me you'd saved my scroll, that helped me see the whole picture about my experiences in Egypt." She smiled. "I was in a magical world inside my rainbow, and I opened up my scroll and read the words I'd written so long ago. Then I knew, with all my heart, that I wanted to speak and share that knowledge again."

Looking around the garden, she said, "I was here before, when I lived in Africa the first time." Sitting up and hugging her father, she said, "Thank you for bringing me here again. I feel completely healthy. I've got so much energy; it's like my body is renewed and my soul is flying."

"Amanda, I'm so glad you're all better now," he said, laughing with happiness. "I thought we'd lost you for awhile."

"I was lost for awhile, searching for myself. But then I found my rainbow," she said. "Everything seemed like it was happening in a dream and somewhere along the way, I reconnected with my spiritual nature and woke up inside myself."

Judy smiled. "Welcome back, Amanda. Your laryngitis is all cleared up and you sound like your talkative, bubbly self again."

Amanda laughed. "Lavender, my spiritual self, had a lot to do with that. She found her voice and she's a writer. She looks into words to see what they really say."

She smiled at Adam. "You were a shaman before, just like you are now. I remember you telling me about the magic within myself, trying to help me heal my body, mind, and spirit. But I was too sick to care then and too afraid to face my fear. I didn't listen to myself—to the voice within."

"You just weren't ready then to hear what you had to say," Adam replied. "Sometimes it takes a long time to let go of fear."

"Lifetimes," Amanda said in agreement. "I wish I'd healed myself the first time but in a way, it seems like now and before are really the same." She looked up at the rainbow. "I'm so happy to be alive," she said joyously. "I feel so free."

Looking at her father, she said, "I remember the map you showed me when we lived in Africa before. What do you say we go to Egypt and find that treasure now?"

"I'd like that," Jim said. "I know exactly where I hid your scroll. As a matter of fact, I redrew the map on the plane when I was flying here." He pulled it out of his pocket and showed it to her. "I thought it was just a dream, but now I know that dreams are real."

Amanda smiled at the rainbow in the sky. "Rainbows are real too," she said.

Fifty-Three

The Scroll of Knowledge

"The present is very different than the past," Jim said, surrounded by the throngs of people touring the pyramids in Karnak.

"If you look closely, you can see the past reflected in the present," Amanda answered. "You can sense and feel the energy of past events."

Jim smiled. "Find a focus in the present, then center in on the vibes from the past. Look within your subconscious for the images and feelings, and the memory will become clear in your mind," he said.

"That's how it works," Amanda replied. "How'd you know that?"

"I read it in one of your reincarnation books," he answered. "And Adam helped me put it into practical use."

"I'm ready to follow my feelings into the past," Amanda said. "I'd like to go to the Temple of Ra, where I studied mystical knowledge. I think that by being there, in the same place, it will help me open up more of my awareness." She took her sandals off. "The temple is over that way," she pointed. "I remember walking there every day, feeling the sand beneath my bare feet."

Standing in front of the Temple of Ra, Amanda saw and sensed her past-life images and feelings opening up inside her. Tuning into the energies of the philosopher she used to be, she softly said, "I remember how it was." They walked through the open-columned hallways, then entered the innermost part of the temple.

In a reverent tone, Amanda said, "Ra was the sun god of Egypt, and this temple was built to honor him. At the time, the Egyptians believed that all life came from the sun—from the light—and Ra was the giver of light to the earth, the giver of life. Within the vibrations of sunlight were hidden the secrets of life and the true knowledge of your soul. If you knew the secrets of sunlight, you knew the truth about the nature of a soul. It was those secrets that I shared."

She was quiet for a moment, remembering. "There's really no secret about the knowledge. There never was. When people are willing to look for the light within themselves, they reawaken their awareness and begin their search for spiritual truth. Every soul has all their knowledge within."

She smiled sadly. "I'm ready to go to the Luxor Temple now, where I was ..." She took a deep breath. "... Persecuted," she said.

"This is still painful for you, isn't it?" Jim asked.

Amanda nodded. "Yes, but I want to completely explore all the aspects of my past experiences in Egypt—to blend them into my present awareness and understanding."

"The Luxor Temple is where your scroll is," he said. "It's several miles from here, but it's a nice day for a walk."

"Even if it were possible to dig out my scroll, I doubt it would still be intact." Amanda sneezed. "It's probably dust by now," she said. "It's a good thing I remember what I wrote."

"I remember listening to you speak about the truth of light and the power of knowledge," Jim said. "You talked about empowering yourself with knowledge, saying that having knowledge is like the light of a sunrise. Acquiring knowledge is accomplished by looking inside your thoughts and experiences to see what they really show, and applying knowledge is what helps you find the light within yourself.

"After one of your talks, you gave everyone a yellow rose, saying a rose is a symbol of hidden knowledge opening up within your mind. You asked us to watch how the rose opens up as it reaches for the light of the sun. You told us to do the same thing—reach for the light of the sun, both within ourselves and in our experiences. You said it would help us to open up our spiritual nature and become more aware of our inner knowledge.

"You were forever saying that there weren't any shortcuts to spirituality, and the only way to really understand and learn was to experience the knowledge for yourself. You asked us to listen to our feelings and look into the pictures in our mind to remember our knowledge."

Amanda smiled. An image of her scroll and the opening words flashed through her thoughts. *"From the pictures in your mind come words ..."*

"Speaking of pictures ..." Jim said. "You told us that we talk to ourselves with words and feelings, but our mind draws pictures of those words and communicates with us through those pictures. You said that we think our thoughts into existence just by feeling them and seeing the images of them in our mind." He smiled. "But you never told us that we were creating our own reality. I guess because back then, no one had come up with that term yet."

Amanda laughed. "We're in the New Age now. The words have changed, but the knowledge remains the same."

"You also talked about the microcosm and the macrocosm, about how the earth is a reflection of the universe. You quoted a phrase, 'As above, so below,' saying that the two separate worlds are parts of the same energy vibration and they only appear to be mirror images because—" He stopped talking abruptly.

"Oh, Amanda, look. I can hardly believe this," he said excitedly. "A reconstruction is going on at the Luxor Temple. Maybe we really can unearth your scroll. This is so incredible. I was one of the architects who helped to design and build the entranceway to this temple. Maybe I could join the crew."

Thinking out loud while seeing a plan form in his mind, he said, "I'll call your mom; she and Gary can get their passports and come out for the summer. I'll extend my leave of absence from my job. This could really work out." He smiled. "It's an incredible coincidence."

Amanda laughed. "There's no such thing as coincidence. It's more like perfect timing—synchronicity. You've wanted to have the adventure of being an archeologist again. It's in your soul; you've dreamed about it all your life."

"It makes you wonder if everything—if every experience and every event—really does happen simultaneously in time and space at various vibrations of energy."

"You amaze me with your knowledge. Where'd you learn about the energies of time, space, matter, and motion?"

"From a philosopher in Egypt," he replied, smiling at her. "Amanda, wait here for a few minutes, will you? I want to find the foreman and see if I can get hired on the crew for the summer."

Amanda sat under a palm tree, looking at the temple. Images and feelings began to flow through her mind and her throat began to hurt. She pulled her knees up to her chest and put her head down, unable to stop the thoughts running through her mind, seeing them over and over again.

"I've been hired on the crew, and we have permission to walk through the temple," Jim said. "I promised we wouldn't touch anything and that we'd stay out of the way."

Amanda slowly raised her head and looked at him.

"Amanda, honey, what's wrong?" he asked, seeing the look on her face. He knelt down beside her, putting his hand on her shoulder.

Amanda's heart was pounding wildly and her breath came in short gasps. "Daddy, I don't think I can go in there," she whispered, her eyes wide with fear. "Too many bad things happened to me in there. I died in there."

"I think that's exactly why you have to go in there now," Jim said gently. "There's still something you need to know."

"Maybe it could wait until my next lifetime," Amanda said.

Jim smiled and said, "There's a karmic debt that I feel I owe you. I became aware of it when I remembered that I lived in Egypt before. I made a promise to you when I saved your scroll. That promise was to help you find a treasure. I thought the treasure was your scroll, but now I think the treasure is helping you find the real truth about your knowledge." He stood up and reached for her hand. "C'mon, Amanda, let's go inside," he said, helping her up. "Let's find that treasure."

"There's no time like the present," Amanda replied bravely, holding tightly to his hand.

They walked past a row of sphinxes that lined the entryway to the temple. Near the entrance, Jim stopped in front of a column. "Your scroll is inside this column," he said. "This is where I hid it."

Amanda touched the column, then rested her head against it and looked at her father. "I remember walking this way. I remember everything so clearly. I knew the priests were going to kill me and I felt so saddened by the thought that my knowledge would die too," she said, crying. "Even though I knew that so many others had the same knowledge that I did, people everywhere all over the world, and that the knowledge wouldn't ever really die, I still felt that everything was lost to me."

"I think it was natural for you to feel that way considering everything that happened to you." He was quiet for a moment. "I watched them kill you, Amanda," he said despairingly. "And I didn't do anything to try to stop them. I felt so helpless ..."

"But you saved my scroll," Amanda said, smiling through her tears. "And you helped me come back to life this time—physically and spiritually."

Entering the open-air, circular courtyard, she let go of his hand and slowly walked into the center by the large, round, flat-topped stone inscribed with symbols. Sitting down on the ground with her back to the stone, she looked at her father. "The priests laid me on this stone and stabbed me through my heart," she said, with no trace of emotion in her voice. "But I was dead before they killed me because I'd decided never to share my knowledge again. I felt that everything I'd valued and respected had been taken from me, and

I'd given up caring. The last thing I saw was the sun shining into my eyes," she whispered, looking up at the sky.

Suddenly she jumped up. "I remember," she shouted, running over to her father. "Somewhere inside me, there was a part of me that refused to die and I put my spiritual knowledge inside the sunshine for safekeeping," she said joyfully. "And that's where I found the key to my knowledge, when I went inside my rainbow dreams. And I remember, right after I was born this time, I placed the key inside a rainbow so I could open up my knowledge when I was ready to see it and share it again."

"When you were a little girl, every time you saw a rainbow, a special light would come into your eyes and you seemed to sparkle," Jim said, smiling. "You knew all the time where you'd placed your knowledge and how to find the key."

Amanda hugged her father. "Thank you so much for helping me to see that. There really is a treasure at the end of the rainbow," she said. "I think that now is the perfect time to see what my rainbow is really all about. And the best way for me to do that is to write a book about my rainbow dreams."

She smiled to herself. Lavender, are you listening? A voice inside her mind replied, "I'll share my pencil with you."

Fifty-Four

Following the Future

"Thank you for inviting me to this wonderful candlelight dinner," Amanda said to Adam. Lifting the cover off one of the wooden bowls, she sniffed appreciatively. "Oh, yum! My favorite. Broccoli. How'd you know?" she asked laughing.

"Just a guess," he replied, smiling. "Have a seat," he said, pulling out the chair for her.

She sat down, then scooted her chair over next to his. Putting her elbow on the table and leaning her chin in her hand, she looked at him and smiled.

"Would you like something to drink?" he asked, producing a bottle of sparkling water from the cooler under the table, along with two champagne glasses.

"How on earth did you find champagne glasses in the middle of the jungle?" Amanda asked incredulously.

"You just have to know where to look for things," he said. "To be honest, I, uh, manifested them out of thin air." He smiled and shrugged his shoulders. "You know how that goes."

"I've seen how the images work," Amanda replied, smiling. "What shall we toast to?"

"How about health and harmony?"

"I'll drink to that," Amanda replied.

"Could we talk seriously for a minute?" Adam asked, refilling their glasses and serving the food.

"Okay. But only for a minute," she said, doing her best to look serious.

"Amanda, I'd like to tell you some things about myself that I didn't tell you before, because ..."

"Adam, can I ask you something serious?" Amanda interrupted.

"Of course. You can ask me anything you want."

"Is the minute up yet?"

Adam laughed. "Yes, Amanda. Time is up."

She breathed a sigh of relief. "Oh, I'm so glad. I don't like getting stuck in a time frame. It somehow warps the joy in life."

"Now to get back to being serious for a moment ..." he began. "Oh, sorry. Bad choice of words." He grinned apologetically. "When we found each other again here in Africa, I was evasive when you asked me to tell you what I've been up to because I thought you weren't ready to see through the illusions. To tell you the truth, I'm not really who I appear to be."

Amanda smiled. "I know that you're really more than a shaman, and that you've completely mastered energy and evolved above the earth realm. So why did you return in physical form?"

"One of the reasons I chose to come back was to be with you again," he said softly, leaning over and kissing her. "That's why I appeared in your broccoli garden when you were a little girl, and it's part of the reason I'm here now in Africa. Would you like some more?" he asked.

"Yes, please," Amanda said, kissing him back.

"I meant some more broccoli," he said, gesturing toward the food and kissing her again.

"Yes, that too," Amanda replied, smiling at him.

"I also returned because I want to help people remember the magic inside themselves and teach them how to master it," he continued. "I've been training for this for a long time. I went to high school in the universe, and I practiced as a throat specialist to open universal communication and to help clear some physical channels."

"So what you're really trying to tell me is that you're an escapee from the western world of traditional medicine." Amanda laughed. "You looked so unnatural in your illusion as a doctor."

Adam smiled. "You do have a way with words," he said. "How's your book coming along?"

"Last time I looked, the pages were putting themselves together and it's nearly complete." Amanda smiled. "I'll let you in on a little secret. I have a magical pencil so the book really seems to write itself."

"You're becoming a master of illusion too," he said.

"So you came to Africa ..." she prompted.

"... to apply the energies of natural healing in an accepting environment. I chose to be a shaman again because I wanted to learn more from the earth and the people here. They're so in tune with their inherent power and their instincts. They truly understand and apply the harmony of naturalness in their life. I'd like to teach other people how to physically attune themselves to their true nature—to flow with the natural harmony of the earth and the universe.

"Since you've returned from Egypt, you've become clear about what you want to do when your time with the Peace Corps is over in six months. You've said several times that you want to help people learn how to understand and apply universal light energy in an earthly vibration of awareness."

Amanda nodded. "In a special place somewhere inside me, I think I've always known that I want to help people become more aware of the light within themselves so they can recognize their own power. I just needed to see that for myself by rediscovering my own power. I want to share all the spiritual knowledge that I learned in my life as the philosopher."

"Since our plans and goals are very similar, I was wondering if you'd like to open a holistic harmony and health center together. Maybe we could do that in Hawaii because nature is so in tune with itself there, and the universe seems so close that you could almost reach up and touch it."

"We can be kahunas," she said. "I like the idea and it will help me expand my spiritual development."

Adam looked into her eyes. "Umm, Amanda, there's something else I've been wanting to ask you." He took a deep breath. "Umm, I don't know quite how to say this," he began.

Amanda smiled. "Yes," she said.

"You don't know what I was going to ask."

"I can see it in your eyes. You were going to ask me to do the dishes," she said, laughing.

"No, that's not exactly what I had in mind. You're really going to make me say this, aren't you?"

"Adam, you look so adorable, like a cute little boy, when you're shy. I love you with all my heart and soul, and I'd love to marry you."

Adam hugged her, laughing with happiness. "You always were better with words than I was," he said.

"You just have to know how to speak the truth," she replied.

"Judy, I'm glad you're still up. I want you to be the first to know. Adam and I are getting married."

"Somehow that doesn't surprise me," she said, smiling. She got up from the chair and hugged Amanda. "I'm so happy for both of you. You're perfect for one another." She went into the bamboo house and pulled out the other folding chair. Opening it up, she said, "Sit down and tell me all about it."

"After I'm finished my work here with the Peace Corps, he's coming home with me and we're going to get married in the back yard, where my broccoli garden used to be. Then we're going to

Hawaii for our honeymoon. While we're there, we're going to look into opening a spiritual center to help people remember universal light energy and to rediscover their natural harmony with themselves." She smiled. "What are you planning to do when we get home?"

"Do you remember the path I kept seeing in my mind that I felt would lead me to my soul's true purpose, and I knew that my future would unfold in Africa?"

Amanda nodded.

"When we first arrived here, I felt as if I'd come home. Being in Africa and sharing peace with people is my purpose," she said in a soft voice filled with emotion. "I'm staying here with the Peace Corps. I've been seeing this clearly for the past few months and I didn't tell you before because it makes me sad to part with you."

Amanda reached over and squeezed her hand. "I'm so happy you found what you want in life. There's no reason to be sad; we'll never really be apart. We're as close as our thoughts of one another. Our friendship is very special, and you've helped me in so many ways to see who I really am."

Judy looked up at the clear, starlit sky. "It's so right for you that your purpose is to share universal light energy," she said. "You see things differently than most people do, and you've shown me ways to look inside myself that I never would have dreamed were possible."

"Do you see that little star twinkling way up there?" Amanda asked, pointing to Orion's belt. "The one that's just above and to the left of the center star? That's my star. That's where I lived before I came back down to earth." She smiled. "Really. It's the truth."

"I believe you," Judy replied. "You always did seem to be a little out of this world."

"I wonder what the future holds," Amanda said. "If I knew then what I know now ..." she began. "Maybe I'd do the same things differently. But then, who really knows? Life is for learning and one of the most important things I've learned is to just be here now—to go with the flow of every moment and enjoy where I am in the present. But I wonder about all the choices and paths we have."

Judy smiled. "You're probably exploring all those choices and paths in other places somewhere else in your reality."

Fifty-Five

The Real Rainbow

Watching the sun come up over the horizon, Lavender said to herself, "School is over today and summer vacation starts tomorrow." Looking into her thoughts, she remembered that Rainbow had said the exam would be given in several parts: There was the physical part that Amanda had to pass, and the written part consisted of her master's thesis and her research report on a past life. And now that she'd found her voice, Rainbow would probably say there was an oral part too. I wonder what questions she's going to ask, she thought, knowing that if she failed to find the answers within herself, she'd fail to find the truth.

A smile came into her eyes as she looked at Amanda's life on earth. I know she'll pass her part of the test. She's remembered her spiritual knowledge and learned how to apply it in all of her experiences, and now she's ready to fulfill her destiny of sharing vibrations of universal light. I wish I could say the same for myself; I wish I knew all the answers about my spiritual nature.

"I don't like these tests; they're so silly," she muttered. "Your fate shouldn't hang on one or two misunderstood experiences or be decided by a few misplaced thoughts. You should be graded on everything together, not separately." But she knew that everything had to be perfect or she'd have to repeat the classes until she'd learned everything there was to know about her soul, and everything else for that matter, and had mastered the complete awareness of all her energies.

"I want to understand the meanings of all my experiences so I can graduate my soul," she said to herself. Watching all of her past/present/future experiences flow into her mind, she saw that she was in three different places at the same time. "I feel as if I'm stuck in the middle of all this, trying to see everything at once so I can understand my true nature," she said, noticing that her thoughts were becoming scattered.

Trying to collect herself and focus her thoughts so she could put them in their proper perspectives and see the whole picture at once, she said to herself, "Somehow I'll just have to get myself centered and find the time to finish writing my thesis before I turn it in, even though it appears that I've run out of time."

Walking resolutely into the Time/Space class, she sat down at her desk. Reaching inside, she found her pencil that she and Amanda were now sharing. Amanda had decided to write a book about her rainbow dreams to discover the truth about her soul. Lavender smiled to herself. I've already written a book, *Somewhere Over the Rainbow*, that she's seen and read in her dreams from time to time, and now that it's almost finished—only the last chapter remains to be written—maybe she'll wake up soon and see the light within herself, she thought.

She shook her head, trying to clear her thoughts. Amanda is awake, she reminded herself, but she thinks I'm dreaming. Reminiscing, she saw that she'd viewed Amanda as her parallel self until she'd seen for herself that she was truly a spiritual being.

I wonder if Rainbow ever thought that she had a parallel self. The thought triggered a conversation she'd had with Amanda not too long ago. She was curious about who Rainbow really is and had wanted to look into it sometime in the near future.

An image of Amanda floated into her mind. She was waking up from what appeared to be a dream about following a rainbow. She looked at the words Amanda was writing in her dream journal. *I've reached the rainbow's end, and I can see for myself who I really am and I know what's real. Knowledge is the power that sets a soul free to find the light within themselves.*

Feeling as if she was wavering on the edge of enlightenment, she saw an image of the sunrise seminar she and Amanda had attended and watched her walk into the center of the sunrise. Looking into the light, Lavender said to herself, "Maybe I can come up with the answer about who I really am before Rainbow gets here."

Some things never seem to change, she thought, noticing that her thoughts were beginning to wander and wondering if she was late for class. "Oh, no, not again," she said as a thought ran unbidden through her mind, remembering the first class she'd attended.

But the thought presented itself anyway. Maybe I'm too early. But then there's always the possibility that I'm too late and I've missed the class. Or even worse—maybe I'm in the right place at the wrong time, or the wrong place at the right time. She sighed, noticing the clock with no hands hanging on the wall. That wasn't here before, she thought. Synchronizing time and space is so difficult and I still haven't acquired the ability of being here, there, and everywhere simultaneously, and at the same time really knowing where I am all the time. Waiting for Rainbow to appear, she looked out the window at the universe.

If I fail these tests, I'll get a longer vacation than just the summer. I'll probably have to reincarnate again until I learn how to synchronize all my experiences. No use feeling down about it, she thought, trying to cheer herself up. Wandering in her thoughts, she realized that she hadn't made any plans for her vacation. It might be fun to practice rising above myself to see if I can get centered, she thought. When I get good at it, maybe I'll follow Rainbow around the universe to find out where she goes and what she does on her summer vacation. A thought sparkled in her mind, like a burst of light.

Just then Rainbow appeared in the doorway. "I think I know who you really are, Rainbow," Lavender said, jumping up from her chair and running over to her. "And I've decided, once and for all, to find out who you really are, instead of just wondering about it," she said, realizing that she'd just rephrased herself. Don't get over-excited about this, she told herself. Don't be jumping up and down and running around in circles. But the thought was so awesome that she could barely contain her energy.

Looking Rainbow right in the eye, she said very calmly, "I'm at the end of the rainbow now, and I'm ready to see all the vibrations of my soul. I'm standing on the edge of enlightenment here, and I don't want to fall when I'm so close to really knowing. Just let me catch my breath for a minute and get my balance. I know the truth is somewhere *inside* the rainbow, not *over* the rainbow."

Looking into the center of her awareness, she saw that she was in the center of a sunrise, holding a golden key to knowledge in her hand. Feeling a surge of energy soar through her soul and sensing her full power opening up within herself, she said, "I remember who I really am—I mean who you really are."

Feeling as if she was waking up from a long dream, she took a deep breath and said, "I know that you're more than who you appear to be, and you seem to know everything about my soul. If I'm expressing the physical part of my spiritual nature as Amanda, then you must be expressing the universal part of my soul through her at the same time. And that means that you're me and I'm you, just as Amanda is me and I'm her, and you're her and she's you, and all three of us together form one essence of energy that I call *me*. I'm the real rainbow."

"Yes," Rainbow replied, sparkling with energy and shimmering rays of sunlight all around and through and within herself at the same time.

Lavender smiled a very special smile, knowing that she'd finally seen the light within herself.

"Now that you know the truth about yourself, do you have your research report and your master's thesis on *Time and the Two Separate Worlds are Really the Same*?" Rainbow asked.

It looks like I blew this part of the test, Lavender thought, feeling a sinking sensation in her soul. "I haven't found the time to finish writing my thesis yet," she answered. "But I have completed my research report," she said, giving the past-life paper to Rainbow. "For authenticity, I wrote it on papyrus paper with a reed pen," she added.

Just then she felt the energy form of her pencil vibrate in her hand and knew that Amanda was writing the final words in her master's thesis. I hope she finishes it on time, she thought. "If you'll wait a minute, Rainbow, my master's thesis will be completed and you can read the words."

"While I'm waiting," Rainbow said agreeably, "What time is it?"

"I can answer that if I answer a simultaneous question about space and synchronicity at the same time," Lavender replied. "The time is now and the space is here." She laughed. "In reality, they're both nowhere."

"Are the earth and the universe really two separate worlds?"

"The earth and the universe are one simultaneous vibration of energy interacting with each other," Lavender said, seeing the words in her mind. "When they're not in perfect harmony with one another, they *appear* to be reflections or mirror images and show themselves as illusions, but they're really the same world."

"Tell me about thought perspectives and image perceptions. What do you think about them and how do you see them?"

"I think they really matter, and I see that my thought perspectives were limited before. I was seeing parts of myself at one time; I wasn't looking at the whole picture all at once. That's why my perceptions of my images seemed to create separate experiences," she answered. "And because my perspectives and feelings focused my perceptions and directed my awareness, that's why I saw Amanda as my parallel self rather than seeing her as the physical expression of my spiritual nature because I hadn't focused my awareness into the center of myself. That's also why I couldn't see my universal nature until now."

Weaving the threads of her thoughts together to form a masterpiece image of her soul, she continued. "Just as a rainbow is centered between the earth and the universe, the spiritual part of who you are is centered between your physical self and your universal self. When you know your true nature, and you center your awareness into all the vibrations of your thoughts and experiences, you blend into both worlds and you can see the whole picture."

She smiled, remembering all the times she'd felt as if she was somewhere between the earth and the universe, between Amanda and Rainbow. I've known the truth inside me and had all the answers from the very beginning, she thought, watching all the pieces of her thoughts, feelings, and experiences fall into place as the picture came together.

"What's the purpose of life on earth?" Rainbow asked.

"To recognize and remember that you're truly a spiritual being, so you can completely understand yourself and apply your knowledge in all your experiences," Lavender replied. "In that way, you evolve into enlightenment—into higher realms of awareness. There are an infinite number of ways that a soul can rediscover and reexperience their true nature but the purpose is the same: To see who you really are and to express your true nature in every avenue of your awareness, in every part of your life."

Rainbow smiled. "What are the secrets of sunlight in relation to the universal expression of your soul?"

Lavender returned Rainbow's smile, seeing the sunlight shimmer and sparkle through her awareness. "Universal light energy is within your soul and around your soul, vibrating in harmony through your soul. The secret of sunlight is knowing that you are the light. And that sets your spirit free to express who you really are."

"Lavender, you've passed all your tests with flying colors. You've understood the reasons for your reincarnation by balancing your past life energies in Egypt and remembering your spiritual knowledge, and you've unearthed the meanings and mysteries of the universe. You've mastered all your energies and graduated," Rainbow said, embracing her. "Welcome home."

Epilogue

Somewhere Inside the Rainbow ...

Brilliant rays of sunshine sparkled through the open window as Amanda woke up. A dream image of a rainbow writing a book whispered words into her mind. Rubbing the sleep out of her eyes, she picked up the pencil that had mysteriously appeared out of nowhere and began to write, "Follow your dream ..."

Reading the words, she saw an image of a butterfly soaring through the clouds and felt as if she was flowing through a mystical mindscape of images, a magical world created with words. As the words drew her into a special place within herself, images of her experiences circled through her mind and repeated themselves in echoes of energy. A pre-birth promise about remembering who she was before, and who she is now, floated into her thoughts and she began to dream.

Walking through a rainbow, searching to find herself and to know what was real, she traveled a ray of light into the center of a sunrise. Seeing a golden key, she knew that it was a key to knowledge that opened magical doors within her mind—doors that revealed the truth about her soul, doors that showed her the way to unearth the mysteries of the universe.

A sudden gust of wind blew through the open window, scattering the pages here, there, and everywhere. Gathering the words together, she saw that the images were weaving a tapestry of thoughts that were magically interwoven and in tune with the expressions of energy inside the book. In the middle of rearranging the pages into pictures, she saw that she was on a high-spirited search for truth and a quest for knowledge that led her on a mystical journey through the earth and the universe, traveling inside the colors of a rainbow.

Watching the images weave through her awareness, she saw that everything was happening at the same time in perfect synchronicity with multi-dimensional vibrations and expressions of energy, even though it had appeared at first glance that all the images were superimposed upon one another in parallel pictures. Taking a closer, second look, she saw that Lavender was dreaming her life. "Wake up," she whispered. "Find a magical rainbow somewhere inside your soul and follow your dream."

Feeling the key vibrate in her hand, she opened the door and watched Lavender walk into the images inside the book. As she walked through the rain, searching the sky for a rainbow, the clouds began to clear and the sun sparkled through the mist, illuminating a rainbow that showed a universal path into knowledge. Following the path that led her within, she found herself standing at the rainbow's end and knew that knowledge is the power that sets a soul free to understand their true spiritual nature.

Watching herself turn in her master's thesis and graduate her soul, she became a real rainbow, evolving into enlightenment as she woke up from her dream. Knowing that she'd found her way home, she picked up her pencil and began to write a magical book to share the secrets of knowledge with other seekers of truth.